Way out in
INDIA

All rights reserved.
No part of this publication may be reproduced
or transmitted in any form or by any means
without permission from the publisher.

© Meryl Urson, 2015

Although none of the people or places described in
this book is imaginary, occasionally the real names
have not been used to protect the individual's privacy.

First published in 2015 by
Porcupine Press
PO Box 2756
Pinegowrie, 2123
South Africa
admin@porcupinepress.co.za
www.porcupinepress.co.za

ISBN-13: 978-1514259955 | ISBN-10: 1514259958

Produced by Porcupine Press
Design and layout by www.wimrheeder.co.za
Set in Minion Pro 11/15
Printed by CreateSpace

Way out in
INDIA

Travels in a Curious Land

MERYL URSON

PORCUPINE PRESS
Johannesburg, South Africa

To Arnie for journeying with me and to my wondering, wandering children.

Acknowledgements

In the writing of this book I have received so much support, firstly from my dear husband Arnie, who provided the most patient technical support to bolster my limited computer literacy. He also listened to my reading of passages, chuckled at the right moments and took the photographs, sitting with me indoors on sunny weekend afternoons, selecting the best ones for the book.

Thanks also to my children, the Vardi family and to my friends for their encouragement all the way, and of course thanks to the team at Porcupine Press, especially Gail Robbins and Clare-Rose Julius for their professionalism, commitment and warmth during the process.

Photographs by Arnold Urson

Contents

Introduction	7
1: Of Grace and Gurus	11
2: Of Palm Trees and Pigs	72
3: Of Waterways and Warblings	108
4: Of Caves and Crystals	152
5: Of Rot and Religion	165
6: Of Tigers and Tall Tales	185
7: Of Palaces and Protests	189
8: Of Passengers and Puffings	222
9: Of Peaks and Pine Trees	227
10: Home Run	244
A Glossary of Indian Terms	246

Introduction

'TAXI?' HE SEEMED A decent chap, the driver, bobbling his head and wrapped up in the deep freeze of a Darjeeling winter. And the car was clearly solid and beloved.

'How much to the airport, to the Embassy Airport Hotel, Friday?'

He gave the fee.

'Do you know where it is, the Embassy?'

We took his half-moon head weave as a yes, and with the date and time on his card tucked into my woolly gloved palm, we plunged into Kungas for a bowl of steaming *momos*.

Wheeling back and forth down the Himalayan hairpin bends two days later, we smiled nauseously. These seventy kilometres would take three hours and more. The little car bumped along as valiantly as the driver's English while tea plantations, rowdy foliage and tidy villages all rolled by in a scroll of dust and colour.

A few minutes from the airport, amid the usual honking and tooting, the driver drew to a sedate sort of halt.

'Driver geography conference,' I whispered to a frowning Arnie.

'Well, he hasn't got a GPS.'

After a futile yell by our man to the nearest stationary colleague, the conference waxed gravely telephonic before the driver turned to us.

'You said Embassy Hotel was at airport,' he intoned, clicking the red phone button. 'It's back to Darjeeling more.'

'You said you know the place,' Arnie countered.

'I know the place now, but cannot take you there.'

'Why not?' My voice wobbled a tad.

'I have to take you to Darjeeling more. Put you on three-wheeler.'

'Three-wheeler?' A squeak escaped me as a jumble of skinny legs and weathered faces pedalled triangularly by, powering passengers along in the chaos of cars and trucks. And then, oh then, there was our luggage to be lugged. I defaulted to pidgin English under pressure. 'How far Darjeeling more?'

The driver waggled his head. I twitched my India twitch and gazed my India gaze, agitated, through the window.

'Darjeeling More,' a roadside sign responded, '7 km.'
'What is Darjeeling More?' I ventured.
'A Johnson.'
'Right.'

At the junction another bawl from the front seat summoned a tuk-tuk for us, with its driver bellowing back, spitting and reluctant to transport us to the elusive Embassy for less than his monthly salary because the price would include an engine.

A fee finally fixed, the luggage was loaded into the rickshaw and we puttered back the way we'd come, ploughing into the clogged and colourful little lanes of Siliguri, the town eighteen kilometres from the airport. Down a particular lane the driver stopped suddenly for no apparent reason, until above a hole in a wall a sign appeared: Embassy Hotel. Outside in the street the locals gathered to gawk at us as we tiptoed over a large pile of mud, surely laced, from the aroma, with something less fragrant.

'I can't do this,' I mumbled, but Arnie didn't hear me. Too many cycle rickshaws were honking their enematic horns that sucked and squawked like donkeys smoking cigarettes.

But then two steps away beyond the Embassy's glass doors, as India does at times, she turned a hundred and eighty degrees, engulfing us in a modest hall of marble – quiet, orderly, cool with a duo of saris rustling behind the front desk.

'Welcome to the Embassy,' the receptionists smiled with that crinkly radiance that crumples resistance. And bobbled their heads – just to make sure.

IF YOU'RE serious about exploring India, expect a few rides like this one and adventures contained in such pursuits as road crossing. It's not for the faint-hearted, this country. It's too kaleidoscopic and contrary for our ingrained systems of order. But if it's adventure you're after, colour, food so delicious it will wrench grunts from you in public, people so sweet that a conversation will taste like kulfi; if it's a surprise several times an hour and the kind of endearing simplicity embodied in treadle sewing machines and bicycle bells that go "tring", then pack your bags

– not too heavily, though. You never know when you might end up on a three-wheeler of one kind or another.

And when people ask you why on earth you'd spend your time wandering the land of crowds and garbage, you'll probably just shrug and giggle – maybe even waggle your head; because why *would* you spend your holidays eating curried everything for breakfast and enduring high-intensity jostling when you could be sprawled out on a beach without hawkers or skiing sanitised mountain slopes?

Ask anyone why they'd visit India, and those who didn't run for cover at the first leper tapping on their legs for alms, will generally smile in a wistful way and cross over to incoherence. So what is it that draws those who love it back to its chaotic bosom?

The first thing is that it is otherwise. That is the last thing, too, and almost everything in between. So many aspects of it are totally foreign to Westerners, from the pavements that we understand are for walking on, which traders clog in cross-legged oblivion; to toilets that we understand as polite porcelain chairs. Quite reconfigured in India to two footholds straddling the depths, they reconfigure *us*, crouching and cursing and realising with disarming suddenness that we've taken our conveniences for granted.

And this is the crux of the matter. When everything is unfamiliar, air, water, food, shelter and everything else, we wake up. I mean, we WAKE UP. Senses are primed. What's that strange smell? What's that man bleating for? (Calm down, he's only calling his scrap metal wares, wheeling his barrow along). Look at the *pink* on that sari! It's making my teeth chatter. And, hey, is that guy seriously going to eat that dosa all on his own? Oh, God, he's crushing it to death with his hand. Where's the cutlery and why is a goat browsing on the pot plants outside the restaurant?

At every turn there are moments like these. After just a few of them the brain starts dancing, and the head starts spinning – and, because of that, you'd better watch out when you cross a road.

I FELL IN love with India vicariously, via tales of a dear friend's long sojourns there from Kashmir to Goa, from palm-thatched beach huts through long train journeys to Himalayan beauty.

And then there was the yoga. I'd fallen in love with that, too, a few years before India seeped under my skin. Iyengar yoga it was and has been all these long years. If you practise this style, you soon hear of the extraordinary life and exploits of its founder, the famous Mr BKS Iyengar – known to his adepts and followers as "Guruji".

For a long time I'd harboured a yearning to go to his institute in Pune, India, to witness him and his family in action, but two obstacles had blocked my way. One was my family. I was a married mother of three young children and the institute's programmes last a month – too long to be away from my precious ones. The second was that only students with at least eight years' experience and a steady ten-minute head balance are admitted to the institute, which, alas, excluded me.

But at last the children were older, my husband came home from his travel-loaded corporate career and I'd become an invert for minutes at a time as a matter of daily ritual.

That first trip could only be described as life changing. There were no wafty Mother India moments or, indeed, fuzzy Father Iyengar ones. The whole experience was like being sucked into the tube of an old-fashioned kaleidoscope, twisted and tumbled and bashed about as the colours changed. Spat out goggle-eyed and gaping, I screeched the marker gleefully over the last day on the calendar and fled home, skinny, jumpy and gasping for clean air and water.

Back on familiar turf, though, the tumbling continued in a torrent of tales and anecdotes to my friends and family, the latter of whom just HAD TO SEE THIS PLACE.

So off we set at the end of that that selfsame year to Goa, which only whet the appetite for further explorations in this exhilarating country. Aside from this trip with two of our three children, the others have all been with my dear husband, Arnie. Do beware, then, if you intend to go: you might hate it and cringe back into your hotel at the first clamour of the crowds or goat's head hanging in a butcher's stall with its brain enhancing the display. But chances are the incense will get to you, or the accents or some unnameable alchemy and, like us, you'll be magnetised back there for no clear reason at all.

1
Of Grace and Gurus

THE GURU WAS IN a mood. 'YOU ARE ALL DONKEYS!' he roared. 'YOU ARE ALL STUPID!' His dentures might have done a little dance then, but without my sweat-slippery specs I couldn't be sure. 'WHAT ARE YOU DOING IN THIS HALL? ARE YOU BEGINNERS? HAVE YOU COME TO WASTE OUR TIME HERE? LOOK AT THIS DONKEY HERE!'

And with that I turned and beheld, if a tad fuzzily, the enlightened hand of Mr BKS Iyengar himself shoot out and grab a slender white British arm, yanking its owner off balance so that she stumbled, thumping down on to her bony bum with one regulation bloomer leg riding up above the other.

'YOU ARE A DONKEY!' he thundered into her pale and blinking face. She didn't look like a donkey to me. She looked like a trimmed Titian beauty with flowing tresses clasped modestly at the nape. 'YOU ARE STUPID! WHY DID YOU NOT LISTEN TO THE INSTRUCTIONS?' Her mouth opened and closed like a baby bird's beak as he bellowed on about 'YOU PEOPLE!' and to a rational adult we froze and shrivelled under the frown of his electrified eyebrows.

The tirade continued for some time with the skew-bloomered woman trying over and over to perfect the pose, her increasingly violent trembling throwing her off balance. There was some rough handling by the guru on the way to the non-result at the end of it, with sharp slaps to her thighs, to her butt, a bit of pushing and pulling here and there to "awaken" the offending parts, until completely distraught, she began to cry, unleashing a further crash of fire and brimstone from some elevation beyond my view. Maybe it was just the myopia.

When the rest of us donkeys attempted whatever it was we were supposed to attempt (I never did quite get it), waves of vocal contempt broke over us, the assistant teachers all flapping about wild eyed and terrified. And so the class proceeded to its end, when more than a hundred stupid donkeys loaded with bolsters, blankets and other yoga props all followed each other dumbly back to the equipment area, trying to squeeze through its portal ahead of each other.

'WELL, THAT WAS uplifting!' I ventured by way of levity back on the street with my companion, Earth Warrior, breathing what felt relatively like fresh air – even if of the urban Indian variety. There a sane and friendly coconut wallah stood at his barrow selling decapitated coconuts and straws to the thirsty students. 'He could double his sales,' I added brightly, 'with a shot of spirits for the spiritual. Look around. Who wouldn't buy one?'

But Earth was having none of it. 'You really are Jewish,' she blurted – relevantly – adding that my aversion was all clearly my ego's problem and my business idea my ethnicity's. And if I couldn't appreciate the yoga institute, I should just go home.

Now there was a plan! I just wanted to hang around long enough to follow the guru's lead and slap her, but remembered his teaching on the true yogi's equipoise and opted for that in the moment.

And so I stayed. It had to get better. And, besides, I was instantly addicted to the juice of decapitated coconuts.

SO IF IT'S spiritual growth you're after in the bosom of Mother India, go ahead. Cautiously. Leaving all preconceptions at home. All expectations. Guarding your brain against washing, your spirit against egos lurking in well-worshipped sages and your sane and worthy self against anyone who dares to deny its existence. If you want to explore spiritual India, there'll be an ashram or a guru, a holy river or a charlatan waiting for you around every corner.

So be discerning. If it gets too creepy or too overwhelming, *leave* and never believe that anyone cares more about your well-being, sanity, safety or dignity than you do.

Researching your journey, you'll find ample examples of seekers who've reached states of ecstasy in the presence of a holy man or woman – sometimes from the effects, I swear, of hyperventilating during so-called breathing exercises. If you dig a bit deeper you'll also hear tales of trauma and even psychosis after a thorough brainwashing by some quack in a saffron robe spouting his or her version of The Imperative Path to Enlightenment. Obviously every journey is different and the seeker also adds her own experiences and expectations to the mix.

After all, you come to India from somewhere and those elsewhere roots, I discovered, run deep and can't be denied. The vision invariably on a journey like this is that you'll traverse a spiritual incline between A and B. India, more than any other place I've visited, has a way of twisting weird zigs and zags into any planned route, which ultimately might hardly resemble the one you envisaged and might never take you to B.

My journey to India in 2006 was nothing less than a *trip*. There were two trips to be precise, the second in 2010, but the first proved of incomparable shock value for my rupees. The deal was that I would travel to the Iyengar Yoga Institute in Pune for a month of yoga. Its official name is The Ramamani Iyengar Memorial Yoga Institute with the inestimable, inimitable, internationally renowned Mr BKS Iyengar having presided at its centre before his death in 2014.

The institute sits in all its octagonal uniqueness in the city of Pune, about one-hundred and fifty kilometres south-east of Mumbai. It is a city of about five-million people, malodorous air, an adulterated river confluence, choking traffic and profuse flourishings of garbage on public display. It did once possess some edifying features, but these have mostly been neglected or destroyed amid the construction of cubes stretched skywards in aspirational facelessness. Without its citizens, then, bustling about with sunny busyness, the city might with reasonable generosity be described as a dump.

That, however, was the least of my problems.

My travel companion, introduced earlier as Earth Warrior, had requested to travel with me on my planned solo journey. She was a fiery sort from my local yoga studio, scrawny and rugged with blazing blue eyes and gravely green principles. I had my doubts about spending a month so close to such volcanic nobility accessorised by a Swiss army

Way out in India

knife, but she seemed sorely in need of company and had done the trip before, which reassured me in a wussy kind of way.

There were previews, admittedly, to the scenes that were to play out between us in Pune, namely some unbridled berating about the cost of the visa company I'd chosen for us in those days of naivety, her muttering about the price of airport coffee on departure day, her disapproval of the disposable cups that contained it and her disturbingly passionate smooching of her partner on the airport concourse.

Our point of entry being Mumbai, we shuffled into its airport at 2:00 am, cheek by jowl with the burgeoning population of India, which also shuffled along in the darkness on the roads. Weaving as well as possible in our taxi between the huge, decorated trucks that ply the road bumper to bumper through the night we trundled along, pointing at the "Horn Please" requests on their tail ends in curly, colourful scripts – to which all oblige, liberally.

Such exhilaration I'd seldom felt before. With plumes of diesel smoke billowing through the windows and my face gleaming sweatily, I grinned at Earth Warrior and stated the obvious: 'We made it!'

She, thrilled at the prospect of a month in the smelly embrace of India, turned beatifically to me for a robust high five. 'Let's go, Sister!' The diesel fumes, strangely, didn't seem to bother her. Neither did the spectral cows that rose skeletally from the darkness at intervals. All along the highway, for that was what it had been at the design stage over a decade before, people traded at snack food stalls, chai stalls and who knew what else stalls? What could people be trading in at three in the morning on the side of an overburdened highway?

This place, this India, didn't seem to sleep and no wonder. A hit of that ginger and sugar in a thimbleful of chai at the roadside could keep even the weariest bouncing through the night, I discovered two hours later.

The only person who seemed to have slept was the hotel's nightwatchman, tooted awake with the rest of the neighbourhood by our driver at dawn. He's a common character in India, the nightwatchman, although he does not actually watch anything. Usually regarded as a low-born fellow, he sleeps on a mat at the entrance to the lodgings, but remains on call for any nocturnal arrivals, departures, lost keys or burst water pipes.

Of Grace and Gurus

'Good night,' I grinned at Earth Warrior as the sun rose and she set up a photo gallery of her beloved on her room's windowsill. Then I backed out of the door to sort of tap-trance down the hotel's echoing passage to my little sanctuary labelled Room 109.

'Passport, please!' a voice intruded into my dream. 'Passport, please!' What? What's the deal?

Just a tip: In India you seldom know what the deal is or when one will detonate. And no amount of freaking out or protesting will make it go away.

This particular deal is a common one for foreigners. It straddles the government's vigilance against infiltrators and Western yoga students; and its penchant for gratuitous manual administration. The former is understandable in terms of the terrorism that has visited India, but the latter speaks to the national devotion to Filling up the Form. It ranks second only to cricket. It's an art form, Filling up the Form. It arises at the most unlikely moments and always in duplicate or triplicate on flimsy paper designed to puncture at the touch of a pen.

Authority in India is another art form, and these two intersect at the point where pen meets puncture and begins to quiver. An integral part of the art of Filling up the Form is the plenitude of questions usually covering murky aspects of one's life, such as whether one might fancy a trip to Jammu or Kashmir, or what one's mother cooked for Sunday lunch in April '64. They're as tricky as the filmy paper they're written on and might well trip one up on a train station platform as the train pulls out.

A bristle of the brows behind the ticket counter on perusal of the ticket-purchasing form, a twitch of the moustache at the ballpoint bullseye might have such consequences. One might even be booted off a Land Rover in a tiger reserve due to the fuzzy brain induced by the vehicle's lack of suspension and writing surfaces, along with wild animals lurking nearby as one bounces off on safari in the dust, form flapping blithely in one's lap.

Blasted from a light sleep with senses primed, I filled out the form, handed it to the receptionist, Dinesh, and thumped back into my bed. But no sooner had the elusive waves of slumber begun to wash in, than a yell pierced the twittering morning. It was a nasal yell, sharp and

Way out in India

desperate, like a sheep's on its way to the heavenly pasture.

I shot to the vertical, convinced that someone had omitted something from The Form and was now keening madly on the pavement for it. But then it came again, more loudly this time, more insistently. On it whined, on and on, until lightly clad in a towel, I emerged on to the room's dusty balcony to spy a man on a bicycle beneath my window in the grounds of the block of flats next door, wailing his head off, while housewives scurried out in their saris towards him.

It turned out he was selling something from a basket in front of his handlebars. A softish white substance it seemed, covered in paper in a hessian cloth and between bleats he displayed samples, tucked rupees into his pocket and cut chunks off for the ladies to buy. I tuned in more closely. 'Pan-e-er! Pan-e-e-r!' was his word and then one plump young woman, her rolls bobbing buoyantly under her sari blouse, noticed me in the towel, grinned up and said 'Cheese!' followed by a gesture that could only mean 'Wrap up, girl! This is India!'

Scratching my head I ducked inside. Wrap up? But wasn't her midriff on shameless display, even to the paneer wallah? Mine certainly wasn't.

'MIDRIFFS ARE NOT a problem here!' Earth Warrior snapped as we strolled through a nearby park on our way to the yoga institute later. Well, I strolled. She marched. We were not in step.

'So where's the problem then?' I panted.

'Armpits. They don't like armpits here. Or upper arms. So I hope you brought some T-shirts with sleeves for classes.'

I had, by virtue of my early training. Synagogue had always meant sleeves, as had any other place of potential modesty.

SO, YES, I am Jewish. Yes, I respect the orthodox who wish to practise their Judaism to the black-coated letter. Yes, I have tried that route myself but turned around on realising that I was standing on an essential foundation of fear. And, yes, my ultimate purpose in coming to Pune was spiritual.

I was unprepared, though, for the depths of my Jewish roots and my intolerance for bullshit. It took the month exploring such matters in India to differentiate between the two.

I was, however, more interested in the body-mind *route* to spiritual progress than in the attainment of any spiritual goal. I'd watched my own life shift and change with the elasticity I'd gained through yoga practice, the stamina, the balance and the strength. I'd seen it in my students, too, because along the way I'd undergone the system's teacher training and qualified after three years to set up my own studio. Every physical change had brought corresponding shifts in their counterparts mentally, emotionally and practically. It was a fascinating journey.

Intrigued enough to follow it to its source, I'd decided to go to Pune. Aware of what I might find there but unsure of what I would, I ventured forth nevertheless with Earth Warrior, her presence as my travelling companion being the first surprise and challenge of the trip.

To understand a journey to this place, one has to know that admission to it is not that easy. With this style of yoga being strict, the conditions for acceptance demand dedication and constant practice, and usually indicate an intense level of commitment to the teachings of Mr Iyengar.

The problems began for me soon after my arrival on realising that another contract unsigned by anyone demanded another commitment – to Mr Iyengar himself. All over the world he is regarded as a guru. With his exceptionally refined and extensive medical knowledge he gained the utmost respect internationally, earning honorary doctorates from renowned universities in the East and West. He was also well known for having plumbed the depths of the human soul during his many decades on Earth and to thousands of his followers around the globe he was an enlightened being.

Well, yes. I got that bit. But, to be frank, I don't *do* enlightened beings. Why? Because who is qualified to judge whether anyone is enlightened or not? The enlightee? His mentor? His disciples? I rest my case.

What I do understand is that anyone half-human, revered repeatedly as enlightened, might be tempted to concur after a time. I withheld my judgement about Mr Iyengar and waited eagerly to see him. I'd had some introduction to him via tales of students who'd visited the institute and survived. He was, they'd said, a hard taskmaster. He used unusual methods to keep students focused. Such as? Well he hit and kicked them

Way out in India

a bit. Ooh, that was heartening. And, oh, he was a bit of a tyrant with a bit of a temper. Hmmm. That was all appealing enough, but apparently his son and daughter, who had taken over most of the institute's teaching, were no different. I couldn't wait for classes to start.

Rearing to leap backwards if necessary, I donned my modestly sleeved T-shirt and set off on that arrhythmic jaunt across the park from our hotel with Earth Warrior for our first class. The fact that I refused to wear the regulation bloomers for the event like a British schoolgirl from a 1940s high-school gym, settled like a stone on her. She sallied forth sporting her trim and hairy legs into the line that spiralled up the staircase to the practice hall on our first day.

The line murmured with apprehension, the walls above the staircase crowded with certificates and citations lauding Mr Iyengar through the decades. I did wonder why they had to be there and not on his lounge walls at home or down the domestic passage. Why did such an enlightened being need to shove in one's face the fact that so many had found him enlightened? I didn't say that to Earth Warrior, though. She was even more bristly than the hairs on her legs.

No one else seemed to think about it. There were honeyed American voices dripping: 'I'm SO happy de be heeeere!' and Indian scarves draped around Western throats and hearts pulsing their way into the mood.

Mine were the exception. I felt queasy. Perhaps it was all that sweet incense wafting from the shrines in various niches. Finally, the line started to move as the previous class exited the hall. Then pandemonium broke out.

The architectural point about this institute is that it was built in the 1970s when Mr Iyengar was beginning to make a name for himself. As a long-pursued institute of his own, it was a major achievement, sparkling in its octagonal glory in a part of town called – tam te daaa! – Model Colony. In this tranquil upmarket suburb full of the ultra-modern phenomenon, the apartment block, billboards on plots ready for construction promised "No Slums in Sight!"

India encroached gradually on Model Colony, however, turning it into a contemporary urban warren where the traffic spews black soot on to the buildings and blares, toots and honks its racket and dirt into the institute's famous practice hall.

Now, also, hordes of students worldwide apply to study at this place, which has proved itself to be only so elastic. It was marginally expanded at some point, but the demand has just kept growing, leaving it straining at its original green bathroom tiles on the walls when class is in progress. Mats at times have to overlap to accommodate the hundred and more who practise in a space meant for fifty. The chronically grubby equipment is kept behind a storage wall with an entrance to the area a little wider than a door frame. So every time a teacher calls for equipment, a stampede ensues as the yogic faithful shove each other out of the way in a frantic reach for, say, a blanket.

This is most fun in the hot months when sweat and curry fumes combine with diesel and incense in a heady blend that can transport one to enlightenment in seconds. And the game only reaches its zenith when one returns to one's mat to find someone else sitting there in the lotus position with the tranquillity of a frog on a lily pad. Then there's nothing to be done there. The instructions start flying through a scratchy microphone from the marble platform at the front of the class. The only course of action is to seize whatever mat is empty and adopt the frog-on-the-lily-pad pose oneself.

So back to the pandemonium that broke out before the first class of our month at the institute: it took more or less the aforementioned form, with newbies like myself learning the drill instantly. Those who landed up at the back of the octagon risked finding themselves staring at a pillar, while someone's hairy toes or horny elbows encroached on their focus and their mats. Ancient overhead speakers distorted the accented English, all in the absence of visual cues, available strictly to those beyond and between the multiple pillars. Hence the stampede.

The hall hushed into successive waves of silence as Mr Iyengar sauntered in. No shuffling for this octogenarian, as he was at the time. As his long creamy robe shushed along the flagstones and his eyes shaded by shaggy eyebrows scanned the hall, disciples in bloomers began lurching forward to fall at his feet, to touch the floor before them with head and hands. The most extreme among them prostrated themselves completely while Mr Iyengar greeted the devoted with a namaskar and his long, silver hair glinting in the white neon light of the practice hall.

Well, yes, I thought to myself, glued to my mat as if my bum had grown suction cups. It had nothing to do with yoga, this stillness. It was merely a form of camouflage. And a determined self-preservation.

Then suddenly the class was in progress, the introductory chants done, the heat rising along with the press of traffic outside. Mr Iyengar's daughter, Sunita, taught. Like his other children, she was in her sixties and, let's say, well fed. Her bloomers bloomed with impressive tremors as she plodded among us and her voice carried stridently through the hall. As always, Mr Iyengar took up his position in his accustomed area of the octagon and kept a wary eye on the progress of the class.

The poses were simple. The approaches to them were not. The whole Iyengar system revolves around precision, alignment and the intelligence penetrating throughout the body to awaken each cell into consciousness. Not so easy. The microphones crackled and the traffic distracted. The light without one's slidey specs was murky. The repeated interjections by Mr Iyengar ruffled the flow until the dedicated, the devoted, the athletic and the experienced were found universally lacking and the guru erupted into that donkey-laden vitriol, the first words I ever heard live from him.

HALFWAY THROUGH THE park after class I jogged a step or two up to Earth Warrior.

'So just explain to me please, Earth, what the deal is with that place. I mean that Iyengar family has a lot of money. More than a hundred students spend several hundred dollars each there every month – and that's just for starters. Surely they could use some resources to create a space that works?

'You know, where people could stretch their arms out in the poses, say? Maybe there could be a working sound system, maybe a functioning equipment room. They could even splash out and create a changing room. Just think, it could have more than one toilet! With a working lock on its door! I'm just wondering if air con would be beyond the budget and computers and things like…'

'You really are a Jewish princess, aren't you?' Earth's voice dripped as much disgust as if I'd thrown up on her.

'…a schedule of fees in a nice frame on the reception wall.' She quickened her pace, leaving me calling after her. 'Hey, Earth, I'm unique – the only stupid Jewish donkey princess the world has ever known.'

She spun around, glared at me and strode off across the road outside the park, leaving me and my ineptitude to negotiate the crossing in my own misguided way.

Back at the hotel I marched up the stairs, swung around the corner of the stone corridor and almost collided with the scrawny, buck-toothed cleaning man in his khaki uniform.

'Oops!' I blurted. 'Sorry!'

But the man just cowered, retreating his twiggy self deeper into his clothes and staring at me a moment as if expecting a blow – verbal or otherwise.

Was this how it worked in India? Did the fat upper castes intimidate the skinny lower ones into submission? The minute cleaning lady behaved the same way, swishing herself and her little sari aside with downcast eyes whenever I approached.

NOT EVERYTHING WAS bad in Pune, though. Some things were positively brilliant. The rooty smell and the colours of the local housewives in their saris gathered around the vegetable wallah's barrow in the early morning, for example. And the food – oh, the food in that vegetarian paradise! Every dish was a plunge into aromatic heaven, with pillowy bowls of rice and unimaginably flavoursome curries. From Aloo Ghobi to Zunka Bhakri, every meal was a banquet, alerting the taste buds to unchartered realms of delight.

And the yoga could induce an appetite! With the classes two hours' long and one's own practice another three, plus the walks to the institute and around the area, the need for food grew to a hoovering exigency.

The German Bakery, a major hangout for yoga students and other foreigners, was one place to get it – although there was nothing German about it and its baked goods were middling at best. How German could it be after all, with Himalayan owners who'd be lost in the Alps amid all those strudels and roggenbrots?

It was in an Indian version of an upmarket suburb called Koregaon Park, whose main feature was the Osho Meditation Resort. This world-

Way out in India

famous place is the reincarnation of the former ashram known as Osho Commune International and a magnet for Westerners seeking the Indian Spirichill Experience.

A controversial, charismatic and self-styled guru, Osho lived from the 1930s to 1990 and was also known as Bhagwan Shree Rajneesh. From his original base in Pune he took his teachings to America in the 1980s and immediately became a favourite there, of throngs of seekers and the media who lapped up his brew of Eastern mystical practices laced with dollops of pop psychology and lashings of sex as a recipe for enlightenment.

The commune he established in Oregon soon afterwards aroused widespread suspicion as the nature of its activities became known and Osho's fleet of Rolls-Royces began to grow. He was finally deported on charges of immigration fraud and fined hundreds of thousands of dollars. Like Moses trying to lead his people to the Promised Land, he led his followers to more than twenty countries, which refused them entry, until at last he arrived back where he'd started: in Pune at his old ashram. The difference was this time, that hordes of foreign devotees began to converge on the place to listen to him speak and to meditate with him.

Although he died more than twenty years ago, the demand for his teachings is as brisk as ever, their popularity no doubt bolstered by the advocation of "free love" in buckets, a favourite recreational activity at the reincarnated ashram. This evolved into the Osho Meditation Resort in 2002, with nary a hint of irony, when an imposing auditorium was built in the generous grounds of the complex to accommodate the evening gatherings. In line with Osho's teachings related to universal abundance, the place is the last word in beauty and luxury, with prices to match. The resort part comes complete with "zennis" courts, a swimming pool, basketball courts, a beauty salon and a boutiquey guest house.

The meditation part comes in the morning and evening, with suitably coloured robes for each. Thus the parade of odd-looking Westerners swanning about the area surrounding the resort, robed either in maroon in the mornings or white in the evenings, when a kind of meditative dance takes place in the auditorium. One of the meditation techniques advocated by Osho was mind clearing through physical activity. Hence a lot of berobed jumping about takes place during the meditation sessions, or dancing, with accompanying cathartic vocalisations, to wit: 'Hoo hoo!'

Imagine a sleek, modern pyramid-shaped hall with up to five-thousand people bouncing around in maroon or spinning like dervishes, all bellowing 'Hoo hoo!' in an effort to purge the emotional toxins.

It's a far cry from the lone meditator sitting by a stream on a rock surrounded by lush foliage. At the Osho complex this is available, too, in its enormous landscaped park-garden. In fact, there's little that isn't available here, from t'ai chi to fencing to gourmet food, to art, to night-time shows and dancing. It's a world apart. You can visit it for a fee just to have a look around, but the first time I tried that the young man behind the reception desk invited me to lunch with him. He was young enough to be my son, so I turned with a polite refusal to stride down the road. The moment the experience tilted to creepy was when I glanced to my right to find him jogging beside me, still insisting on lunch together.

'There's a place for good thali, Madam, just over there!'

My sandals transformed into trainers on the spot, transporting me at speed across the multiple lanes of traffic and into the crowds.

A strange place it is, this meditation resort, attracting all kinds of people. During my first stay in Pune I met two old American women in separate situations who'd lived there, worked there to earn their keep and left there, penniless after thirty years apiece when they could work no longer.

I met some Israeli travellers, too, who liked the level of resort luxury that they couldn't afford elsewhere. And then there were the weirdos – and plenty of them, too. They'd hang around at the German Bakery across the road from "the Osho place" attired in their maroon robes, eating hamburgers and engrossed in their laptops or cellphones. Speaking to a few of them, it dawned on me that when parents spoke about their children going off to India to find themselves, this was where they might land up. It made me shiver.

On our third day in India, Earth Warrior insisted on breakfasting at the German Bakery. So off we set in a black and yellow tuk-tuk across town for the experience. The tuk-tuk itself is an experience, in essence a mildly powered motor tricycle with a body that seats the driver in front and a maximum of three passengers (theoretically) behind him.

Way out in India

It's a doorless contraption designed for short rides and easy access. In Pune it's usually a tad infirm, rackety, rickety and has been known to feature a view of the road through a hole in its floor rusted around the handbrake. Tuk-tuks swarm around India as a cheap and easy mode of public transport that takes you precisely, and sometimes imprecisely, to your destination – ours, thankfully, being the well-known German Bakery that day.

And *that* was a ride! The tuk-tuk began to ruffle my feathers when it magnetised towards every other vehicle on the road. Then, as if the magnetism repelled at the last moment, it swerved dramatically towards someone else. Its bouncing challenged even my armour-plated sports bras to a painful degree and as if gasping in fright wasn't enough at every turn of the twenty-minute journey, I was gasping the grey gunk that passes for air in Pune.

Then there was the matter of the little street urchins turning themselves inside out at the traffic lights where the traffic only stops if it backs up – which it does all the time. Otherwise there are no lanes, no rules, only a cacophonic traffic dance whose rhythm only the locals can hear. And amid this veering, lurching mob, the grey-faced street urchins performed their circus tricks from sunup to a surely leaden exhaustion at sundown.

With matted hair and robot eyes, they'd juggle a few battered balls and drop backwards into arches from which they'd rise up on to their bare little feet again. They'd fold themselves in half and wriggle through tiny hoops in heartbreaking monotony, before clustering their fingertips to touch their empty stomachs in the universal Indian gesture of hunger.

Their tricks, however, also extended to reaching their fragile yet agile arms into the tuk-tuks of foreign women in the direction of bags and purses, sometimes inducing a fishwife screech and a slap from a flabbergasted initiate heading for the German Bakery.

'You don't have to scream at them, you know,' Earth Warrior enlightened me. But it was too late. I'd revealed my hysteria, a more extreme version of it for the lack of blood sugar caused in part by her unpredictable start to the morning, and, in more minor ways, by oxygen deprivation and a credit card almost bound, with a passport, for an impromptu tour of Pune.

The German Bakery for all its fame was a nondescript place that buzzed inside, nevertheless. Among the Osho followers there were all kinds of patrons, notably students of all stripes. Attending one or the other of Pune's educational institutions, they'd come to this Oxford of the East, as it's known, for the quality of education there.

By the time we reached there I could have golloped a dozen pastries, but Earth Warrior had other ideas. She was going shopping. At a hippie heaven upstairs, with handmade paper, Tibetan singing bowls, enough incense to suffocate a herd of sacred cows and a rainbow of tie-dyed garments hanging just beyond the crystal forest that, she insisted, I just had to see.

I began to stagger behind her, marvelling at this beaded talisman or that mass produced Buddha-on-a-perch when suddenly she spun around, eyes aflame.

'You don't have to follow me everywhere, you know!'

BINGO! My signal to fly down the stairs, order a main, a side, a Himalayan version of apple strudel, a lassi and whatever else the kitchen could provide.

But carrying my tray around the place, I found every seat taken. Every seat that was, except for one at a table beside a dusky man of about my own age with long, frizzy hair, smoking.

Ignoring the shower of nicotine seasoning as gallantly as I could, I scoffed the sustenance like a tuk-tuk chewing up roadway. In mid-munch the dusky man turned to me.

'Is my smoke bothering you?' His voice was husky and he raised an eyebrow as he turned away to blow out a stream of smoke.

Huh? Something guttural about his accent threw me off balance: 'Is my smoke baddaghing you?'

He must have taken my quizzical silence as a yes, stubbing his cigarette out and turning back to me.

'Where are you from, by the way?'

'South Africa. You?'

'Originally Israel. Oghiginally Isghael. But I've been here a long time. Ten years.'

HALLELUJAH! HE'S FROM MY TRIBE! I could have shrieked across that German expanse. I could also have hugged him on the spot,

Way out in India

so familiar and comforting was that accent to me.

'So what are you doing here?'

I explained my yoga quest, whereupon ensued a discourse on (a) the illusory art of guru worship and (b) the complicated business of religion. He'd done it all, a pious Jewish background, rebellion, swamis, sadhus, saints and gurus and left it all behind, save the essence of spirituality outside any rigid form coupled with some of the practices of Judaism – for their beauty.

'By the way,' I offered, 'I'm also Jewish.'

He pushed the ashtray away to examine me more closely, my green eyes and brunette hair, my longish limbs and neat Anglo-Saxon ear studs. 'So from where are your grandparents?'

'Great grandparents. Lithuania.'

'Ah, so you are African. But you speak Yiddish?'

'A few words.'

It struck me then on my seat at the German bakery owned by Nepalese, trading Yiddish insults with an Israeli and laughing, that my agenda and I were parting company.

'Oh and there's my friend.' Which may have been an overstatement to describe the glitter-eyed figure in teenage boy shorts a few metres away from us, gripping a tray with white knuckles and glaring at me, before huffing off to attend at last to her own hypoglycaemia.

'She is your friend?' He stared after Earth Warrior and shook his curly mane.

'Well – ah, we're travelling together.'

'She's very angry, that girl.'

And it was only day three.

He turned back towards me. 'Can I ask you a question?'

Oh dear. 'Sure.'

'Do you know that tomorrow is Yom Kippur?'

I did, I confess. I did know that the next day would be the holiest day of the Jewish calendar. But I'd assumed I'd excuse myself from the twenty-five-hour fast, being immersed as I would in similarly beneficial practices at the yoga institute. Anything would have been preferable to forgoing food and drink completely in that heat sans oxygen so far away from home.

That was not to be, however. The next day was a public holiday, I learned from him. So there'd be no practice at the institute, spiritual or otherwise.

'Yes, I did know about Yom Kippur.'

He threw up a pair of welcoming hands then. 'Well you must come to the Bet Knesset tomorrow then.'

The synagogue? Holy Whoever! 'What's a Bet Knesset doing here in India? Where is it?'

The man sipped his coffee, smiling. 'You don't know? India has had Jews here for centuries. Thousands of years, in fact. Some have been here since the Kingdom of Yehudah – Judah.'

My head buzzed. As far as I'd been taught, Judaism had been peopled primarily by robed biblical figures in the Middle East, followed by black-coated Ashkenazis from Russia, from Eastern Europe. More sketchily I'd been aware of the Sephardim from Spain and North Africa with their delectable Mediterranean cuisine. It beat our gelatinous gefilte fish hands down.

But now here was this man introducing me to a whole other part of my world.

'What's your name, by the way?'

'Hebrew or English?'

'Hebrew.'

'Me'ira.'

'Ah – Giver of Light.'

'Yours?'

'Ariel.'

'Lion of God.'

We shook hands before he hailed the waiter for another coffee.

'You know, Me'ira, the Jews here were mostly very rich. They never had problems with anti-Semitism. And many times in their history, here, they were very close to the rulers and the princes.'

I took a sip of lassi, not knowing what to ask first. 'So what did they do here?'

'What do Jews do everywhere?' he shrugged.

'Buy and sell.'

'Of course. They were traders. Some came here running from the

Way out in India

Spanish, eh…'

'Inquisition?'

He nodded. 'They had good relationships with Europe. They traded in spices, especially pepper. Very expensive, pepper – like gold. And then the others, they came from Iraq in maybe sixteen-something, seventeen-something. They were also running from anti-Semitism. Do you know, they spoke Arabic?'

'I didn't know they existed.'

'Come on, Me'ira. Haven't you heard of the Sassoon family?'

'Vidal Sassoon?'

'Who?'

'Vidal Sassoon. He was a famous hairdresser in London in the seventies or so. Very rich. Hairdresser to the stars…'

Ariel shook his curls. 'Does it look like I know any hairdressers? Anyway the Sassoons of Bombay left India after Independence. They were afraid of persecution and communism at that time. Virtually the whole community left. Over some time, of course.'

'But there are enough to keep the Bet Knesset running?'

'Well,' he said as we sipped our coffee, 'yes. But the community is very small now, nothing like before. These Iraqi Jews – they were called Baghdadi Jews – were so, so rich, you could not imagine it. They used to trade in textiles also and you know what else?'

I shook my head.

'Opium.'

My cup wobbled a bit as I set it down. 'Opium?'

'So much opium – to the Chinese. The thing was that the Iraqi Jews used a lot of opium money to build things.'

'What things?'

'Schools, hospitals, the houses for the children without parents.'

'Orphanages.'

'And many Bet Knessets. The one here in Pune is the biggest one in Asia – outside Israel, of course.'

'So is that where you go for Yom Kippur?'

He shook his head. 'Nah. The Bet Knesset where we will go is the Lubavitcher one. You know the Lubavitch?'

'Of course. Everyone knows them.'

The synagogue that Ariel was referring to was an American-Israeli transplant, established next door to the Osho Meditation Resort in true Lubavitcher style, to mop up any spiritually seeking Jews who might have lost their way and called in for help from their own tribe.

'But even so,' I frowned, 'I'm not crossing that road to get to any Bet Knesset.'

He tilted his cigarette box on the table thoughtfully. 'It's no problem. You cross like a cow. The cow doesn't look. It just walks.'

That was encouraging. And preferable to spending the public holiday with Earth Warrior. She'd fumed lavishly on the way home about the outrageous irresponsibility of picking up Indian men in restaurants, especially since I was married. And on my first day out! What else was I planning to do?

'He's not Indian,' I smiled. 'He's Israeli. And I'm going to spend tomorrow fasting at the synagogue, where he'll be waiting for me.'

That shut her up for a bit.

THE SYNAGOGUE ITSELF was a house, large and once white, but otherwise nondescript, with two little boys playing in the gravel driveway with their *payyot* swinging along their cheeks in the sunshine. Ariel was leaning against the gatepost waiting for me, clean shaven and spruce, with his locks caught in a ponytail and a *kippah* perched on his crown.

'*Chag sameach*,' he greeted me solemnly. 'You are in the right place.'

'I know.'

Since Yom Kippur entails a full day of prayer, the service was already in progress when I arrived. It transported me instantly back to my childhood synagogue and almost every other one I'd attended since then. It followed the Ashkenazi tradition from Eastern Europe and Russia, which tends towards significant uniformity in the order of the service and the tunes to which prayers are chanted or sung – throughout the world, evidently.

The chairs were white plastic, the floors white tiles and the rabbi's wife layered in white cotton from head to foot in the Yom Kippur tradition of purity, with a kind and welcoming smile for me. The other women ranged from tanned Israeli travellers, young and carefree, to the

Way out in India

old lady mentioned previously, who'd spent her adulthood immersed in Osho's ashram. In between there were some corporate wives from Israel visiting their husbands, who were in the IT field. There were Jewish students too, hippies and tourists. They'd all stopped their lives for a day whose theme was forgiveness sought and bestowed through reflection, prayer and fasting.

So mine were not the only Jewish roots that ran so deep beneath the secular surface, I nodded to myself, looking around.

It was hot in that place that served as a community centre and the rabbi's house. In the break between services Ariel met me outside the door.

'So what do you want to do now, Me'ira?'

Aside from food and drink, my craving was for a cool green space in all that grimy murk. I'd heard of the Osho estate's enormous park, along with public access to it being restricted to the late afternoon and early morning. The rest of the time it was open only to those with a "meditation pass".

'No problem,' Ariel shrugged. 'Come with me.'

After a short tuk-tuk ride we arrived at the gate of the park.

'What now?'

He pointed a finger into the air. 'I talk. You don't talk.'

'But how will we get in without a meditation pass?'

'Me'ira.' He thrust his chin towards me. 'Your skin colour is meditation pass.'

As we approached the gate the guard glanced at me, his moustache bristling with authority, his hand extended with its pearly ring glinting on his baby finger. I felt a muscle twitch in my jaw.

'Meditation pass.' His gaze slid towards Ariel who gestured to me. I shrugged.

'She left them at the resort.'

And sure enough the gate swung open without a Form to Fill Up and a stretch of green expanded before us like an endless inhalation. Here and there under the trees lounged groups of Osho-ites, chatting, reading, dozing and every now and then one would appear as still as midday, sitting cross-legged in silent meditation.

We wandered slowly through that verdant heaven, tempered by the sun and the kind of clear emptiness that fasting can induce. I'm sure the hit of oxygen also played with my mental state, a stunned stupor after the experiences of the previous few days. At last we came to rest on a bench under a mango tree. But then the flies came, in swarms.

'Do you want to go back to my house rather?' Ariel smiled.

Well. I wasn't sure. I had no point of reference for this kind of thing. But one fly too many landed on my nose and that was that.

'I live on a balcony,' he said as we flagged down a tuk-tuk. 'It's really beautiful and the others there are good people, you will see.'

Others? That was reassuring.

VILLA LAXMI, WITH its knee-high grass and a cannon rusting in its front garden, was a sagging mansion housing one of the most unique homes I've ever encountered – Ariel's balcony. Round the side of the villa we creaked up a staircase and landed on the first floor where an ancient locked door led to a small lobby off which led other rooms. From one direction the floating fragrance of earth signalled sandalwood soap and the presence of a bathroom. Its floors were of marble and its doorknob of brass. Then Ariel opened another antique door and suddenly we were in his balcony home.

It stretched the length of one-quarter of the courtyard that it overlooked and, at its opposite end, led to a flat part of the mansion's roof. There an outdoor kitchen had been built. The sun warmed the concrete counter which smelled faintly of cumin.

Another bathroom served this balcony, as well as some sort of slapped-together aerie on a higher part of the roof.

'One of my friends stays there, but he's in Israel right now.'

'So the kitchen and bathroom are yours then, for now.'

'Oh, no,' he said. 'Everybody uses them.'

I wondered who everybody was and where they might be, presently.

'A lot of Israelis stay here,' he explained. 'Some of us have been here for a long time, but there are always others coming and going. You'll meet them.'

We were standing at the doorway to the outdoor kitchen, where the pantry stood, splendidly wood-panelled, open and redolent of rose

Way out in India

water and cardamom. Studying the panelling, I realised that it was not a pantry at all, but had been built as a lift, no doubt to ferry the original owners of the mansion one mere storey upwards to the cooler air and shade of this balcony.

I wondered aloud about these former residents who'd lived in such luxury and named their villa after the Hindu goddess of wealth.

'Yeah,' Ariel sighed. 'Now it's for poor people. Maybe fifty, sixty of us live here. Some rent one room, some rent small apartments like this one. The Indians have a lot of people living in one room.'

And sure enough, glancing over the balcony to the rooms on the opposite side of the courtyard, a tumble of children and their grandmother squeezed out of one of them to gather round the outdoor tap while the old lady bunched her sari to fill a large plastic bucket, her grey plait falling almost to the ground.

Along the balcony's ledge Ariel had planted all manner of pot plants, which cast a cool green light over the furnishings. And above the line of the plants, when one sat down as we did then on a pair of cocoony cane chairs, the veil of a neem tree softened some of the afternoon sun.

I remember talking to Ariel about his family quietly and one of his friends breezing through with a pile of books and a "shalom" once or twice. I think I remember Bob Marley being mentioned as Ariel's ultimate guru of choice, but I don't remember dozing off.

When I woke up into the dimmer light of sunset I couldn't remember where I was or figure out if I was still dreaming. On peering around I found Ariel nowhere in evidence and for a moment I panicked. Now what?

But soon a whiff of cigarette smoke wafted towards me and his voice croaked from the cooler end of the balcony and over the edge of the magnificent antique four-poster that some of those wealthy former residents had abandoned.

'So you had a good sleep, Me'ira?'

From my vantage point I could make out the lotus pattern painted on its inner canopy that mirrored the lotus carvings at its head and foot. I nodded, a touch sheepishly.

'I would offer you some tea,' he said, rising, 'but the fast is still continuing and it's nearly Ne'ilah.'

Ne'ilah is the closing service of Yom Kippur when it is believed that one's fate for the forthcoming year is sealed finally. Its solemnity is usually magnified by the communal privations of the day, the synagogue filled with pale, sluggish worshippers hungering for food while a faint odour of dehydration hovers in the air.

And after Ne'ilah the storm breaks. The community bursts into joyful song and an exuberant exit and dispersal afterwards.

'Me'ira! Me'ira!' Ariel called to me over the heads of the crowd, lest I disappear back to Yogaland like a Jewish Cinderella. 'We will go to meet the others at the bakery!'

The German Bakery had some longer tables down one of its walls where the group gathered. Some were from the villa, the friend with the books from the afternoon, a man named Veda and his Japanese-Brazilian girlfriend who bowed to me. Sarit was a sports coach at a school in Israel, to which she'd emigrated from Russia a few years before. She was staying at the villa for a few months, using it as a base for her travels with Devorah, a nurse from Jerusalem. The two IT men on contract in Pune from Israel were Ilan and Eitan, one from Turkish ancestry, the other Polish. We were quite a mix that night, sharing tea and muffins, since the Ashkenazi tradition and the immediate accessibility of the German Bakery's muffins suggested pastry as a fast-breaker before anything else.

That was just fine with me, smiling and tasting all the flavours shared and passed around. I felt so strangely young then, so safe among these people, my people, despite my firm footing outside the boundaries of strict religious observance. It was as if the religion that bound us had washed over us that day without saturating and sinking us, and had left us all clean and clear in the same way.

ARIEL STOOD BESIDE the tuk-tuk he'd summoned for me after dinner, his smoke mingling with the city fumes.

'You can come to the community centre any night, Me'ira,' he assured me. 'There's always dinner there and table tennis. Sometimes chess. A good argument every night – on any subject you like. No appointment necessary.'

I sighed as the tuk-tuk puttered away. A sanctuary in all that chaos.

Way out in India

BACK AT THE hotel Earth Warrior was waiting for me, thumping on my door the moment I arrived.

'You'll have to watch it with those Israelis of yours!' she glowered. 'When the yoga gets serious you won't keep up if you go gallivanting around town 'til all hours like you did today.'

I looked at my watch. It was 8:34 pm. Then I looked at her glaring eyes and decided I'd reserve my debating skills for the Jewish Community Centre.

'Thanks for the advice,' I smiled wanly, just yearning for a shower and my unyielding mattress with matching cement pillow.

JUST A NOTE on Indian showers, to get the subject out the way – and bathrooms in general: they are as foreign as can be. That is, unless you're in a fairly upmarket tourist establishment, but even then there are exceptions.

Showers in India have no doors. Or curtains. It's an interesting design flaw whose chief benefits may be a regularly sprayed toilet seat accessorised by unwitting toilet paper droopily moistened at intervals. Depending on design, other advantages may be a thorough spraying of the toiletry shelf with complimentary rusting of aerosol cans. The floor, too, profits from the arrangement, being soaked constantly and entertained perhaps by the half-witted user who lets his pants into a puddle upon the call of nature, slipping, sliding and cursing afterwards about the ordeal of negotiating this procedure.

And Indians don't believe in plugs and therefore in baths. They believe in running water, which I found out at the domestic store down the road from the Pune hotel.

'Do you sell plugs?'

'What is that?'

'Sink plugs. Basin plugs. Bath plugs – to stop the water running out when you wash your face in the basin.'

'We do not use that system here.'

'Seriously? Well in that case the big plastic bowl will have to do the job.'

Also, in most Indian bathrooms you'll find a large bucket in the shower, usually of the ten-litre variety. Beside it you'll usually find a little half-litre jug. You'll also invariably find a tap at hip level in addition to the shower head. Indians and Earth Warrior fill the main bucket, soap themselves, then rinse off by dipping the small bucket into its bigger sibling and sloshing the water over their heads. The beauty of this system is its environmental lightness, but it can get cold in winter. The other beauty is that if you're doing your own laundry, the bucket serves the purpose very well.

Of course, when it comes to bathrooms, there's that other question of endless curiosity to Westerners: is it true that Indians… you know?

The short answer is "yes" and, unless you're staying in at least a mid-level hotel, don't expect to find toilet paper within reach. The aforementioned little jug is pressed into service for this function, along with the fingers. Oh, yes. But only of the left hand. The right hand is used for eating and passing items to other people.

Beside the toilet you'll usually find a tap with a pipe running out of it. In many places the pipe has a spray mechanism attached, which then negates the need for the little jug. But sometimes you do wish proprietors had stuck with the jug option, since the spray raises questions about (a) what was sprayed where and (b) why the floor needed to be sprayed into the sort of puddly mess that's been known to creep over the edges of sandals and land one at best stinkily and at worst dangerously in a disgusting splash. If the proprietor is frugal with electricity and the building frugal with toilet windows, as many are, the likelihood of this eventuality rises. (Just a tip for your packing list: bring your own initial roll of toilet paper, a headlamp and a bottle of hand sanitiser.)

The intrigue grows if the toilet happens to be one of the many squat specimens in India. To prepare for ablutive functionality, the best course of action is Achilles tendon stretches well ahead of the trip. And a dedicated sorting out of creaky knees.

This is India after all, home of strange and spicy foods, which have a habit of inducing toiletward sprints at short notice. Of necessity, start practising various necessary moves: the rolling up of the pants move and the dangling of the handbag round the neck move to avoid the aforementioned contact with the slosh on toilet floors. For many places your physical conditioning should also include a practice of prolonged

Way out in India

breath suspension. And in case you're wondering, toilet rolls are available these days at the little kiosks that dot every city, but off the beaten track, you're on your own, mate.

But I digress.

AFTER CLASS IN this early part of our month in India, Earth Warrior would lead me to one or other of her familiar old haunts where the waiters were friendly, the tables grimy plastic and the food transcendent. Within days familiar Western women's faces from the institute would appear at these eateries and soon we began to gather at the bigger tables to share war stories or tales of bliss from our time beyond the hallowed portals of the institute. We shared more ordinary stories, too, since we were only ordinary, but from the outset Earth Warrior shifted uneasily among these women and began to pull away. I enjoyed being with them, breaking naan dripping with butter and passing the dishes around for sharing.

One of these women was Cecily from New York. Cecily was plucky, sixty and tiny and she'd contracted the Pune version of Delhi belly after about three breaths in India. Cecily had been teaching this style of yoga for three decades and had been practising it for years more, but that made no difference to her status in the Pune hierarchy. She was a mere foot soldier like the rest of us, gravely in need of ego surgery. To address her digestive condition she'd made the mistake of using the "own practice" session on the first morning to follow the prescribed sequence of poses. One of these required a supine position with backward folded shins as well as a bolster to lie on and various other props.

The props of Mr Iyengar are a subject on their own, but suffice it to say that any yoga props used around the world today were probably his idea and design originally. He was ridiculed for using props in the early days and called "The Furniture Guru" for his use, for example, of wooden benches, blocks, wedges of various sizes, canvas straps and the aforementioned bolsters.

It was just such a little wedge that Cecily needed to create alignment in her reposing pose, and she used it as prescribed. Then she lay down, closed her eyes and prepared to allow for some yogic healing.

Of Grace and Gurus

Unbeknown to Cecily though, a "gentleman" had arrived at the institute for private tuition with Mr Iyengar. He must have been quite some honcho of a gentleman, maybe a government minister or the like, since his vehicle, parked outside, was a military one all sploshed with camouflage. Several soldiers with serious weapons and slanted berets attended him outside, while inside Mr Iyengar got busy unknotting him with a gaggle of assistants all pulling his limbs this way and that, while yet another lackey videoed the proceedings.

The gentleman himself seemed entirely disembodied and gazed out of the window to whose grille he was trussed with several of the aforementioned canvas straps in an Iyengar-style effort to straighten him out. I must mention here that there were no bloomers on this god. His kit was dress pants and a dress shirt buttoned to the throat, pressed to a typically Indian crisp, with the customary holey white vest as the under layer.

We'd all been herded away from the gentleman by Administrator Charming, closely corralled by an imaginary line and instructed to continue our individual practices, pretending that they didn't require the extension of limbs.

With Cecily's practice involving only a quiet corner in which to lie, she was oblivious to the manoeuvrings going on in the central area of the hall.

Then, suddenly, low guru growls began to rumble from the gentleman's area. Assistants began to flutter. Where was the little wooden wedge necessary for the gentleman's alignment? Where could it be? Supple brown hands began to fiddle through the shelves of equipment. The guru's shaded gaze panned over the jumble of bodies, until at last it alighted on the little item wedged under Cecily's tiny butt to keep her crooked hip straight.

'THERE IT IS!' he ranted, striding over to Cecily and landing a kick in her butt, whipping her over on her side while she grimaced in pain. 'WHY WERE YOU HIDING IT?'

Huh?

'WHY WERE YOU HIDING THE WEDGE?' he bellowed at her.

I'd been under the distinct impression that all that smacking around was specifically and exclusively for educating parts of the body

Way out in India

that required a few smarting wake-up calls. But this was a different application altogether and I wondered how it might be explained as a teaching tool, or while preaching about the yogic equipoise that had been so thunderously shattered by a missing piece of wood as big as a biscuit.

Of course, there was no answering the guru for Cecily or anyone else. She lay on her back goggle-eyed and clutching her hip while he stood over her barking on as the room froze over again.

I wondered if she'd even understood him, since being bashed out of a meditative state by a bushy-browed guru yelling: 'Vy ver you hiding de vedge?' might not have induced immediate clarity.

The only person in the hall who seemed unaffected by the fracas was the gentleman who, still trussed to the grille, maintained a mien that bespoke either an evolved state of serenity or contemptuous dissociation. It was difficult to tell.

THE SUCCESSION PLAN at the Iyengar Institute has had some hairy times, with Mr Iyengar announcing sometime in the 1990s that he would be teaching less or nor longer. It is whispered that furious rivalries then began in earnest, between his man in Europe and his eldest daughter, Geeta. Geeta Iyengar, or Geetaji as she is respectfully known, is not a woman to be messed with.

Formidable, sharp and severe, stoic, Spartan and pious, she has had an enormous load thrust on her shoulders from a young age. With her mother dying suddenly when she was about thirty, she assumed the Iyengar matriarchal mantle overnight and since then has held that role, in addition to her others as teacher, healer, writer, administrator, housekeeper and who knows what else?

She is not a well woman and never has been. Her start in yoga arose from various serious health issues, which were alleviated by the practice and very early on she committed her life "holy and soully" to yoga. She still wears only white saris and has been single throughout her years. She's known to have inherited her father's fierceness and a good dose of his brilliance, but her interest in women's health has been one of the main jewels in her crown.

So it was with some intrigue and trepidation that I anticipated class with her.

It began on a sweltering evening with a hush spreading over the room as she shuffled in stiffly, clad in a white cotton bathrobe. There was the same falling about to touch her feet among the students as there'd been with the guru and the same flocking of the assistants to her side to help her from her robe, attach her microphone and support her up the few steps to the low marble platform that forms the focus of the practice hall. There she was seated cross-legged on an elaborate arrangement of bolsters and blankets to accommodate her arthritic body.

She was large and imposing as she gazed out slowly over the mass of students, all neatly cross-legged and mesmerised. With her sharp eyes and hooked nose she resembled an eagle. The class began with the usual instructions for quietening the mind and with the chants. Her voice croaked with age and depletion and, at the end of the chant to Patanjali, the "father of yoga", she added: 'Bow down to Lord Patanjali.'

Now hang on! Who was this Patanjali chap to whom we were now supposed to bow down? There was a beautiful statue of him at the front of the class in some dark metal decorated with what appeared to be copper and bronze. We'd always joined our palms and chanted an invocation to him at the beginning of every class, to acknowledge and thank him, as one teacher had explained, for his work on mind, body and language.

As far as I'd understood, he was Sage Patanjali, which was all very well, but which nevertheless had always elicited a slight squirm from me at the moment the chant began. Jews don't use the praying palms gesture at all, so the minimal knee jerk may have had something to do with that. However, I read it as a salute to a learned man of another culture.

But now he'd morphed into Lord Patanjali and we were to "bow down" to him. No.

I asked a few Indians who Patanjali was exactly, but the answer was never clear. One woman said he was a demigod, which made me wonder if I should maybe demi-bow down to him like ballerinas do with demi plies. Another opinion came from one of the top teachers, an American who'd embraced Iyengar yoga about forty years previously in every aspect. Her answer was that if he was a positive force, what was

Way out in India

the difference?

The difference was that I would not follow instructions blindly when it came to spiritual practices and it bothered me that people seemed to have no problem doing so. Maybe we *were* just a bunch of stupid, gullible donkeys after all. Geeta Iyengar seemed to think so.

She addressed us as "them" – which was a tad disconcerting in the beginning, before it began to irk me.

'Some of them have got the back foot turned out. They must turn it in!' she'd urge. 'That madam in the red T-shirt, she must turn the foot in!'

Who was she addressing in this manner and why? The assistant teachers? The hot and heavy air? The other form of address was "you people" – a herd that seemed in Geeta's perception to embody all the ills of the modern Western world, from Attitude to Zero Respect. Funny that. The hundred and more of "us people" comprised Indians and others from continents as diverse as Europe, North America, Asia, Africa and Australasia. We were of all ages and professions, races and religions, too. Among us were parents and grandparents, as well as the very young and supple-bodied. And yet her surpassing intellect seemed oblivious both to our diversity and the whiff of insult puffed into the room by her term of address.

But when the young madam in the 1940s gym ensemble turned the foot the wrong way, then Geeta swooped in like the eagle she so resembled.

'The young madam in the blue bloomers,' she yelled and began to cough. 'Stand up.'

A beautiful young Indian woman rose amid the mass of seated bodies. 'Aren't you Prithvi?'

The girl nodded, twisting her wedding ring, with her chin dug down and her gaze pulling up towards the platform. 'Yes, I am.'

'Well, why haven't you been to class then?' The question was entirely rhetorical. 'I told you to come to class twice every week. Look how you are standing. Look how you are doing the poses. I am so tired of teaching people like you who don't appreciate it. It's like casting pearls before swine.'

Her voice rose to a breaking croak which descended into a fit of tight coughing again, that would not abate. An assistant picked her way swiftly through the bodies to offer a drink of water to the hacking old lady racked with rage.

Meanwhile the girl stood there in her little blue bloomers and a golf shirt, her long plait hanging down her back and her head dipping down lower and lower like a schoolgirl's before the headmistress's desk.

The tirade continued for a while until Geeta's strength and our precious tuition time ran out. The gist of it was that she'd devoted her life to teaching numbskulled ingrates like us who had in effect robbed her not only of her time, which had been entirely wasted, but of her health, of her yoga virtuosity and her positivity.

It was an astonishing performance, which left me veering unsteadily on the walk home, between disgust at her arrogance and victim stance and a cringing empathy with her pathos.

Make no mistake, the teaching of Geeta Iyengar was brilliant, subtle, knowledgeable and creative, but in that class and every other I've taken since with her, it's always overlaid with this anxiety, this apprehension of aggression and judgement. One of the most memorable moments with her came during another tongue lashing, when she claimed that no one had ever learned anything from the Iyengars, EVER!

I wondered why. Maybe it was the teaching methods. But who would venture to voice that?

EVERY MORNING WE wended our way to the institute and back for a self-practice session of three hours and every evening a two-hour class. The former was a free-for-all with bodies twisted, inverted, supine or balancing every imaginable way, while Mr Iyengar practised in his corner attended by a handful of assistants. What he could still do in his late eighties and the suppleness of his spine was astounding. Elegant arched back extensions of quite some extremity appeared to flow right through him in perfect alignment, with his face a mask passive enough to induce envy in the Buddha himself.

All the while, though, and quite mysteriously, he kept a beady eye on the students. Every now and then he'd call for one to be brought to him for correction, at which point the tide of students would sweep towards this event to watch his genius express itself in straightening or balancing the momentary culprit.

After each success he'd stand back beaming like a used-car salesman who'd restored the gleam to a wreck. Arms akimbo, he'd turn left and right to the assembled company to ask: 'And who else can teach like that?' The question was not rhetorical and inevitably one of his top American teachers would chant like a teacher's pet gushing her times table: 'Only you, Guruji,' with the inevitable fawning grin. Some of these women were in their sixties and were still falling in nauseating adoration at his feet the way they'd done for forty years. The only thing besides will that kept me from a full-blown bilious attack in that place, was the single ladies' toilet on the premises with its door that didn't close properly.

At issue here was the fact that Guruji is not a used-car salesman peddling a few good ideas on the side. He is a purveyor of egolessness and humility, restraint, culture and dignity. These little sessions of solicited adulation led to a crux-level question: if I followed his teachings devotedly, would I also end up in fits of temper calling my students stupid donkeys and seeking compliments on my ability at the age of eighty-eight?

If so, I asked myself: 'Dear and worthy self, please remind me what I am doing in this nuthouse, turning myself upside down on a grotty mat in a lather of sweat, at the mercy of people I respect only in patches. Please remind me why I am here.'

The question tormented me day and night. How was one to view all of this? If the rest of the yogic population, which constitutes millions in the modern world, saw this man as royalty, I felt like the kid in the crowd squeaking: 'But the emperor has no clothes on!' The only thing was, nobody seemed to be listening – in public, that was.

One day, as we were waiting in the simmering haze of tension for class to start, like schoolchildren all lined up on the spiral staircase leading to the practice hall, one of the other South Africans attending the institute that month asked me how I was enjoying my time there.

'Not at all. I hate this place,' I replied.

She squirmed uncomfortably but forged on. 'Really? Why?'

'Because it's a monument to an ego.'

She smiled, then, in a tut-tut kind of way.

'It is,' I insisted. The people above and below us were beginning to shift uneasily. 'Just look around you at these walls. Why are they covered in all these certificates and citations? Is this the home of an egoless being? Do you think Mother Theresa's set-up looked anything like this? Or Gandhi's?'

Mercifully for her, the door of the practice hall flew open and the previous class began its egress.

But, after that, on the odd occasions when I chose to have dinner with just one other student and these issues arose, there'd sometimes be a whispered concurrence with my conclusions, which reassured me that I was not imagining things.

The other issue was which way to turn this matter. BKS Iyengar and his family I would absolutely not regard and worship as religious figures. They are not political figures, either. They had fallen from grace in my estimation as spiritual leaders. So I had to view them in economic terms, according to the law of supply and demand, acknowledging that there is only one Iyengar family and thousands of people worldwide who want to be taught by its few members. They are a limited commodity and keep their teaching even more limited by housing themselves in that cramped and decrepit old dump.

In economic terms, then, the students equal clients. Now where else have you seen clients treated this way? At a hair salon *de jour* by a prima-donna hairdresser? The point is, a hairdresser is a hairdresser. He's *supposed* to use colour with a flourish and blow hot air. This family business is about as far from that as can be and I had a hard time reconciling the claims of these teachers with their conduct.

In contrast to the self-practice sessions, the classes were completely structured. Even in these, though, one's practice was very careful. This was not only for precision's sake, which should have been the case, but for the sake also of avoiding humiliation at the hands that held the power.

SUNDAYS WERE BLISSFULLY free after the gruelling physical schedule of the week, but the adrenalin kept running in an effort to keep alert in this foreign land, in this otherworldly institute and, besides,

Way out in India

there was a lot of exploring to be done.

Initially I accepted Earth Warrior's invitations to scout bits of the city, mostly little shops that sold Indian cooking equipment or linens. Not being much of a shopper myself and horrified by the thought of trundling home with an overweight bag full of tablecloths, I contented myself with the spectator sport involved in the exercise. Every now and then I'd find something irresistible, such as the sandalwood soap whose fragrance had wafted from the bathroom at Villa Laxmi.

These excursions with Earth Warrior, however, began to wear thin after a short while. For one thing, she was constantly annoyed by the pace and manner of my movements and by my choices. They were either too fast or too slow for her, too clumsy in the shops or too generous with the merchants. I crossed roads too hesitantly, leaving her scowling on the opposite side and I frequently missed sights she pointed out to me as they whizzed by, as sights tend to do in the swirl of Indian life.

So quietly, I began to venture out on my own to the various attractions of Pune. The tuk-tuk driver would always assure me he knew where the place was, only to head off in the vaguest of general directions and then to yell to other drivers in the traffic for specifics. I came to call this process the tuk-tuk driver geography conference – to myself, of course. But what else could I expect? With no street names anywhere in sight and a suspected high rate of illiteracy on the part of the drivers, how else were they to find their way around?

I saw some interesting sights this way, though, probably the most engaging of them being the Aga Khan Palace. Built in 1892 by the Aga Khan, one of a long line of wealthy Muslim imams, it is set on a vast forested parcel of land. Aside from being such an impressive mansion with its Italianate arches, red tiled roof, multiple spires and frilly plasterwork, Mahatma Gandhi was imprisoned there by the British after the launch of his Quit India movement. In the grand and airy comfort of these surroundings he was kept from 1942 to 1944. With him were distinguished nationalist leaders and his wife, Kasturba, who died there, as did Mahadeobhai Desai, Gandhi's secretary for thirty-five years.

The spacious rooms and wide doorways with their fanlights delicately carved, contrast distinctly with the simplicity of Gandhi and with his reason for inhabiting this place. The architecture fairly sings of freedom and abundance, but not of the kinds that interested Gandhi in any way.

A self-pinching moment arrives at the palace on seeing the room assigned to Gandhi, its original pink carpet and the minimal furniture that he used during his time there. The contrast between the room and its sparse furnishings couldn't be sharper. It is a sizeable room with two imposing arched doors on the far side. One of these, as I recall, leads to what would have been a modern bathroom for the 1940s. A huge painting of him with his wife, Kasturba, graces the wall between these doors. It is a striking painting in its own right for a number of reasons, one of which is that he did not spend much of his life with his wife and was certainly not often depicted with her.

The painting also portrays the Gandhis in an unusually tender and intimate position. They are both clearly older in this canvas and Kasturba obviously ill. He sits on a mattress on the floor, leaning against a pillow propped against a wall. Kasturba's head lies across one of his skinny thighs. His right hand rests on her abdomen, with the mattress and both Gandhis draped in white cotton – the hand-spun cloth or khadi, which was so much a part of his life. Her eyes are closed, his downcast. In front of the mattress stands a low writing desk topped by a porcelain vessel in royal blue. On the mattress lies a book with a grey cover.

The startling thing is that as the eye travels down to the bottom of the painting, a triangle of pink carpet spreads away from the mattress. If the eye travels beyond the lower border of the painting's frame, that selfsame mattress, pillow, book, carpet, writing desk and vessel spring to life on the floor on which one stands. The only elements of the painting missing are the Mahatma and his wife. And how one feels their absence! His plain wooden sandals or chappals stand just beyond one of the doorways, as if he might appear, slip his feet into them and start speaking in his high, reedy voice.

I wondered what he might say as I meandered out towards the back garden of the palace to see the shrine where his ashes are kept. A tiled hexagonal structure on a low plinth, its whiteness stands freshly against the green lawn around it.

Ambling down the driveway towards the city chaos outside afterwards, I couldn't help drawing parallels between this prison and the stark island one in which Nelson Mandela spent most of his years in confinement. The self-effacing modesty of both men was one of the traits that elevated them so far beyond their outstanding achievements.

Although Gandhi is widely regarded as the spiritual father of modern India, he was not a saint. His unwavering commitment to the poor and marginalised took years to develop, so that the notion of his supporting the British in the Anglo-Boer War as a stretcher bearer seems a notion of someone else entirely. Mandela, too, had some questionable moments in his time and said himself: 'I am not a saint, unless you think of a saint as a sinner who keeps on trying.' The point was that neither of them ever claimed to be perfect and never blew their own trumpets.

That hexagonal shrine in the garden of the Aga Khan Palace reminded me of the octagon I was attending every day, with its reception hall full of golden awards on proud display and its spiritual leader lecturing on pride, proclaiming that it comes in two convenient types: ignorant pride for some; and enlightened pride for the rarefied and more equal class of others.

I wondered what Gandhi or Mandela would have said about that.

I WONDERED ABOUT this quite a lot and found my mind roaming away during the endless introductions to the classes that Prashant Iyengar gave. He is the guru's only son among his five children and, at the time of my first visit to the institute, he was sixty years old. A brilliant man in shorts and an old-fashioned holey white vest, he struck one as slightly odd at first, which impression remained and still does. It was difficult to pinpoint his oddness, or to understand what exactly made him so.

Gradually it became clear that although he taught strictly – very strictly – using sudden vocal crescendos to indicate our ineptitude and all the usual failings attributed to students in these parts; if one cared to analyse the teaching exactingly, subversive aspects began to appear. So subtle they were, that one could easily have missed them. So ambiguous was some of what he said, that it was not immediately apparent that he was teaching in direct opposition to his father's sacred cows.

One example would be the guru's demand of entering and exiting the poses slowly, staying in them and adjusting them continuously and minutely until the best result was reached. In most students' practice the poses are so challenging that the adjustments continue until the end of the holding time, so that one seldom reaches the point of stillness about which Guruji speaks. Prashant's demand, by contrast, was to adjust nothing and to move in and out of the poses quickly.

I pondered this and other examples as well as Prashant's life. As the only son of BKS Iyengar, it is rumoured that he'd wanted to follow a musical path in his youth. He was apparently a violinist of great talent. Yehudi Menuhin, one of the greatest violinists ever, found his way to Guruji in the 1950s as a student and, after a while, recommended that Prashant follow this dream. The story goes that Guruji forewent his restraint at the suggestion in favour of an almighty rage, which caused a rift between the two men for some time.

It is also rumoured that Prashant wanted to marry in his youth, but that Guruji forbade this path, too. And then at some point the young man was involved in a motor accident whose injuries to his right arm put paid to his musical dream for ever.

It is not clear how and why he committed his life to teaching yoga, but he did and is still treading that same stone floor crowded by students to this day. Decades later, he still lives in a room in the institute building, having at some point moved out of the family home about ten metres away.

His style of teaching usually involves a lengthy philosophical prologue, convoluting its way to a conclusion, by which time the seated students may well have lost track and stiffened into pillars of concrete. At this point he generally lets rip a volley of instructions for the group to split into three or four, with each subgroup attempting a different pose. The volley is typically so rapid and Indian-accented that subtitles would be useful to prevent the inevitability that follows: some poor souls misunderstand the instructions, or are caught without the equipment for a certain pose because it has run out.

These people, like children in a game of musical chairs when the music stops, freeze blankly, awaiting their fate. This is, of course, the predictable verbal torrent, enumerating all the faults with "you people" who are dull and stupid and infinitely more concerned with shopping malls and restaurants (no kidding) than with yoga.

Often a kick or a slap will send the poor unfortunate packing, to join in at a weird angle for lack of space; or Prashant's attention will be drawn by some other miscreant too stiff to present a decent pose after sitting still and cross-legged for forty-five minutes. The real musical chairs start when the groups have to rotate between the poses and some groups have more people in them than others. He calls the groups "batches" and yells when the batches are to change poses. His face in such moments could easily grace a newspaper article depicting war or natural disaster as his voice cracks in the kind of rage that should only ensue from either of the above.

But, I suppose if you've lived in an institute compound that is your whole world your whole life and you've had to give up your dreams, you have your store of anger and frustration and know nothing of those of your students and little of the broader world. You assume that the failure of a yoga student to present himself instantly with the appropriate equipment in a decent pose constitutes a crisis. I couldn't get my head around it.

BY THE end of a few of these classes, I HAD to escape that whole milieu. After a hasty retreat from Earth Warrior, I slipped on my sandals outside, hopped on a tuk-tuk and rode to Koregaon Park and the Jewish Community Centre.

I hadn't bargained for a leftover downpour from the monsoon season, so I arrived steamy and drenched and just in time for some falafel and hummus in what felt like another world. Just inside the tiled entrance to the place I slipped off my sodden sandals and proceeded inside, where Ariel was engaged in a debate on a point of Torah law with an orthodox young man from New York in a black hat and coat.

'Ah, Me'ira,' he smiled, waving his cigarette, 'welcome. Come and have something to eat.'

I did, gratefully, wolfing down the Israeli fare pungent with garlic while the conversation crackled back and forth. In front of the cabinet that housed the Torah scrolls, Sarit played a fast and sweaty game of table tennis with one of the rabbi's children. It was a mix of stimuli a little rich for the blood.

And when the argument had concluded inconclusively between the New Yorker and Ariel, he turned to me.

'And why have you taken your shoes off, Me'ira?'

Was this another debate? An Israeli style challenge?

'We are not Indians,' he added. 'We don't take our shoes off like Indians.'

I gazed about my surroundings for a suitable response.

'Oh, yes, we do,' I insisted, wiping my mouth with a paper serviette. 'We are in the presence of the Torah scrolls, which makes this a sacred space. Remember Moses taking his shoes off in front of the burning bush?'

Ariel just shook his head and smiled, then paid me the ultimate compliment: 'You argue as good as any Israeli. You want a game of table tennis after Sarit and Yonni are finished?'

I did. I needed to work off some adrenalin. After that Sarit, who'd played in the Israeli national team, gave us an impromptu tutorial. She was a good teacher and a pleasant person, who, when she was around at the centre, would always be happy to play a few remedial sets with me.

But then Ariel, babysitting that night for the rabbi and his wife, summoned the boys for their daily lesson in Jewish learning, which was how he earned his living in India. From a Yemenite Jewish background, he was trained in Jewish thought and orthodox living the way race horses are trained to race. He'd become a kind of mentor to the boys.

'And maybe you will learn something also, Me'ira.'

So I settled down in a corner of the room on a white plastic chair, while Ariel sat round the table with the four boys aged about ten to fourteen. The lesson was to be on the subject of *kvod habriot* that evening, literally the "honouring of creations" – in other words, honouring the dignity of others and sparing them humiliation or embarrassment.

This was no trifling matter, Ariel explained to me in English. It had a whole set of laws dedicated to it in the Jewish legal system. If one was found by the Jewish Court to have humiliated or embarrassed another, damages were payable to the offended party and even a high-status person is liable to one of lower status, should the former embarrass or humiliate the latter.

The boys were spellbound by Ariel's tale of Moses rebuking the Jews

– indirectly, to save them embarrassment – for the sins they'd committed during their forty-year trek through the desert. I wondered then what early lessons Mr Iyengar had learned to make it acceptable for him and his family to treat the students the way they did.

BY THE TIME I got home that night to the now familiar sight of Earth Warrior breathing smoke at my approach up the stairs, I felt much lighter and saner than before. I also – fatally – omitted to remove my shoes after my muddy return to the hotel and mistakenly stepped over the threshold of her room in them.

'What the fuck are you doing?' she lashed out. 'What's the fucking matter with you? Look what you've done to my floor!'

Her face resembled Prashant's during the more harrowing moments of the class earlier. But I couldn't see any blood or fire anywhere except in her eyes, so turned silently back to my room to fetch one of the cloths I'd purchased from the domestic shop down the road and proceeded to wipe away my footprints.

NEXT MORNING, THOUGH, she had simmered down to sweetness again as she leaned freshly bucket-bathed on one side of my doorway.

'I think we should discuss the theme of Prashant's class yesterday,' she suggested. 'What would you say it was?'

'Bullshit Baffles Brains.' I hadn't pulled on my own equipoising bullshitty armour for the day yet and shot straight from the hip. 'Nothing more complicated than that.'

Earth Warrior snapped herself to the vertical. 'Do you know you have a major problem?' she sneered. 'You have the gift and privilege of learning from a man of Prashant's calibre and this is all you can say?'

We were galloping down the steps and out into the street by then.

'And what exactly is the calibre of Prashant?' I panted. 'And why are you so defensive of him? Do you know that you're just one of the little cookies in one of his cookie-cutter batches? The man hyperventilates at the sight of a skew mat on the floor and has no experience beyond the walls of that dump of an institute, but feels qualified to spout all the judgemental bullshit and philosophy 101 that he does.'

She didn't get it. She just fumed on: 'You are a spoiled Jewish brat. You know that? You've been full of shit from the moment we got here. I've had to babysit you through every moment of every day and I should never have allowed you to follow me here!'

Pardon? Did I miss something? The fruit wallah wheeling his barrel along the road stopped and turned to stare at us as her words mingled with exhaust fumes and pineapples.

I'd booked my solo flights quite happily, months before she'd even considered the trip. I'd also parted cautiously with its details in her direction in intuitive anticipation of just such a scene.

'Not so,' I countered.

Earth Warrior was not sure how to deal with that one, so she forged on: 'You find fault with everything and everyone.'

Not so. Besides the institute's teachers, India had offered a cornucopia of colour and interest to me.

'You're so focused on those Israelis of yours that you've forgotten what you're here for.'

Not so. But I had veered off to explore a different path towards the same ultimate destination.

'So why don't you just go back home to your nice little rich, polite, Jewish life and leave the rest of us to appreciate this place?'

By this time, as was her custom, Earth Warrior had crossed the road and was shrieking at me for all she was worth, turning Indian heads to gape at her ruddy face and thin, flailing arms.

When I caught up with her, it was the end. I inhaled deeply and coughing, invoked my inner yogi to announce with suitable modulation: 'From now on, Earth Warrior, our trip together is over. You will go your way and I'll go mine.' Then I turned a corner and at a clip took a different route to the institute.

From then on I greeted her civilly whenever our paths crossed and for a while she'd smile and seem ready to initiate a conversation. I was not. The place and pace had worn me down to a rasping chest infection and I'd lost so much weight that my pants were falling off, even when belted. I had to conserve my resources and Earth Warrior consumed more than I had to give.

Way out in India

IT WAS AT that point that I decided to visit the Kare Centre for a weekend, an ayurvedic retreat centre near a lake about an hour from Pune. Since this place had been recommended by many of my colleagues who'd survived the Pune pilgrimage, I decided to go there, wary though I was of the heavy punting it got from our Pune hotel's owner via primitive pamphlets slid under the doors of the guest rooms. The same pamphlets, assuring the potential guest of Iyengar yoga as part of the Kare package, appeared in the institute's lobby. That doubled my doubt. But, feeling so grim and suffocated, I forged on.

Compared with the trip there, my ailing lungs were nothing. Wild enough to induce cardiac arrest, I wondered why I'd exchanged one set of health hazards for another. Sharing the taxi with a sweet yoga student from the UK, we bonded over grimaces at the suicidal speciality of the driver – roaring around the road's many bends to beat the speed of sound, then upping the ante to simultaneous overtaking.

To his sound track of continuous hoots, toots and parps backed by Indian hit songs at high volume, he alerted everyone and often no one to our presence on the road. At last, a lot more wrecked than when we'd left, we stumbled from the car at journey's end while the driver sucked his teeth in sullen protest at our mumbled and tipless parting from him.

The place soon soothed us though, quiet as it was, well wooded and overlooking Lake Mulshi down below. As is the case everywhere in India, though, the air still smelled of smoke with an eternal haze hanging like a voile curtain never fully drawn. This comes courtesy of the universal Indian practice of burning garbage, since there is little in the way of public sanitation systems to take care of it.

The centre itself was spotless and breezy with an open-air "hall" overlooking the lake for meditation sessions and other gatherings. In typical Indian fashion, it was simple but colourful, with green supporting beams, red floors and lines of terracotta pots in which waved identical palms. In its centre a lounge suite squatted with a coffee table holding a magnificent arrangement of flowers.

'Impressive,' I wheezed.

'They might have some impressive guests here,' Elaine murmured in her crisp British accent as we strolled away from the reception area to view the lake.

Which was when I spied none other than Guruji himself emerging from the dining area, leading a procession of the entire Iyengar clan. That was when I realised why Iyengar yoga was so much part of the place. The family probably had a stake in it. But that was not my concern. My concern was that I was breathing shallowly, dizzy and urgently needed to lie down.

These facts I relayed in an increasingly oozy sweat to the beautiful young lady in a yellow sari and medical coat, who turned out to have six years of education behind her name, along with the title "Dr".

She'd earned it studying ayurveda, an Indian system of healing involving not only medicines made from natural substances, but also diet, exercise, meditation and massage. The Kare Centre took care of all of them, in my case ushering me solicitously into my room for a nap with a little cup of pills to swallow beforehand.

I woke up in a profound state of disorientation to a soft knock on the door. A kindly woman stood outside looking worried when I cracked it open, wrapped in a sheet.

'It's time for your massage, Madam.'

Dressed in my insistently descending pants and a T-shirt, I followed her to the massage section of the building overlooking an immaculate garden. Beyond the reed blinds at the windows a lawn stretched to the edge of a terrace, where another line of terracotta pots stood like soldiers all topped with feathery plants nodding in the breeze. Between the two a small pond hosted pink lotus lilies, the perfect signal to descend into the dreaminess of a massage.

But first there were the formalities in this strange little room. The kindly masseuse balanced a clipboard on her padded abdomen, instructing me to undress fully.

'Fully?' I gawked at her for confirmation.

'Yes, everything off please, Madam. Panties also.'

Then I was to stand before her in my thin and quivery nakedness, attempting to stay up as my blood pressure fell down.

Deftly she tied a piece of string around my waist, then swished out a white cotton rectangle from a pile and tucked it into the string, front and back. Terrific. I was now shivering in a nappy in a forested valley in India.

Way out in India

'Please, Madam, take a seat.'

The seat turned out to be a low and beautifully carved little chair with a high back in the centre of the room.

'And what is your good name?' the woman enquired, passing me a towel to wrap around myself.

Serious?

'Meryl Urson.'

'Hello, Merylurson,' she smiled.

'Hello,' I smiled back. Then unable to resist I said, 'What is your good name?'

Being unpronounceable to me and my brain being so foggy, I forgot her name immediately.

'And what is your family name, Merylurson?'

It was only after speaking to some Indian guests a day later that I understood the meaning of "good" in my "good name". It was a touch disappointing, I have to confess. Having registered on many radars in India as stupid, lazy and worthless, I'd quite liked the idea that I was assumed to have a good name. But alas, no, as it turned out. My good name was Meryl, the way yours might be Petunia – or John for that matter.

I didn't dwell on it then, though, because after a brief glance at my check-in record and her instructions for my treatment, the woman stood behind me to begin a vigorous massage of my scalp as I sat in my nappy on that hard little chair. Well *that* woke up the brain. It felt a bit like that wild car ride earlier in the day, but with a touch more blood flow to the head and no apparent danger. And it saturated my hair with some delicious smelling oil, which, I learned later, was of toasted sesame seeds.

Then it was time to lie down on the bed. Well, "bed" would be pushing it. It was a wooden plinth, dipped in the middle like a sagging mattress, with wonderful carved detail around its head and foot. Other warm and fragrant oils were dribbled over me in a way that felt far-away familiar.

Tactile images swam through my addled head: of vegetable chunks for roasting on my kitchen counter at home with the bottle of olive oil poised in my palm and a glass of chilled white to hand. As the woman raised another little bottle above my body, it released a trickle of warmer oil whose aroma blended superbly with the first. And then the massage began, a basting in oils, a skilled and gentle unknotting of the culture shock I'd chosen and frozen into my body for that month of my life. A silent, soothing healing rolled me backwards and forwards in my nappy on that dipped old cradle until I fell asleep and awoke to the kindly woman rubbing me down with a towel.

That night I slept for twelve hours straight, hungering the next morning for a truckload of toast, eggs and good roasted coffee. That was not to be though, since the kitchen – under doctor's orders for each guest's diet – produced mainly bland food, most of it in dainty portions. I wolfed it down in an instant, burning my fingers on the metal cup sans handle that held some kind of bitter tea, conscious of the delicate manners of the other patients around the table.

It was a good thing, then, that I'd bought an economy-sized bag filled with little packs of biscuits, which, I soon realised, were meant for babies and toddlers. This famous brand, Parle-G, is an Indian institution that's been around for about a hundred years. Priding itself on its distribution network, it can be found in its universally recognisable packaging in the remotest corners of the land. I carried those little yellow packets of biscuits constantly, handing them out to persistent beggar children who touched their clustered fingers to their stomachs and then their mouths in the tragic Indian gesture of hunger.

But after that meagre breakfast I scavenged them for myself, multiple packs full of sugar and wheaty goodness, if the wholesome stalks and radiant little girl on the packaging were to be believed. As an addition to all the treatments, the biscuits worked a treat. My interest was piqued when my new friend, Elaine, and her brand-new breakfast friend from Frankfurt suggested that we investigate the mid-morning yoga class.

Talk about a downer!

The yoga studio on this beautiful site was all kitted out with Iyengar equipment with an overdose of photographs of Mr Iyengar as a much younger man poised in magnificent poses. As antiquated teaching tools go, they are effective, but I've never worked out why Mr Iyengar didn't inspect those famous photos more thoroughly before their distribution all those decades before. It would have saved him the dubious wonder of students for all posterity staring at them, not only to review the poses,

Way out in India

but intrigued by those loincloths whose edges could have been tighter at times.

The class we all attended was a mixed one. Elaine and some others were experienced students. Our class included the athletic novice from Frankfurt, a large old woman in a sari, a sufferer of multiple ailments, a senior Iyengar teacher from Chicago battling his digestive system, and a demure young Indian couple on their honeymoon who'd not done yoga before.

The teacher was a tyrant in the true Iyengar mould, who seemed to take to the task of teaching the way a sugar-cane worker takes to harvesting, except a touch more fanatically. The guy's tongue was a scythe, lashing and slashing, belittling and humiliating everyone in the room as he whipped around, swinging instructions in all directions.

Elaine's face stayed impassive. She'd learned that skill in Pune, since she'd been the "donkey" flung about by Guruji during that first shattering class. Chicago lay grey-tinged in a restorative pose on a bolster in a corner, and the woman in the sari was castigated for coming in a sari. Then, after gaping mutely in response, she was ordered to another corner where a young assistant attended to her. The honeymoon couple looked aghast, then peered at each other shrugging with sly upturned palms on which could have been written: WTF?

I attempted to follow instructions, but the dizziness returned, so I melted to the floor as elegantly as possible.

'And why are you sitting down, Madam?' The teacher towered above me, arms akimbo, jaw thrust forward. 'Did I say to sit down?'

'No.' I wondered if I was supposed to add 'Sir'.

'Then why are you sitting down?'

'Well it's difficult to stand up. I had a fever that's come back – I think.'

'You think? You think, Madam? Get up.'

I creaked to my feet in a swirl of dizziness. Then I'm not sure what fell first, me or my defeated pants.

I think I remember a sort of cross between a gasp and a grunt from the idiot teacher, but I didn't hang around to consider the matter. I gathered both of us up before the first tear fell and stumbled back to my room to hurl the pants across the room for letting me and themselves down and to dump myself into bed. Under the covers I could still hear that voice calling after me: 'Where are you going, Madam?'

I was glad I hadn't responded.

At lunch the honeymoon couple didn't venture anything about their introduction to Iyengar yoga, but invited me to stroll to the lake with them afterwards. They were both professionals and enjoying their honeymoon until this morning's events. Duly horrified, they asked me if it was always this way.

'Comes from the top,' was all I said before we proceeded to pleasanter subjects.

The rest of the weekend at the Kare Centre was filled with the food in bigger portions I'd requested – lots of wholesome, healing food served and savoured with gusto. Aromatic massages abounded between friendly chats, gentle consultations and restful lollings. By the time we had to leave, I felt restored and was sad to go. Elaine and Frankfurt embraced lingeringly in the driveway as Chicago fairly leapt into the front seat alongside our new, sane driver, to share the journey home with us. I stood beside the car waving both hands, not only to show my gratitude to the staff lined up for our leaving, but to prove that my pants would stay up on their own.

LIFE BECAME EASIER after that. I felt a little stronger. I came and went without reporting to Earth Warrior. I ambled at my own pace through the park on the way to class, stopping to smile at the assembled grannies in saris in the lotus pose on the benches. The trees attracted me, too, painted as they were in thick bands of red and white halfway up their trunks.

'To denote their ownership by the Indian government,' nodded a neatly pressed man taking his constitutional in dress pants and trainers.

At night Earth Warrior stopped attending the dinners with the women from the institute, but I have to admit to a pang I felt for her one night as we all passed by a restaurant, chatting and giggling, and saw her nibbling a lonely roti, lit forlornly inside the window.

AT ABOUT THIS time I also started nibbling alone on some nights.

Way out in India

Well, devouring would more aptly describe the process. With the fatigue wearing me down and the hunger extreme after evening classes, I decided to try a cheap and very Indian way of eating. A notice on the window of the hotel reception desk advertised "Tiffins: Rs50.00".

I'd heard of tiffins before – that they were some kind of lunches delivered to working men in Mumbai through a network of delivery men called *dabbawallahs*. There were thousands of these lunches cooked and packed by wives and mothers after their husbands and children had left for the day. Then the dabbawallahs would fan out across the city to collect them from each home and, through a complicated system involving every kind of conveyance imaginable, deliver them to the correct customer – still warm – by lunchtime. It was an amazing phenomenon from many angles and I couldn't wait to try it.

The hotel's tiffins, apparently, were cooked by an anonymous lady in the block of flats next door. All I had to do was get my order in during the morning and presto – a hot packed dinner would be waiting for me in a tiffin box on my bedraggled arrival from class.

The tiffin "box", in its commonest form, is a steel cylinder of round tins all stacked on top of each other with a handle holding them together. A spring catch on the handle releases all the tins from the tower and, as each is opened, a delicious aroma wafts from the individual dishes, which retain their heat for up to three hours.

The tiffin menu usuallly consists of dhal – a lentil dish of soupy consistency, rice, a few floppy and folded chapattis and some kind of curry. The whole is a fragrant feast, with a lot of sauce mopping and mouth wiping along the way. The idea is to return the tiffin to its source for washing and repacking, creating both a green system and employment for the cook and delivery man in one package.

I began to enjoy these tiffin dinners for their convenience, deliciousness, cheapness and the solitude they allowed me in my little room after the racket and bustle outside. I so appreciated the effort put into their flavour and variety until it began to wane and glories such as wilted curried onions would stare at me like deadened eyes from the bottom of the curry canister.

One night, as was my custom, I opened the tiffin, absorbed the bouquet like a connoisseur and tucked right in. Big mistake. In seconds

Of Grace and Gurus

the tiffin had me rearing from my chair, sending it sliding in all its plastic chicness across the room. Grabbing my keys and hoping that no one would see me in my fire-breathing dragon disguise, I hurtled downstairs to Sweeties on the corner, which stocked everything from nail clippers to rice.

Only two words issued from me between flame breaths: 'Curd – please.'

Translation: "yoghurt – in a punnet". Think cottage-cheese container. The moustached shopkeeper turned slowly towards his fridge, glancing at me over his specs all the while as I leaned forward to blemish his display case with my vapour.

Flinging a handful of rupees at him and, under intense chilli power, leaping upstairs, I slammed my door with an echo that would have magnetised Earth Warrior in seconds a few days before.

In all the history of India a punnet of curd has not disappeared down a gullet so fast, along with accompanying grunts every time a cooling blob hit the belly fire below. Once the smoke had cleared I sat down at my desk on which stood the tiffin stacked to attention in shame, its handle firmly clamped. Then into the chapatti canister I slipped a note requesting mercy in future, that I almost signed with hot regards, but decided on calming down, that warm ones would do.

After that the mildness and aromatic sophistication of the tiffins surpassed all others to the point where I had to fight the urge to dine alone every night.

LIFE ALSO BECAME more cheerful because two more Jewish holidays arrived on the calendar on the two weekends following Yom Kippur.

The first of these was Sukkot. It's a joyful festival celebrated to mark both the harvest season in Israel and to acknowledge the wandering of the Jews in the desert for forty years after the Exodus from Egypt.

One of the central traditions of this festival is to build a temporary shelter resembling its biblical antecedents at home or at synagogue. Its main feature is its roof of palm fronds. In this sukkah, as it is called, the family or community take their meals. And what festive meals they are! Foods traditional to the particular community are eaten, songs are sung

Way out in India

and the sukkah is decorated with fruits hung from the ceiling, drawings by children on the walls and other such colourful pieces that lend a feeling of jollity.

At the Lubavitcher Centre the festivities were in full swing by the time I finished class and tuk-tukked my way across town. The evening meal had largely been eaten and songs were being sung with percussive accompaniment by the rabbi and other men bashing the table rhythmically between hearty glugs of vodka.

Once I'd enjoyed a slice of challah, Ariel sidled over to the picnic bench behind the one I was sharing with some others and nudged me.

'Hey, Me'ira,' he whispered. We were back to back, so I turned around. 'I have a surprise for you. Leave as soon as you can. Wait for me outside and I will follow you.'

It didn't take long for him to meet me on the noisy street.

'What's going on?'

'Come. Let's get a tuk-tuk. I've got something to show you.'

I couldn't understand his instructions to the tuk-tuk driver but in a minute we were manoeuvring across town in the hot Pune night. One of the tuk-tuk's features is that its shape prevents passengers from seeing where they're going. The roof is too low, so to see anything from the back seat one has to adopt the kind of crouch-and-compress position designed to make a yogi weep.

For that reason I didn't see the imposing Lal Davel synagogue until we were there. This is the largest one in Asia outside Israel, built by David Sassoon of the famously wealthy Sassoon family. Its red bricks and Victorian architecture loomed out of the smoky darkness, stamping its magnificence against the night sky. At first glance it looked like a church with a clock tower, Gothic pillars and windows, but I'd seen it on too many Google searches in the tacky Internet café with the wobbly chairs down the road from the hotel by then to be fooled, and in a moment we were standing at the gate.

The security was a simple matter back then, in the innocent years before the Taj Hotel bombings. A lowly born fellow served as a guard, instructed only to ask 'Are you Jewish?' to any would-be visitors.

'Of course,' Ariel replied, pulling his kippah from his pocket and planting it on his head. 'We've come to visit the sukkah.'

Then he turned to me: 'These people eat late. They originate from the Mediterranean but are like Indians this way also.'

The sukkah was around the back of the building, down a long, dusty driveway. Golden light escaped from its palm-frond roof and open doorway. From that rectangle of light the sound of unfamiliar singing overtook the hooting of the traffic as we approached. At the entrance we were gawked at momentarily before being welcomed inside. Once my eyes had roved the room, I understood that we must appear as strange to these people as they appeared at least to me.

First, they looked completely Indian. The older men were dressed in suits with all the rings and dark-dyed hair that goes with being middle-aged and middle-classed in India. On many of their heads embroidered fezzes served as coverings. The women wore saris, beautiful saris with their dupattas draped over their heads while their nose rings winked in the glowing light. Everyone seemed to be smiling warmly and looked us up and down, the strange pair who'd appeared from the night. At least Ariel was as dark skinned as they were, but his hair was frizzy and I – well, I came from another planet.

The strange thing was that while the songs and prayers were chanted, I recognised every Hebrew word. Just the tunes were different and sung in that unmistakably Indian nasal way. Some of the hand gestures used during prayer I'd never seen before. They resembled the mudras of Indian dance or yoga. The appearance of the sukkah was also familiar but entirely different.

Some of the motifs in the wall decorations, like the Star of David, were universally Jewish, but the Indian-bright colours and shapes challenged my right brain to absorb them as streaming from the same DNA as my own. Hanging from the ceiling were not oranges but coconuts, their scent permeating the air along with what was it? Incense? The men's rose-water hair oil? I couldn't place it but had never smelt it amid the mothballed formal suits of the old women in the shul at home or the expensive perfumes of the younger ones.

After prayers the traditional *bracha* or blessing on wine was chanted by the hazzan (cantor), along with that for the bread. In the Western world the bread is the inevitably plaited and deliciously soft white challah (a bread eaten on the Sabbath), but here it was flat and round, whether

Way out in India

in the form of chapatti, paratha or something else, I never did discover. When the food came streaming in on platters after that, there was nary a herring in sight. Golden samosas filled with curried vegetables wafted around on trays with other spicy finger foods, spreading their aromas through the glowing sukkah. In Hebrew, Ariel explained to a trio of the community leaders where we were from and, in English, I gave my own account.

The triumvirate seemed to strain to understand Ariel's Hebrew, which was when I realised that even to an Israeli ear, his Yemenite accent sounded very particular. The guttural sounds dove much deeper into the throat, giving it an Arabic sound. The whole conversation was so otherworldly and exotic to me and the Lal Davel synagogue so resplendent in chandeliers, marble and Corinthian columns on our own personal little tour of it afterwards, that the entire experience became almost too intense and I suddenly longed to lie down. Fighting fatigue, I wondered about the fate of this place and others like it. Decades after its thriving communities had scattered and the cost of maintenance had soared, how were the remnants and descendants of all that wealth to preserve all this beautiful history?

For the weekend after celebrating Sukkot, Ariel invited me to celebrate the combined Jewish holidays of Shemini Atzeret and Simchat Torah. The former is really just the eighth day of Sukkot, but its special significance is that it includes prayers for rain. In Israel now, as in ancient times, rain is gold.

Simchat Torah is celebrated the day after Shemini Atzeret and is essentially a celebration of the Torah. A year is required, traditionally, to read the entire Torah, with each week devoted to reading a different portion or *parsha* of it. The festivities held to mark the end of the full cycle of reading constitute Simchat Torah.

And they are jolly! This is no solemn Yom Kippur with fasting and mournful prayers in minor keys. This holiday is full of dancing and clapping, smiling and joy. Approaching the Chabad-Lubavitcher Centre, as it is formally called, I could hear the singing from the street, whose jollity resounded throughout the service.

At its end it was time for one last meal in the sukkah, with everyone passing the big jugs of juice to each other with rosy smiles as the rabbi chanted the blessings over wine and bread. Again the vodka bottle was passed – to the men only of course – and again the rabbi's wife in her modest wig and cotton layers spooled dish after dish on to the table.

Again I sat there wondering which part of my spirit belonged on a yoga mat and which belonged here. And although there was something as comforting and familiar as a blanket in this setting, my internal weather system itched under its weight. I found myself relieved to be on the road between the two on the way back to the hotel, however uncomfortable that road might have been.

With or without Earth Warrior's company, the institute was squeezing my spirit to suffocation. Its dryness, authoritarian approach, disgusting equipment and cramped conditions in the heat all saturated my capacity. So that one sunny afternoon, after a wilting game of table tennis, Ariel pronounced me too depleted to carry on. And what did Sarit think?

Before she could answer, he turned back to me with a question: 'Why don't you leave this yoga and we all go travelling to Hampi for a few days?'

'Hampi? What was that? Where? What about the classes I'd be missing? What about…?' My default reaction was to refuse. It was all too overwhelming to contemplate. But the month was drawing to a close and the thought of spending the rest of it within the confines of the institute's walls without seeing any of the rest of India appealed about as much as a philosophy session on the Bhagavad-Gita.

'Hampi? It's a beautiful place. It's in a valley and all around is farmland. The Hindu kings had their headquarters there about five-hundred years ago so there are lots of ruins around. Beautiful. Architecture. Art. Amazing rock formations. The village is full of colour. The whole place is a World Heritage Site. You will see. We go by bus.'

Because I'd delayed leaving for Hampi a few days later by insisting on attending the Diwali celebrations at the institute at which Guruji himself was to speak, the other Israelis had all gone on ahead of Ariel and me. On the bus, he would be the token swarthy foreigner while I would wave the solitary Western flag.

To anyone familiar with Indian systems, the fact that the bus was leaving from a vague spot outside a bank somewhere across town at 10:30 pm would not seem strange at all. But, to me, standing on what

Way out in India

would have been a pavement if its bricks hadn't deserted it in an apparent effort to cross the road, it was a touch unnerving. In the first place it was difficult to discern the bus in all that smog.

But lo and behold, a few minutes before the appointed hour, the bus came rolling up to the designated nebulousness and a few minutes later we were off into the night, on a distinctly middle-class journey, complete with air conditioning freezing us towards rigor mortis and a Bollywood movie playing at full volume on the screen in front.

The only amenity lacking was a toilet, which, I discovered, would not materialise for a good few hours and would then take the form of a patch of tarmac of the passenger's choice. I sighed down into my seat, stared at by whichever Indian eyes could reach me, and said a little prayer of thanks for Ariel as my guide and protector who'd warned me about bringing a blanket and refraining from drinking too much before the trip.

Nature did call nevertheless in the wee hours, when a lot of squirming interrupted an already interrupted sleep.

'Stop moving around so much, Me'ira,' Ariel frowned. 'We will stop soon.'

'How soon?' The Israeli version is invariably relative to other imponderables.

He turned up his palms, turned down the corners of his mouth and shrugged. 'Soon is soon.'

Huh.

What he didn't tell me was that we would stop in the middle of the highway where the vendors trading in oily snacks were the only demarcation between the two sides of the highway. In the smoky gloom traffic roared in every direction and the valiant little lights of chai stalls shone dimly in all that murk. Well, dimly enough for me, but then again I would have squatted under Las Vegas neon by that point. So in a flash, as the token full-bladdered female, I leapt off the bus, found the darkest spot I could for the operation, bared my shameless Western bum like a full moon and wondered vaguely what the Indian traders might tell their loved ones the next morning about their lunar apparitions the night before.

In the middle of the proceedings a plaintive voice wailed into the darkness: 'Me'ira! Me'ira! Where *are* you? The bus is leaving.'

Comforting news during a comfort break.

As I swung back on to the bus at the last minute, multiple pairs of dark eyes followed me while Ariel hissed with a nicotine breath: 'Don't do that again Me'ira. You made me frightened.'

I wasn't sure what choice I'd had, but apologised anyway, sanitised my hands most heartily from my little bottle, wrapped myself in my blanket like a corpse and sank into a fathomless sleep.

When I blinked my eyes open, we were in Hospet, a bustling little agricultural town and the nearest hub to Hampi. Donkey carts loaded with stacks of hay shuffled along the roads. Men on motorbikes overloaded with bananas attached to their branches wove through the traffic. Tractors yoked to trailers carrying sacks of rice chugged and hooted at nobody in particular.

'So this is where we get off and find a tuk-tuk,' Ariel announced.

As we approached Hampi, it began to reveal itself in an expansion of green, gemmed here and there with its legendary boulder formations of every design nature could have conjured. Some clustered in clans, some stood as solitary sentries while others piled themselves hill-high. Mysteriously rounded, they echoed the rolling landscape luxuriating in its abundance. Rice paddies unfurled under the sun while banana and coconut palm fronds waved pliantly in the wind. Such a balmy richness pervaded the atmosphere that the area's choice as a sacred spot for the Hindu rulers all those centuries ago came as no surprise.

With so much of nature's energy producing such fertility in this area, inspiration must have flowed easily for the creation of the intricately carved temples and royal structures whose ruins abound in this place.

The first we saw as we crested a hill with a panoramic view was the Virupaksha Tower. And what a tower it is! Fifty metres high, it builds to a pinnacle in the common style of Hindu temples, but its scale in these surroundings is impressive. As the showpiece at the heart of the temple complex, it dwarfs the ruins around it and the bazaar bustling a short way away.

At last we were in Hampi Bazaar, which although unashamedly touristy, nuzzles the surrounding boulders and offers up hearty doses of interest and colour. A bohemian atmosphere pervades the place along

Way out in India

with a rural quaintness and the pungency of cow dung, incense and spices. To complete the sense of plenitude, a lovely brown river slithers along in the sunshine.

But sweaty and tired, hungry and thirsty, apprehensive and a touch irritable, I was grateful for the distractions of trinkets and sadhus or holy men raggedly bearded and robed in orange, meandering along the cobbles with their begging bowls. Unlike me, Ariel didn't seem to feel any urgent need to shower and change, eat and drink, or even find our Israeli friends. Maybe he knew he didn't need to, for as we turned a corner, there they were, sprawled out on bright cushions on the floor of a restaurant in the bazaar, some smoking hookah pipes and some breakfasting on idlis.

'Thank God,' I whispered to myself before flopping on to a cushion to land in a jumble of smiles and a gabble of Hebrew.

Then Sarit, pushing her bowl of *upma* towards me for sharing, changed to English. 'Before you go anywhere else from here, you must sign in at the police station.'

Oh, yes, I'd forgotten: The business of Filling up the Form.

The police station was a funny, little flat-roofed building in bright turquoise with a few plastic chairs sunbathing outside and two lines of laundry drying under a palm tree – to enhance its air of officialdom. Policemen must rejoice at being posted to Hampi where the job description mostly involves cricket viewing on the station's TV set. To spice things up a bit there are occasional forays to frighten stray sloth bears away from the temple ruins or catch the odd dope dealer at the riverside. If things get too quiet there's always the apprehension of unwitting tourists who have failed to Fill up the Form on arrival in town. A handwritten sign on the station wall warned of all these dangers and ended: "*Thank's for co operate*".

Rounding a corner of the bazaar, a sharp flute-like sound pierced the air. It came from a man seated cross-legged on the paving tiles playing a calabash flute, while before him out of three flat round baskets rose three hooded cobras. Although they danced to his tune, they seemed – creepily – to be watching us through the eye-like markings on their hoods. To his music they ascended and coiled and I wondered who was more mesmerised – the three cobras or I. Of course, there was a fourth basket for rupees, poorly placed for business purposes, among the other three.

'So, Me'ira, are you going to put something in there?' Ariel challenged me.

'No, I'm staying right here. You are. You're the guide.'

The first step to sightseeing in Hampi is the renting of motorbikes to get around the ruins at leisure. This procedure involves an amble down the road where various men stand with a bike or two and their sales pitch: "Bike"?

And so we were off, two to a bike to see the ruins.

That's not hard in Hampi, since they are everywhere in every shape and size. But it was the amazing Vittala Temple that we sought, the most famous of all the ruins a few kilometres from the bazaar on a dusty road bordered by rural simplicity at its lushest.

Sited on a vast campus, the Vittala Temple's claim to fame is its unique status as a musical instrument. Seriously. It was Ariel's heaven, this temple, its slender columns whose joints, he enthused, are cleverly hidden amid the carvings. Here flower garlands wreathed their way around one column, there horses chased each other eternally around another. Elsewhere, Chinese traders haggled with Indians, while Mughals brandished swords in perpetual readiness for conquest.

The extraordinary thing about these columns and about the temple is that the pillars are carved to various girths so that when tapped, they emit particular pitches. When tapped in turn, musical notes issue from the temple, which also exhibits many a carving of musicians, drummers and dancers.

By the time Ariel explained the next feature to us, he was just about dancing a jig.

'The thing is,' he twinkled, 'that the sound is amplified by the valley, the porous stone of the pillars and also the density of the boulders all around. So when this music was played in the temple, the sound travelled for one kilometre. Can you imagine the rulers and their friends sitting on silk carpets with the best incense burning and fire lamps and this music playing all across the valley. Fantastic!'

Just then a local guide carrying a stick with a rubber knob on its end struck a few pillars in turn. In the resonance everyone froze in wonder until it faded away.

Way out in India

IN THE LITTLE coracles that cruised the Tungabhadra River, life was but a dream. Essentially floating bamboo baskets, sealed these days with plastic and bitumen, these traditional flat-bottomed paddle boats are used for fishing and ferrying. With the rhythm of the oarsman's paddle dipping and splashing on our little afternoon cruise, a dopey state ensued, so dopey that it was hard to tell if the sheep floating past in the next coracle were imaginary or real, or if it really *was* possible to transport three motorbikes across a river in a basket.

The rest of our few days in Hampi were spent in just such pleasant pursuits, exploring the ruins, taking an impromptu swim in a nearby lake fully clothed, watching the landscape reveal its treasures: a graceful woman in a sari, her head piled with firewood; a Rajasthani woman in pink, blinged to the nostrils like a storybook Gypsy; a batch of dung patties used for fuel, drying on a rock in the sun; a school of young boys gleaming at play in the river; and an old man and his grandson cradling a day-old goat in his arms, resting in the shade of a ruined farm gateway.

And my spirit soared. With no institute or institution to mould or scold me, I felt as happy, benign and connected as those boys leaping and diving in the water. The next day, a Saturday, it would be over, I mentioned to the group.

'But it's not over today or tonight,' Ariel beamed. 'So let's all go up Matanga Hill to watch the sunset.'

It was a gentle uphill walk through boulders and greenery to the top of Matanga Hill, which lay about half an hour east of Hampi Bazaar.

As we reached the top of this hill, the curtain rose on the extraordinary theatre of sky and clouds dancing their golden dance towards the sun's descent. We counted the stars as they added sparks of silver to the spectacle. At the arrival of the third one a husky voice began to sing the Hebrew song, "Lekha Dodi" – the traditional song for welcoming the Sabbath. It was Ariel's voice with its deep guttural accent, which was joined voice by voice, accent by accent, until we were all singing along to the same tune.

THE BUS RIDE back to Pune was a basket of thoughts: of boulders, of boats, of carvings and of cobras, which all stayed with me throughout the last week of my month at the institute.

It was difficult to concentrate on the classes there since my spirit was split between the other side of Pune and my family in Cape Town to whom I longed to return. On the eve of my leaving we all gathered at The German Bakery for one last meal.

'So, Me'ira, what do you have to say to us?' Ariel asked after we'd shared all the dishes.

'It's going to be hard to say goodbye to all of you,' was all I managed.

'Ah, Me'ira,' he frown-smiled, 'who's saying goodbye? We're all here enjoying dinner together and we haven't even thought about dessert. Let's get the menu.'

ON THE LONG journey home there was a lot to digest about my visit to spiritual India. From two books I'd read along the way by two American women on just such journeys, I'd learned that there is no shortage of scandal and greed among the gurus and swamis who take gullible spirits into their hands. Financial and sexual in nature, such scandals are often just part of the regular package of incense, robes and chanting.

In that way the Iyengars have kept an impeccably clean slate and still do. In some of Guruji's writings, he recounts the imperative of cultivating his ferocious manner in his youth to deter the stampede of women worldwide, eager to derail him from his path. Powerful, feline and magnetic in those days, one could understand the women's impulses. Just a glimpse of those sixty-something devotees fluttering their eyelashes at his octogenarian self, gave me some idea of what he might have encountered earlier on in his journey.

And as far as the vast sums of money are concerned that pour into the Iyengar coffers, a significant portion of it goes to the development of Guruji's home village, Bellur. A school at which yoga is woven integrally into the curriculum, a hospital and several other facilities have thus far been built and Guruji was particularly insistent on educating girls.

The Iyengars still live clan-style in the same house they built in the 1970s, a few metres away from the institute building. For all their fame, it's a modest house with one or two little cars parked outside. At the time of writing, a lift had been installed around the back of the institute building so that the ninety-five-year-old Guruji no longer had to use the stairs.

The plenitude of paradoxes I'd experienced on this journey turned my brain as upside down as a head balance. The more I thought about them, the more I wondered if the shock of initiation into India hadn't messed with my mind. Maybe warring with Earth Warrior had skewed my view of things, or the exotic blend of hippiedom and Judaism had scrambled my reason.

I had to know these things. So, three years later I boarded another plane for Mumbai and rolled through the diesel-clouded night to Pune again – same procedure, same hotel, but to meet a different cast of companions for that round of the bout and to be introduced to the idea of Guruji's ferocious granddaughter Abhijata succeeding him and his children one day. The result: "Same-same, but different", as the Indians say.

I had to know, in short, if it had been my numbskulled obstinacy or my stress-induced hysteria that had befuddled my conclusions about the place. But after another month enduring the same institute scene and scenes as previously, I deduced safely that it wasn't. And I will never go back there again.

But what about the yoga? Was it a load of garbage to be tossed out because its most eminent teachers couldn't behave themselves?

After a lot of soul-searching and researching, I concluded that it was not. The teachings are largely valid, if not as flawless, as the Iyengars claim and their devotees believe. They are more than valid. If imperfect, they are brilliant and Guruji was truly exceptional in the depth of his knowledge and in his ability to create a systematised version of it that is practical and beneficial to all who wish to use it.

Three tasks lay on the route to the resolution of these questions. The first was to learn to trust myself as my own best teacher, with a cautious regard for instructions and philosophies, however forcefully disseminated. The second was to peel away the teachers from the teachings and follow the latter objectively, disregarding the power of the personalities delivering them. The third task was to free myself of the system's taboo against seeking answers outside its imperfect confines.

Should you venture into the realms of spiritual India, I'd suggest that you do the same. Don't be afraid on your journey either, of turning unexpected corners to find yourself mirrored there in unforeseen guises and don't believe any guises of unworthiness in which others may want to cloak you.

My personal guise happened to be a surprisingly sturdily connected member of my Jewish family tree, whose roots shared mine but whose branches had proliferated beyond my narrow knowledge of them into exotic and alien realms. To my surprise and delight, like the roof of my home, they sheltered and comforted my tattered spirit on its quest in unwelcoming surroundings. Such treasures may await you, too, on your travels, if you chance to lift the lid of spiritual India.

2
Of Palm Trees and Pigs

AT THE RELUCTANT END of our sojourn in Goa there was one more place that Ahmed our driver insisted we visit – the Basilica of Bom Jesus.

'The what?' Arnie whispered to me in the back seat of the car, as Ahmed's jolly good music jingled from the radio.

'A church,' I muttered.

'Oh, Christ. Is he serious?'

I sighed. 'Just relax. He's not trying to convert us. He's Muslim. And we might offend him if we refuse.'

'How can we offend him if he's Muslim?'

Ahmed peered at us in the rear-view mirror. 'This is a very special church, Sir. It has the body of Saint Francis Xavier in it.'

'A body?' That was Michael, our teenaged son. 'A real body? Cool.'

Nothing like a corpse to settle things. So that was it then. The Basilica of Bom Jesus it would be.

Once at the site Ahmed waved us towards the basilica, assuring us that a guide would meet us there. This is how it works in India: at any worthy site, local freelance guides gather. They're invariably polite, well informed, articulate and a pleasure to support. As soon as we approached the entrance, a neatly dressed man greeted us, bowing his silvering head slightly and offering to guide us through the basilica, towards which he waved – disconcertingly.

There seemed to be something missing in his anatomy, some part or parts that should have held up his arms. They drooped forwards, dangling like dead fish from his shoulders, requiring him to fling them disturbingly at approximate angles to point at anything – a frequent occurrence in his profession. Every time he did, our four heads followed the arc of the fling, which would fall in a sudden vertical flop, leaving us perplexed and gazing along its trajectory for the notable object.

In this more or less visual manner we learned the equally strange story of St Francis Xavier, who must be one of the few people in history with an afterlife to rival the vigour of his earthly one. Not that that had lacked any oomph. If you were a missionary trained by Ignatius of Loyola in the mid-sixteenth century and sent sailing off to the East to gather in a heathen flock, you were bound for adventure, a permanent suntan, exotic diseases and an early grave.

St Francis Xavier, now the patron saint of Goa, checked all the boxes, dying on Sancian Island off the Chinese coast in his mid-forties. That was about when the morbidly juicy bits started. Although he was buried on the island, someone – inexplicably – had him exhumed and reburied in Malacca, now part of Indonesia, in a grave perplexingly too small for him.

To squash him into it, his neck was broken, as was noted by his successor who had the grave opened four months after Francis's burial – in order to pay his respects. The successor, aside from noticing his predecessor's cervical state, was struck by something else: St Francis in death had not decomposed, his corpse having retained all the unblighted freshness of its missionary days.

These astonishing remains were then sent to Goa for a somewhat itinerant period before being housed finally in the Basilica Bom Jesus in their canonised form. Every ten years they are displayed to the public. That is, what's left of them.

Chunks of St Francis have gone missing over the years in various incidents, the first of which involved a bite in 1554 by a Portuguese woman caving in to a craving for a saintly toe. A few decades later Rome reckoned it could do with a slice of right hand, which is now venerated there in the Church of Gesu. Then Japan, not to be excluded, claimed the rest of the hand for its Jesuits before others began to burrow in, leaving St Francis Xavier with a truncated intestine whose missing bits found homes far and wide.

Even his splendid casket is no longer whole. Formerly encrusted with jewels, it hovers above eye level in silvery monochrome amid the basilica's gilded altars, waiting for tour guides to point at it or fling their arms in its direction while tourists gawp at its murky glass windows and

Way out in India

St Francis sleeps in eternal fragmentation.

It was a fascinating visit, all the more intriguing for the obvious question left hanging over it at the end. About the tour guide and his missing bits. Whodunnit? A Portuguese cannibal woman perhaps? Deltoid-hunting Japanese Jesuits? Or perhaps Rome through a carving knife tucked in some priest's cassock. The mystery crackled all the way back to the Margarida.

THE MARGARIDA BEACH Resort was a euphemised hotel where we'd been shacking up in Goa, quite a distance from the beach and the general concept of a resort. Nevertheless, we'd snuggled into the place, as you would into a favourite but faded old shirt. The owner, a dour man proud of his establishment, kept everything to a grim kind of minimum, counting the sheets and towels himself on their way to the laundry. It was a sizeable property, the Margarida, with a long potholed driveway and its most persuasive feature, a pool.

Up close, though, its rooms hungered a bit in their sparseness, with just a length of some satiny cloth thrown over a sheet as an echo of a blanket. But that hadn't mattered since the portico's passages had beckoned wide and shiny for a gleeful bit of skidding between outings. And the showers had boasted an interesting arrangement of electric wires attached to the shower heads.

'For hot water, day or night,' the receptionist had intoned with stoic avidity.

I'd noticed on arrival that our bathroom door hadn't quite worked in all the usual ways, but that – for some reason – had been all right, too. I think it was the *susegad* that pervades the area, a Portuguese term for an unflustered calm that might well translate as "chilledness" if there was such a word.

And the waiters were sweet, young men who'd approached us in their neat black trousers and white shirts as we'd stood blinking in the sunshine on our first morning there. What did we want to do, they'd asked us. Where did we want to go?

'You must get a scooty,' young Fernando had recommended.

'And bicycles,' his friend Basilio had added.

It just so happened that Fernando had saved up his cash for two motorbikes to hire out to Margarida's residents on the side. And Basilio, a student of business "manadzement", as he'd called it, knew someone just along the road who hired out bicycles.

This was business in Benaulim, a relatively quiet little town down in south Goa, far from the tourist stampede to the season's northern party scene. For company we had each other and two of our three teenage children, at their fractious best on arrival in Mumbai, sniping at us and each other until the Goa they saw from the taxi's windows piqued their curiosity and perked them all the way up.

Lushly tropical with winding roads and a fluid blend of Portugal and India, the place sang with warmth and colour. With chipped and rusted signposts leading us along and the colonnades and tiled roofs presenting pinches of Portugal, we opened the windows to let in the smell of earth and coconuts along with breezes from the sea. Tuk-tuks puttered by, motorbikes whizzed, some bearing boys in bandanas waving at our kids; some, whole families and one, a pig strapped to the back.

Buildings thatched with palm fronds flickered in and out of view, while at the roadside stalls clothes danced in the breeze like revellers high on freedom. Fresh cashews tempted, too, and pineapples, alongside my old favourite from Pune – decapitated coconuts full of quenching liquid – all on the red-earth roadside leading into and out of the centre of town.

Interspersed with all this, placid rice paddies stretched out in the morning sun, hosts to cows and kingfishers and the odd egret like a swirl of cream in a spinach curry. And every now and then in the undergrowth or garbage a pig or two would be rooting. Here and there colourful shrines bejewelled the roadside. Instead of housing Hindu deities with blue faces, though, Mother Mary and Jesus himself reincarnated in Indian technicolour peered from inside their shelters. And being the festive season, the colour carried on. Tinsel drapings, fairy-light twinklings and banners full of wishes swirled up the sparkle quotient. It was Christianity as a party – full, joyous and as far from the solemn, cloistered notion of Catholicism as possible.

The purpose of our visit was to cure me of a recent addiction, since back home from India after that first stay, I hadn't been able to settle. She

Way out in India

had insinuated herself into my system like a virus, with symptomatic wafting in block-printed cottons and sliding into sandalwood soap baths for dreamy transportation back there again.

A lot of sighing and sinking on to embroidered cushions from Kashmir had accompanied the malady, along with "in India" inserted into every conversation – until even *I'd* got on my nerves. When my husband had resisted yet another curry at the local we fondly call Bollywood and I'd responded with an anguished: 'What do you *mean*, "how about a pasta for a change"?' he'd asked what I'd reckon would cure the condition.

I'd given the question some deep thought for four seconds before delivering the solution: 'I'm sure a family holiday to India would do it. Then you'd see for yourself what it's all about.'

It was his turn then to look stricken, the way a man does envisioning enveloping crowds and emissions heaving in a blur of heat and choking.

'But we could go to Goa!' I enthused. All the Indians have Portuguese names there.'

'Like Pedro Ferreira?' I got the feeling he was stalling.

'Yes!' I gushed, 'and Afonso Goncalves. Luis... Teixeira, Maria... Duarte.' He held up a hand. 'And there are lots of churches there! Cathedrals even.'

His face fell the way it had on our first trip to Europe, when he'd OD'd on churches, courtesy of my guidance. 'Okay, pretend I didn't say that. But it's India Lite, this Goa. In fact, it's hardly India at all.'

'So why would we go there then?'

'For the palm trees. For the pigs.'

'Pigs? Churches? And their relevance to us is?'

'Okay, scratch the unkosher bits.' He folded his arms across his chest with a twitchy sort of frown. 'So far the only selling point is the palm trees and Cape Town's not short of those.'

How could I explain the lure of this sandaled place that had enchanted me through an author friend's tales of writing a book in a "cocohut" on a palm-shaded beach for months on end? Accompanied by stray dogs, a thesaurus and a dictionary, he'd sustained himself on lassi, lentils and joy while the sea swished its soundtrack to the scratch of his pen.

In desperation I quoted my friend to my husband: 'He says you'd love it. So would the kids.'

'Would I need a thesaurus?' he grinned.

The deal was on.

JUST AS SMOOTHLY we wrapped up the deals with the waiters' contacts, rolling in on our wheels half an hour after the mention of them, to the sand-floored lean-to at the nearby home of a handsome man in a Hawaiian shirt. Smiling as he tapped petrol from a large plastic bottle through a hose, he then funnelled the fuel into the motorbike's tank.

And we were off, the beach the obvious first stop on this so far marvellous trip. Beach life in Goa is what the Taj Mahal is to Agra – its chief asset and its magnetic lure to one and all.

With the Arabian Sea dancing in lively currents and lapping on to the shore, a unique seaside theatre plays endlessly through the days. A cushioned lounger becomes the best seat in the house for viewing all the characters who wander into the water and across that sandy stage as the visitor, in a sun-saturated stupor, lets the mind meander with them.

But theatre's no fun without fuel in the stomach and among all the fun-for-the-whole-family activities to choose from on holiday, getting famished together is not one of them. Which was why the line of "beach shacks" along the sands delighted me so. In short, they averted a war. Essentially thatched restaurants open to the elements with names like Johncy's, Pedro's and The Mahal, they beckon in all their colourful airiness, welcoming visitors with cold drinks or beer and the most delectable food. With palm-leaf matting and bamboo cane everywhere, bright tablecloths provide the backdrop to fresh fish dishes, vegetarian adventures and such sauces as chilli, coconut and tamarind. A Goan speciality called xacuti, a red coconut sauce combined with chicken, meat or veg became my addiction *de vacation*.

The other attraction at these beach shacks are the free loungers and umbrellas outside, a clever touch for business, since anyone who lolls there for any length of time will want a cooling drink. And food, finally. And, as the sun arcs across the sky, the bill mounts up.

We had a few visitors for company on that beach, who turned out

Way out in India

to be more audience than actors since they slept through the whole afternoon show – in the shade under the loungers – twitching their ears now and then and only waking up for a sniff or two if anyone around us ventured into a biryani dish or fish curry from the beach shack.

Just as dozy, the portly Russians on vacation, freed from snow and woolly bundling, bared themselves to the sun in soporific bliss, enhanced no doubt by a robust flow of Kingfisher beer.

'You awake, Katya?' Boris seemed to be asking with a sudden surge of energy and a vigorous nudge to his partner's arm.

'Huh?'

'You want to swim?'

'Huh?'

'Swim.' He pointed at the Arabian Sea.

'Da.'

So off they plodded into the water, leaning on each other in a wobble of sweaty inebriation. I watched them, concerned about the currents I'd heard of and the warnings about swimming "wasted" as one guidebook put it. But from plodding they plunged, leaping and splashing, having a whale of a time.

'You having fun?' I was sure Boris was asking.

Katya tilted her face towards heaven. 'Da!' she shrieked. 'Da!'

On their way out they fairly strode through the water, coming to plonk down beside us with a lot of satisfied grunting and seemingly dead sober smiles.

'You want drink beer wit us?' Boris offered in a rare departure from the notorious unfriendliness of the Russians.

The few sips of beer only enhanced the already intriguing procession, a portion of which had taken to the sea. There a bouquet of saris and spangles bloomed giggling in the shallows. From girls to grannies, the group of about thirty waded as the little waves sloshed up to soak salwaar-kameez pants and the hemlines of saris. Shiny black plaits wriggled in the sun as elbows clutched handbags hanging in for the jaunt.

An ice-cream man cycling by with a cooler box balanced on his handlebars was swamped suddenly by the sodden-hemmed circle, keen for a sweet and frosty cooler. When they subsided, another sight rose that sat all of us up, even the Russians.

Before our eyes a mother in a sad-looking sari trailed two little girls, raggedly fancy dressed, across the sand. All of them carried bamboo poles, a tyreless bicycle wheel, a few copper pots, a drum and some rolls of stout rope. Herding the children along bearing a flat metal plate and some plastic balls, another woman brought up the rear. While we watched, the four of them conjured a rough structure with the rope strung tautly between two bamboo A-frames stuck into the sand.

In an instant a child was hoisted aloft, the mother's drum began to beat and the little girl ambled the length of the tightrope holding a shorter bamboo pole for balance. The drumbeat announced this wretched, alluring spectacle that kept to its rhythm, with the second child raised to the rope for her introduction as spectators began to gather.

As the drum beat on the girls traversed the rope in turn, sometimes rolling the bicycle wheel along it, sometimes with copper pots mounting trip by trip on their matted little heads. Sometimes they even pushed one foot along in the metal plate and juggled the jolly plastic balls and still the drum beat percussion to their grim-faced grace.

Accompanying percussion came from the waves breaking gently behind the tightrope contraption, while fishing boats bobbed a jaunty dance on the water. Then yet more percussion clapped its softer hands as each child finished a trick, to be swung on to the sand again. The final percussion came in papery whispers as the girls presented the metal plates to the motley assembly that had gathered for their show.

Then suddenly it was over, the troupe straggling on to repeat the performance up and down the beach until the sun went down. Then the ocean washed in to cover the holes where the sharp bamboo poles had pierced the sand.

'Let's walk,' I said afterwards, unable to sit still.

Ruth and I, strolling along, happened upon a sizeable catch being unloaded from a fishing boat that had just returned from the sea. Vast black nets were spread along the mud while stout men in shorts swung into action to divide the haul – a flapping mass of silver trodden by calloused feet in places. Big bellies heaved as the men yelled to each other, gathering the fish into smaller nets for transporting along the beach. These they slung over thick bamboo poles which they shouldered in pairs, striding up the shore in the sunny, salty breeze.

There the women met them, baskets swinging, bodies floral-wrapped from waist to knees, rich rolly midriffs exposed under their sari blouses with heads cushioned by folds of bright scarves. In a bustle of colour and silver the fish, mostly still by then, were transferred to the baskets in handfuls for their homeward journey. Meanwhile the men, banded now into a team, heaved the boat on to dry land with a dozen pairs of shoulders to the stout mango-wood poles of the outrigger. With skin gleaming, the headman called commands to the slippery crew to push the boat in unison up the slope while seagulls cawed and palm fronds lining the beach waved in welcome.

With baskets full and nets empty, magic hands spread them out on the sand in all their copious stringiness while Ruth and I continued our stroll. The whole operation seemed an act in a play on that first afternoon of beach theatre in Benaulim.

The fishing boats made superb pieces of scenery by being colourful, traditional and charmingly wooden, with names like Infant Jesus and Precila Rebecca-Princess Diana.

I wondered about this beach theatre. Who precisely were the actors and who the audience? Were Ruth and I intriguing someone that very moment, the middle-aged Western mother and her pale teenage daughter with silver "jewels" strung across her teeth? There was no shortage of Indian staring at Westerners, directly and lingeringly as they practised their yoga half-naked or played vigorous games of beach soccer. With no taboo in Indian culture regarding staring, they drank their fill of the foreign pink creatures with undisguised fascination.

I couldn't tell if the water buffalo was watching us after a hard day's tilling in the rice paddies, as it settled down in the shallows for a wallow and a soak towards sunset, its two minders tending to it like a tractor in a barn for a wash. A tractor's not sacred the way this chap was, though, with his curly horns and his tongue flicking into the salt splash. Rugged, young farmers the minders were, commanding their charge with no more than a twiggy stick to the flanks and a yank on its tail now and then.

Days rolled into each other this way with us falling quickly in love with the place and its residents. Conversation tends to flow in an absence of movement and, besides chatting to our waiter, Luis, and his friends between lime sodas and lassis, we got more acquainted with a host of others who'd pitch up around our little camp at the beach shack.

The hawkers were some of them, very young traders in trinkets and textiles who'd trudge the beach all day with their wares. Expert at selling, they'd catch one's eye and ask very casually: 'How are you?'

If you answered at all, they'd approach with the usual enquiry about country of origin and the family ties of the group. Then they'd set down their wares and unfurl a pop-up shop like a trick, stocked with bright, shiny things like an infinite ribbon of handkerchiefs pulled by a magician from his hat.

Many of these hawkers were pretty, young girls, who although cheaply dressed in long dresses or saris, always bore a touch of glamour – in tinkling bracelets or dangling earrings or a scarf startlingly combined with the colour of a dress. Some would walk in twos or threes and surround us with multiple shops all disgorging their wares simultaneously on to the sand or the loungers.

They began to get on my nerves, quite frankly. They were invasive. They had no respect for our space or our privacy. They were persistent. Their goods were essentially useless to us.

So I lay low with my hat over my sunglassed eyes, my book shielding my face and pretended they weren't there. But they *were* there and the more I tried to ignore them, the more my gaze was drawn to these watermill women plodding the sands, until I could not figure out what was heavier, the book or the effort of holding it in place.

And so I abandoned both. It didn't take long before a young girl came by with her bundle. Delicately built with a shocking pink dress and a golden ring in her nose, she flashed her smile, wide and white at me.

'How are you, Madam?'

Between table mats and handbags bearing the image of Laxmi, goddess of wealth, I asked her how she was.

'I have a headache,' she said simply, sinking down on the edge of my lounger in that familiar Indian way. 'The sun is too hot and I didn't sleep good.'

'Why not?' I asked.

'I was worrying about my business.'

'This business?' I gestured at the merchandise.

Way out in India

She nodded. 'I have to send money home to my family and the business is not so good now.'

'Where is your family?'

It turned out that her family, like most of these young peoples', lived in Karnataka across the state border. With tourist gold known to lie on the beaches of Goa, they trickled in constantly for this kind of work from a very young age without knowing the local language Konkani, or English for that matter.

'How old are you?' I asked her.

Again she spread out that smile. 'I'm fifteen.'

Ruth shot up in her seat, all fourteen privileged years of her. Michael shifted the towel off his face to peer out.

'Have you got brothers and sisters who earn money for the family also?'

'Only one. We have five more but they are too small.'

'So do you buy all this stuff and then sell it?'

She shook her head. 'No, we work for a man. He buys it. We sell it. We get commission.'

'And do you all work for the same man?'

'Some of us do. Others work for another man. Those girls work for the same man.'

A group of three came wandering past, squinting their eyes at us, at our hawker girl.

'How are you, Madam?'

I nodded perfunctorily, but they didn't go, rather they circled closer – which, in Indian terms, is pretty close.

'We have beautiful clothes, Madam. You must buy from us also. Not only this girl.'

'I'm not buying from this girl,' I said, since I wasn't.

'Only talking,' she added with a sudden edge to her voice.

'Only talking,' one of them sneered, turning sideways towards her friends, revealing a pregnant belly.

'Only talking,' another repeated, cocking her head and picking up her bundle as a signal to move on.

Our girl pressed her fingers to her temples when they'd left.

'They've got babies,' she offered.

'Babies?' It was my turn to shoot up. But they were babies themselves.

'That is why they are so angry all the time. They must buy food for the babies. And clothes. And they don't sleep in the night-time because of the babies.'

'Are they married?'

'Yes, they are married but the husbands drink all the time. Don't want to work. And the one with the green sari is getting another baby.'

I sighed. My children twitched. My husband lowered his newspaper.

'How old are they?'

She shrugged. 'Eighteen.'

'But you are not married,' I smiled.

She smiled back. 'No, but next year I will get married. My family have husband for me.'

'A good man?'

She didn't know. She didn't know him at all. All she knew was that at sixteen she'd go home and marry a stranger her parents had picked for her. Then she'd come back to Goa and ply the beach as before.

'Does your daughter want some pens?' she asked.

A sparkling set of four or six pens was produced, all spangled with glitter.

'Yes,' I said, 'she wants the pens.'

With a deft movement she shoved them under my towel. 'Don't show,' she said, 'the other girls are watching'.

I couldn't see the other girls anywhere. How could they be watching?

'And what about a handbag for you?'

'Yes, I'll take the handbag, too.'

And the bracelets that jangled. I wanted them all stashed under my towel.

Suddenly we were surrounded again by the pregnant girl in green who looked a little green herself, with her friends a close triangle.

'Only talking. Hah!' she sneered, cocking her chin at the bulge under the towel. 'Hah!'

The three of them hung around in the growing silent tension until at last Arnie came to our aid, sitting up, rattling *The Times of India* and frowning tightly – the alpha male, agitated.

Like wary-weary cattle they turned and plodded away, while with our girl we began negotiations on the back of the restaurant's bill using a glittering pen from our package.

EACH PRECIOUS DAY spent like this presented the kind of new sights and conversations that keep travellers addicted to travel. Each day would end at Margarida Beach Resort's redeeming pool. Surrounded by palm trees and characters, and immaculately kept, it was the perfect way to cool down after the hot ride home.

Just over the property's boundary wall a building site had blossomed and towards sundown the builders there would wash themselves the way Indian labourers do: under a public tap. Stripped only to shorts or loincloths, they'd revel in the water, some brushing their teeth and once again the fascination was mutual between the locals and us, all involved in that universal mammalian ritual, cooling off with water after the heat of the day.

One day when the sea was too rough for swimming, we returned early from the beach to spend the afternoon at the pool. Soon lulled into that silent musing state approaching open-eyed dreaming, a rustle and raised voice drew us all up to the vertical.

The voice was the hotel owner's directing three or four stringy men with shrivelled brown teeth around the pool area. Weathered and wearing only short dhotis, they jumped to his orders and their supervisor's. In his hand each labourer carried a short and primitive rope harness. Strung around the waist of each was a machete in a sheath.

After a bit of barking by those in authority, each labourer approached one of the skinny, soaring palm trees that surrounded the pool. With a quick whipping motion he lashed his harness around his feet and clambered up the trees. In a flash all the labourers were grasping the fronds higher up as they pressed the soles of their feet to the trunk. Cutting notches above them with their machetes as they climbed, they created the necessary footholds for the task. Before our eyes they reached the tops of the trees' trunks where they slashed the bunches of coconuts loose with the machetes, with volleys of thuds on the earth heralding the arrival of the bounty.

Once each tree's harvest had drummed to the ground, the plucker, or *paddekar*, would scamper down the tree again with the agility of a monkey, only to tackle the demanding work of the next tree. An ambling band of women in lacklustre saris meandered along under the sun, each bearing a basket woven of dried palm leaves to collect the harvest.

I only learned later that in Thailand and Malaysia coconut harvesting is indeed done by monkeys, the intelligent macaque variety. As was often the case when witnessing low-caste people working in India, one got the feeling that they regarded themselves as an inferior primate breed. They didn't respond to our greetings while watched by their superiors, but would display such sweet and childlike smiles in their absence, that one wondered what consequences might befall them for simply being witnessed returning the greeting of a foreigner.

There seems to be no concept of political correctness in this country in this regard, although the caste system was legally abolished so many decades ago. The Paravan community from which the coconut harvesters are mostly drawn is openly referred to as "the backward Paravan community" in a *Herald of Goa* article of August 23 2009.

But, perhaps change is approaching, since the article referred to the dearth of coconut harvesters in the current generation of Paravans. Rising school attendance, a falling birth rate and high levels of migration to the cities have begun to ensure that the scene we witnessed will probably have died out largely by the time our children are our age. The younger men seem to value themselves too much to undertake the risks and physical demands of this work, even though the government has offered training and insurance as an incentive to keep the skill alive.

In quite a spin about the lower yields of coconut trees infrequently harvested and the resulting falling revenues, the Coconut Development Board and others have begun to offer enormous rewards for anyone who can invent a coconut harvesting machine. One figure bandied about was ten-lakh rupees, the colloquial equivalent of one-million rupees – more than a human coconut plucker earns in a decade.

With India on the march the way it is economically, there's such a sense that so many of the charmingly simple, traditional skills will gradually disappear. Of course, to the outsider's eye, the artisans and craftspeople lend India its amazing colour, while they themselves often suffer terrible privations. For the traveller, though, the poignancy of this

Way out in India

idea leads to reflections on the transience of life itself – often too busy in the West, too noisy and automatic an entity for the meditations induced by travel.

TO INDUCE A deeper version of this state in Goa, I decided to avail myself of the *shirodhara* treatment offered by the Margarida's ayurvedic masseuse, along with a full body massage. In the shirodhara treatment, a vessel containing warm oil is positioned above the forehead. Through a small opening on the vessel's underside, it trickles in a continuous stream on to the centre of the forehead, where it soothes the nervous and hormonal systems into sublimation.

The full body part in the little poolside pavilion went swimmingly. Margarida Beach Resort's masseuse was young, very young and pretty and shy, like a little flower with steel in her stamens. In a way that I couldn't explain, I felt happy for her that her touch was so sure and so strong. The plinth was slippery wood as at the Kare Centre near Pune, but there was no nappy this time – just me sliding around under a sheet drawn back in parts, until the time came for the shirodhara treatment.

Then the young woman covered me, asking in broken English that I wait. She was going to fetch an assistant. I nodded drowsily, until in she padded on her bare little feet, followed by a heavyset fellow, fully moustached and smiling at me lying naked under my oily orange sheet.

'Man will hold oil,' she announced. Man waggled his head encouragingly. Client did not. Was Man going to hold curvy brass vessel of oil above client's head for an hour? And where would Man be when Client got up?

There have probably been more effective versions of the shirodhara treatment given and received before, primarily through the simple device of a ceiling hook to hold the oil vessel, which would eliminate both the client's tension and the need of a man for the treatment's duration.

I dressed hurriedly afterwards in my swimsuit and sarong, eager to get out of that building and my coating of oil and into our weird electrical shower. But the door to our bathroom was locked, with a plaintive wail issuing from behind it.

'Ruth?' I called, fiddling the latch which stood stubborn under my slippery fingers. 'What's the matter?'

Some fuzzy lament was the matter, which got fuzzier and more screechy every time I repeated the question. Ultimately, I established that my daughter was locked in the bathroom and had been for some time.

To which my response was to hurl myself sideways at the door, leaving an arm-shaped oil print on its impervious surface and a bruise on my shoulder that tingled in protest.

'And where's your father?'

Her voice rose an octave or two. 'I don't know. I called him and called him but no one answered.'

'And where's your brother?'

'I don't know!'

'Well, I'm going to find someone to get this door open, so get your clothes on.'

A sniffling tempered the meek 'Okay' from behind the door.

Striding down the passage, I stopped outside Michael's room and knocked.

'I'm in the bathroom,' he mumbled. 'I can't come to the door.'

'You, too?'

'What do you mean?'

'Ruth's locked in our bathroom. Can't you come and help me get her out?'

A grunt and a moan floated out through the window into the echoing passage.

'No.'

'What do you *mean*, "no"?'

'Er, just hang on.'

I hung on. What was he *doing* in there?

'What are you *doing* in there?'

His voice squeezed out an explanation: 'I'm squitting and vomiting and crawling on the floor trying to work out which end to point at the toilet first. So sorry, but I can't help you right now.'

Charming.

Racing back to our room, I flung open the door to the balcony to see

Way out in India

if help was available from below. And there was my husband, cap over his face, blissfully asleep on a lounger with a Kingfisher beer glowing amber beside him in the sunset.

Approaching him was our waiter Basilio, bearing a large spanner, a screw driver and some other businesslike tools.

'Sir,' he seemed to be saying, 'your family's in trouble.'

Arnie shot up, tipping the beer over.

'What? What's going on?'

Then the two of them marched towards the building, Basilio leading the charge up the resounding steps towards us.

It was a red-eyed young woman who stood aside as the door blasted open with its own brand of drama, to meet her oily mother, dopey father and the handsome young waiter who'd come to her rescue. When Michael joined us later downstairs and Basilio offered him a snack, he refused.

'Ah, because you have poo problem,' he nodded with a sage kind of sympathy. 'You must drink a lot of water, then.'

For my part, I was only too glad to be rid of that oil which I'd showered off – leaving the bathroom door ajar – for the sake of everyone's sanity.

Although it hadn't been life or death by any means, the sudden stress in Goa seemed a contradiction in terms. It was soon smoothed away, though, by our little rides to and from the beach, passing rowdy palettes of bougainvillea while dodging potholes and stray chickens or cows. Funny old Ambassador cars rumbled by the rice paddies, while an occasional bird of prey circled overhead. Here and there, we took brief excursions down unknown roads to rows of racks made from bamboo and palm where hundreds of fish lay drying in the sun.

ONCE OUR BOYISH-LOOKING Michael had been for a few trial runs on the motorbike, we agreed that he could ride me from the beach to the hotel to collect something I'd forgotten to take in the morning. In raising children, the value of certain moments is not realised or appreciated until afterwards. This was one of those.

We set off from the beach towards the hotel and stopped to observe a sugar-cane vendor pressing the juice at a roadside stall. The pressing contraption was a cross between an antiquated sewing machine with two big wheels and an ancient washing machine with rollers to squeeze out the liquid. This was then served to passersby in glasses, who unwittingly, happened to be us. Very soon the vendor insisted that we taste the green and frothy substance.

Oh, dear! I, for one, was not keen but reluctant to offend the vendor by refusing, equivocated. And how was one supposed to explain that the foreign microbes on his glasses washed in the same bucket of questionable water the whole day might cause us a difficult decision about which end to prioritise while crawling around on a bathroom floor later.

Michael, though, was keen, even as a bathroom-crawling veteran. And so we drank the sweet, delicious juice, though I do confess to having recited a heavy-duty blessing in silence over it first. It must have blitzed the bugs, since there were no adverse effects to speak of afterwards.

We rumbled on, towards the village, noting the cows grazing in the fields, one among them clearly an albino. It all looked so lovely and peaceful until the albino took exception to us and began to charge. With all his sixteen-year-old nerve, Michael accelerated while the animal chased faster and faster. Kicking up dust not far behind us after a harrowing hundred metres or so, it seemed suddenly to lose heart, leaving us laughing hysterically at the picture we'd seen of a white bull, red puffs at its feet, galumphing after us beside a green rice paddy.

To ease the shock, we stopped in the town for a jolt of sugar at a place advertising "Chocolate Kokis", cookies that did enough of a tranquillising trick to get us to the hotel. All was going smoothly on the way back until we stopped at a crossroads in town, wondering if it was a stop street or not, or if such a concept exists at all there, when an elderly man in a pressed shirt and tie with neatly oiled hair approached us.

Peering at Michael over his spectacles, then at me, he raised an eyebrow and waggled his head. 'Legal age?'

'Of course, Sir!' I smiled sweetly, then gave Michael a leg-nudge. 'GO!'

I THANKED HEAVENS for his quick reflexes – and his strength – a

Way out in India

few evenings later when we'd assumed before we'd known better that we could venture out at night on the two bicycles and the motorbike to find dinner. The beach restaurants were not far, we reckoned in the peachy dusk. The weather was balmy and the sky clear. So why not?

I'll tell you why not. There are no street lights in Benaulim. There are lots of potholes and bends in the road to negotiate in the dark. There are lunatic drivers, some of them drunk. And there are the feral dogs, which move in packs of up to ten and enjoy nothing better than a dinner of human calf, the more appetising for its rapidly pumping action on a bicycle pedal.

At sixteen, Michael was stronger and faster than I was, so, above the barking in the dark, I yelled at him not to wait for me but to get the hell home as fast as he could. The dogs stayed with me and my sparkly purple Indian Princess bike as long as they could keep up, canines bared and eyes aglow. The adrenalin was gushing. I hadn't spent all my school years standing up to urge my gearless bike up hills for nothing. The muscle memory kicked into my forty-something legs and somehow I managed to make it back to the holey tar driveway of Margarida Beach Resort unscathed.

Michael was there, bent over, hands on knees and panting. Arnie was, too, and had been for a while, jingling the motorbike's keys with Ruth wide eyed beside him. 'Well, that wasn't too bad, was it?' he beamed.

I glared at him and thundered upstairs, careful though not to slam the bathroom door when I reached it. I'd had enough drama for one night.

THE WAY THINGS work in India is that among the billion and more citizens, there are plenty of people to offer tourists their services. Some of these are the taxi drivers who beckon from the roadside. If you take a taxi anywhere, the driver will often offer you his business card for future trips. If you are satisfied with his services and take the card, you are then assured of hassle-free rides for as long as you're in the area.

So it was with Ahmed who became our driver for the rest of our stay in Benaulim.

His Tata Indica, although not new, was spotless and treasured with all the trimmings that that involves in India. It starts with blankets covering the seats and plastic covering the floors. There's also the mandatory ornate tissue box on the back shelf of the car and the piece de resistance, the religious icon on the dashboard. Ahmed had all the above, the tissue box being a faux wood and gilt affair of notable bling.

His religious dashboard icon was slightly unusual for the region – a golden decal encircling a Koranic verse.

'Are there a lot of Muslims in Goa?' Arnie ventured, gesturing to the icon as we set off with Ahmed to a restaurant called Dinha's.

'Not so many,' Ahmed replied. 'Mostly Hindus and Christians are here. Catholic. You know Catholic?'

'Oh, yes,' Arnie nodded.

'Are you Catholic, Sir?'

'No.'

Ahmed turned the aircon up to freezing, a common Indian courtesy to the welcome visitor.

'So what are you, Sir? Hindu?' He chuckled lightly.

'Er,' Arnie began, 'we're Jewish.'

A silence accompanied the hum of the air conditioner while Ahmed gave his moustache a pensive pull. 'Jewish?' We held our collective artificially cooled breath. 'What is Jewish?'

A family-wide exhalation ensued at some length, not that we were Jewish-neurotic-paranoid or anything. Anyway, what was Jewish? Where did it begin?

'Er,' Arnie ventured again, but Ahmed interrupted. 'Who is your Man?'

'Man?'

'Yes, your Man, Sir.' He waggled his head with an outward rolling palm for emphasis. 'Muslims have Mohammed. Christians have Jesus. Who is the Man of Jewish?'

Arnie turned to me and the children, his eyes bouncing helplessly from one to the other. Who was our Man? Abraham? Isaac? Jacob?

Eventually, of his own accord, for reasons known only to himself and with lightly chattering teeth, he settled on Moses. 'Moses,' he said, moving swiftly into translation for Ahmed's benefit: 'Moosa.'

'Moosa is the Man of Jewish, Sir?'

Way out in India

'Sure!' Arnie beamed. 'He was a great man, don't you think?'

Ahmed seemed to think better with wailing females warbling at high volume, to which he tapped on the steering wheel, pondering the question of Moosa with an occasional suck on his teeth.

These evenings being driven by Ahmed were some of the most memorable and relaxing I can recall from my multiple trips to India. We'd arrive at the dusky beach freshly showered and drenched with the delicious fatigue of a whole day's sunning and swimming. The drinks were chilly, and the food hot and oozing aroma.

We'd ladle our curries on to cushions of sticky white rice, sharing and tearing pieces of flat breads served in baskets. These we'd fold into scoops for the sauces, smiling in the candlelight at the name of some dish or other. "Chicken lollipops" was one of these, whose drumsticks were shaved to the bone at the bottom, then baked tandoori-style. "Loveable sandwich" was another, though we never did find out what it was. Afterwards we'd trudge out through the sand to the parking lot, where Ahmed would wave to us from the door of his Indica and we'd all pile in for the trip home.

AND THEN IT was Sunday, with church bells pealing ardently to remind us of that, while we sat in Margarida's sunlit garden, enjoying big chunks of watermelon, drinking tea served by Basilio and wondering what to do with our sunburned selves for the day.

Michael, a bit peaky again, nibbled vaguely and mumbled, while the rest of us decided on a bit of old-fashioned moseying.

We moseyed towards the church in the centre of town, an imposing edifice in crisp white with yellow trim, its generous gable flanked by two bell towers. At first glance it could have graced a Portuguese *praca* but then those little twiddly bits around the gables and bell towers spoke of India and again the internal kaleidoscope rolled to fuse the two.

Approaching the church, things suddenly got busy, with family parties in their Sunday best bustling about in and on all manner of vehicles. Perhaps it was a wedding. But where was the bride? A flash of white tulle whizzed by on a motorbike, the bride a little girl of about twelve with dainty shoes to match her dress, her veil blowing over her face while she stood between her father's feet.

It blew into his face, too, as, frowning in his suit, he negotiated the family's way through the churchgoers gathered in the dust outside the church. Quite a task that was, since behind him sat the bride's little sister, her head bowed into her father's back and behind her balanced mom, side-saddle and resplendent in a peachy embroidered ensemble, her pantyhose glinting in the sun.

As we strolled further across that dusty entrance area, several more little brides appeared from inside the church, all bearing their confirmation certificates and giggling among their families with excitement. Flanked by mothers, sisters and aunts, many colour-coded in home-made outfits for the occasion, they smiled for the cameras, their little tiaras glinting, while the men stood behind them, puffed up and sweating in the claustrophobia of suits and ties while the sun climbed higher for a better view of proceedings.

An old bow-legged beggar stood at the church gate holding out his bowl, but no one noticed him in that swirl of colour. Maybe his camouflage worked too well, his skin and rags a perfect match for the dust all around.

ON OUR RAMBLINGS about the town with the slender Ruth sandwiched between us on the motorbike, we succumbed to the beckoning of a shopkeeper standing in the doorway of his jewellery and textile emporium. Such shops are common all over India and are invariably owned by Kashmiris who leave their troubled state to trade elsewhere, always offering the customers Kashmiri tea aromatic with cardamom, while they delight in unpacking vast varieties of textiles, which they drape over their counters. Shawls and tablecloths appear, bedspreads and cushion covers, until the desire to buy any of them sinks under the bamboozling weight and colour of all that fabric.

And then there are the *carpets*. The zenith of a Kashmiri textile dealer's workday is the sale of a high-grade, handwoven carpet to the unsuspecting customer. The carpets are an art form, ancient, labour-intensive and requiring uniquely refined skills. The sales pitch starts at the lower end of the range and rises with the display of the more beautiful

Way out in India

and valuable carpets. Assistants swish these magnificent pieces from among piles of others, laying them on the floor and, in the case of certain silks, twirling them about to make the fibres change direction slightly and with them the carpets' colouring. It's an impressive performance.

The pressure to buy bears down on the customer in inverse proportion to the soaring sales pitch, which inevitably includes the assurance of insurance and safe shipping – to pluck those excuses from the startled customer who, half an hour before, never suspected her own deep desire for a carpet from Kashmir. Sweat begins to bead and ooze all round, drying into proprietal disappointment at the customer's grudging concession to the peace-offering purchase of, say, a table runner.

Kashmiris have textiles in their blood and will regale a customer at length about their various grades of wool, silk or cotton, invariably flourishing out examples of each for the customer to feel and appreciate. Or even more commonly, the senior salesman will summon "the boy" for the task, setting him clambering up ladders and rooting in low drawers.

In Indian businesses of any kind there is always at least one "boy" who is sent chasing about constantly to please the customer. Prime Minister Modi himself was once one of these – a "tea boy" to be specific. These boys are the magical elves of the Indian small-business world, producing anything from a pack of tissues to a cricket bat at a stern nod from the shopkeeper.

'Do you have any of those white cotton embroidered shirts by the way?' you might ask the Kashmiri shopkeeper.

His dark eyes might cloud, his brow furrow and his moustache bristle. 'No, Madam. Not really. But wait! One minute. I'll send the boy...'

The boy scoots out through the front door while your teacup steams with a fresh dose of cardamom. He returns a few minutes later, shiny, breathless and bearing a bundle of the requested items to be splayed atop the rest of the stock for your perusal.

It's amazing where these boys sometimes go to get the stock. Often it's to a nearby shop with either a family connection or a reciprocal arrangement with his employer. But other times it's up an impossibly spindly ladder into a storage attic that one didn't notice above the shop. Yet another boy destination is a storage hole in the floor called a "go down" behind the counter of an indoor market shop. It should rather be called "hell" for the occupational hazard of suffocation in the heat and stuffiness down there.

The boys are not young children but usually teenagers who inhabit the lower perches of the business pecking order. In restaurants, boys clear the tables, often dressed in khaki shirts and shorts as part of the British colonial hangover. The main tool of their trade may be a two-tiered stainless-steel tray arrangement, the two trays held together by curving steel strips that form into a central handle above the upper tray. The boys dash between the tables, swinging their trays and wiping down tables with damp cloths in a hundred and fifty shades of grey.

The Kashmiri traders of Goa also commonly trade in silver jewellery and gems sourced mainly from Nepal nearer their home state. Most of the jewellery is very beautiful, but I asked the shopkeeper: 'Who buys the swollen bits of bling under the counter?'

'That is for the Russians, Madam. Not for you.'

It was interesting talking to these men with big brown eyes and long eyelashes. Essentially an itinerant workforce, the Kashmiris leave their mostly Muslim state to live as a minority wherever the trade winds blow fortuitously. In the case of the Goan traders, that means packing up and leaving for Ladakh in the north when the monsoons come to the south. Every year they get home to their families for a month or two before the whole loaded caravan rumbles out to trade again.

The presence of these Kashmiris and the Nepalese who run so many Goan restaurants made us curious about the tiny spot of Goa on the south-west coast of India, its culture and its history. When we explored it, we were amazed to learn how much drama, wealth and power had passed through it on its way to the present.

For about two-hundred years, from about 1350 onwards, the rule of Goa passed between various Muslim sultanates and Hindu kings. Then, in the fifteenth century, a royal dynasty decided to make Goa its capital. Its rulers were the powerful Adil Shahs of Bijapur who realised that commanding the area's rivers and natural harbours would secure their dominance of the lucrative spice routes of the time. They lasted only eighteen years, though, because the little gem had caught the eye of the successful, swashbuckling and seafaring Portuguese who, after defeating

Way out in India

the Shahs in 1510, conquered Goa and made it their own for the next four and a half centuries.

From language to religion, the former Muslim capital was transformed into a European colony. Thriving on spice and power, the Portuguese set about the task of colonising the hearts and minds of the population, demanding its conversion to Catholicism. Whatever means deemed necessary were used for the task, including the newly minted Goan Inquisition. Among the tales of fabulous old Goa, those of savage tyranny are more quietly told, if at all.

In the accustomed manner of conquerors living off a land, the Portuguese did so lavishly – in the name of God. In return they multiplied the wealth of the little colony and educated its people, a valuable legacy for all those descendants of converted Ferreiras and Garcias whose state to this day still retains income and literacy rates among the highest in India.

By the time the Portuguese left Goa in 1961, their culture and religion had been so closely interwoven with that of the locals that a new culture was born – the warm, vivid and intriguing Goan heritage that draws travellers to its shores again and again.

The Portuguese did not leave easily, though. They were prepared to fight for Goa and fight they did, but with a depleted army scrambling about in Africa attempting to stem the tide of the movements for independence in Angola and Mozambique. Noting the opportunity, the Indian army advanced on Goa, seized it and proclaimed it part of India.

An old Portuguese fort somewhere nearby on that dreamy coast told some of this story. It thrummed in the heat, opening its splendid views on to reflective internal windows. These looked on to the ocean and all the vast violence, riches and history that had crossed it in centuries past. Their other view was that of great powers rising and falling as inevitably as the waves far below us.

IT WAS WITH some animation afterwards, that Ahmed drove us to the brisk little town of Margao, for it was there that we would explore on our own and he would visit his relatives until we called him to drive us home.

Situated a little way inland, Margao is the main hub of southern Goa whose busy atmosphere extends its emotional distance from the beaches. People stride along the roads checking their watches, cobblers sit on matting outside shops, their knees splayed out, clasping ailing shoes between the soles of their feet for repair. A Muslim man in a fez and long shirt marches by, his hennaed hair bleached orange by time and sun, while a jostle of schoolboys in British-style uniforms swagger and push their way past him, their hair bouncing with after-school glee.

The covered marketplace of Margao was a must-see, people had said, an intense cliché of colour, pressure and other people's elbows. After a brief excursion into its hyperstimulating arteries, we escaped it, gasping and grasping our few token purchases and heading unanimously to a nearby park for a slug of oxygen.

It was there that we decided to visit one of the region's famous old mansions of Portuguese Goa, more specifically, Casa Menezes-Braganca. Near the park's entrance a few futile phone calls were made to establish opening times and directions, while the heat rose, literally and emotionally.

'Is that Casa Menezes-Braganca?'

'Huh?'

'Casa Menezes-Braganca?'

'Huh?'

My point, precisely.

But never fear in India. Help is always at hand. This time it took the form of a portly driver resting in his tuk-tuk in the shade of a crocodile bark tree a metre or two away.

'Where you want to go?' he asked, grunting to the vertical on the side of the road.

'Casa Menezes-Braganca?'

'Huh?'

'Casa Menezes-Braganca?'

'What is this place, Madam?'

'Big house?'

'Big house. Ha! Yes, Madam. Come, I take you.'

'But there are four of us.'

He waggled his head encouragingly. 'No problem.'

Way out in India

No problem? Three of us at the back would already be a squeeze.

'Young man sit with me.'

Where? Where was young man going to sit in that tiny contraption?

And so it was a memorable chug from Margao eastwards to Chandor over the twelve or so kilometres, with Ruth squashed between Arnie and me, and Michael perched up close to the driver on the front seat with the latter leaning into his steering wheel at an angle, his plastic sandals beneath his seat, his smile stretching with each passing kilometre.

'Big house!' he beamed, stopping somewhere seemingly random suddenly and decanting us on to the dusty roadside. 'No problem. I wait for you here.'

Braganza House did not disappoint. A splendid specimen of an old Goan mansion still owned by one of the state's former landowning families, it's an example of the astounding wealth of this class in its heyday. Favoured by the Portuguese royalty of the time, members of this level of Goan society were commonly granted land by the king. The land on which Braganza House sits was among such grants and the house, between two and three centuries old, is only one of several in the luxuriant village of Chandor that was popular with the grandees of the day.

The opulence of the house was not immediately apparent in the foliage of its unkempt front garden, but a glance around the long Portuguese-style building, with its twenty-four towering windows, left no doubt about the status of the place.

This particular house has two wings, east and west, belonging to the descendants of two branches of the same family.

'Left should be left!' the driver giggled amid more head waggles. 'Right is right.'

'Huh?'

It took a few repetitions for the riddle to resolve, all of us shaking our heads and heading right.

The front door was opened by a stern old matron dressed for a meeting with the Queen, down to her pantyhose and pumps, regardless of the heat. She greeted us formally and minimally, sizing us up with a slight sneer, as if the children might erupt into a fit of teenage partying to swing raucously from her Venetian chandeliers.

Yes, we could tour her home but the rules were strict. We were to follow her and do as we were told. No lagging. No photographs.

Yes, Madam.

The house was astonishing in its beauty and lavishness, its vast rooms airy and bright from the light of all those windows, expansively sized and capped by fanlights of exquisitely curving designs. A "sunroom" led out to the back garden through several arched doors, the room hosting the ghosts of the past still enjoying its lightness, with spectral servants perhaps serving cool drinks on its polished table. A music room housed an old piano and delicate chairs, while four-poster beds fit for royalty graced the bedrooms. A dining room for a big Catholic family blessing their fortune, then feasting on plenty, boasted a glorious table, while all around Ming vases and marble floors complemented rosewood furniture of rare beauty.

Then suddenly a ballroom opened – a *ballroom!* – vast and empty. And vast because it was empty, its aforementioned chandeliers somewhat dulled by dust and redundancy. Still the phantoms danced across the floor in silks and satins, while the music played and wraith ladies sat fanning themselves on the curvy-carved couches along the walls.

Although these mansions were built in the Portuguese style, a few of their features were uniquely Goan. One of these was the oyster shell window screens that let in a light delicate and diffuse, while the sun hammered down outside. The frames of these screens were of wood inserted in long vertical bars between the segments of oyster shell. Usually painted a bright colour to complement the rich hue of the house, the frames offered stability while the translucence of the oyster shell light ensured privacy when the screens were closed. A small hole, presumably for air, was left open in the middle of each screen. The craft of creating these windows has almost completely died out, leaving examples like the ones at Braganza House as fragile little pieces of a history worth preserving.

The decor of the house was eclectic, with antique pieces from China, Macau and all over Europe blended to create an artwork of a home. The mirrors were Belgian, the carpets Turkish. The whole impression was of being whisked through a dream of endless elegance, abundance and something else – a precarious, previous grace from before the time

Way out in India

when the Indians seized the lands of the Portuguese, leaving them with these huge mansions without the means to maintain them.

Still clutching the remnants of her family's favoured past, the hostess's bearing was arrogant rather than regal, the clan's shredded power having come to rest in her frail old hands. Its tools were her haughtiness and her prerogative to rush guests through her treasure trove, as if their feasting eyes would gobble up the lot, leaving her in penury.

There was no official fee for viewing Braganza House, but Arnie's offering of a fan of rupee notes placed in a porcelain receptacle on a little table at the end of the tour was met with the lady's contempt. A sombre speech from her followed, regarding the costs of maintaining the mansion so valiantly, so immaculately, with these tours being her sole means of doing so. Duly shamed, he disbursed a wad more, before she ushered us out into the sunshine, all slightly dazed by the experience and the notions it evoked again of power rising and falling, through layers of resistance as crusty as oyster shells towards pathos, so inevitably.

Outside, the driver waggled his head happily.

'You like house?'

Yes, we liked.

'Better you left the left one. Not so good.'

After Braganza House the only treasure left in Ahmed's chest for us was the Church of Bom Jesus with its denuded coffin, dismembered saint and disjointed tour guide, whose valiantly attempted wave at us signalled the disagreeable reality of ending our Goan odyssey.

It was hard to leave this place for many obvious reasons, one more being that the journey home would qualify as gruelling, involving as it did a nerve-wracking shuffle through the Mumbai traffic, a tedious layover at the airport until a 2:00 am departure and a ten-hour flight.

ONCE EVERY AIRPORT official in uniform had peered at us from under his peaked cap and banged another stamp on our papers – as is the common practice at Indian airports, be warned – we were checked through to the waiting area where we waited. And waited. And drank dreadful sugary thimbles of chai from the kiosk there, with chilli-bombed potato chips for comfort as the night wore on. And on. It was a long slog to 2:00 am with increasingly scratchy children, one in particular drizzling a tear or two on the dusty tiled floor.

At 1:15 am the airport curtain went up on a sudden drama, announced through the Indian system of sending an employee in a shirt, tie and dress pants to address the weary would-be passengers, clutching their carry-on and longing for sleep.

'There is a problem with the aircraft, ladies and gentlemen,' he announced brightly. 'The technicians are doing their best to repair it, but it will not be leaving at 2:00 am as planned. We will keep you informed of their progress.' He waggled his head jauntily, then attempted to leave the area, but the suddenly converging mob trailing their wheelie bags wove into a tight circle around him, foiling that plan until the poor man found an opening and made a dash for it, wiping his brow with his handkerchief flapping like a white flag under the neon glare.

In his wake a young heap of auburn curls collapsed weeping into my lap, overwhelmed, exhausted and worrying about missing the first day of the school year close to dawning a far way down south.

It was a long night of replays, the scene only differing in the pitch of the crowd wound as tight as a sitar string while the sky turned grey outside, along with the pallor of the man in the shirt and tie assigned to declare the ground-bound tidings.

When the sky turned pink, he stood before us once more to deliver the verdict. 'You will all be accommodated at hotels until the aircraft is repaired, ladies and gentlemen.'

In the pandemonium that followed, I feared for his life, forgetting the futile mopping of my tear-soaked jeans as I strove to see if he would get out of that mobbing in one piece.

How he managed it remains a mystery to this day, as do the machinations that found us swanning into a five-star cavern with grand marble staircases at 7:00 am. A lofty flower arrangement graced a table on that shiny expanse of concourse while, flanking the first staircase, two cylindrical lamps rose in all their phallic brazenness to the height of three men. From a restaurant nearby the aroma of a breakfast banquet beckoned the children to peer gobsmacked into the dining room.

'Can we *afford* this?' Michael asked Arnie who educated him swiftly on airline liability.

Way out in India

Which was how our children came to pad on thick carpets and sleep in high thread counts, indulge in fine feasts between staring out of their palace window at the slums just below, squirming and asking questions of us and the universe about how all this could be so.

We tried to answer them by stepping beyond the hotel's gates where a mob of beggars and touts besieged us, one an unofficial taxi driver offering to take us in his rattly old Ambassador wherever our hearts desired.

This iconic car, the Hindustan Ambassador, has become one of those endearingly old-fashioned reasons one falls in love with India. First manufactured in 1958 and based on the British Morris Oxford III, it has remained steadfastly its solid little self throughout the decades, having hardly changed at all since its debut. Sadly, these cars have started disappearing from India's roads and soon will become part of its history, since their emission standards fail to comply with stringent new laws aimed at curbing pollution.

We trundled along Mumbai's roads in our faded green model dodging trucks, tuk-tuks and the odd plodding cow. In the middle back seat and in my voluntary role as human shield to protect the sleepless children from each other, I'd unwittingly chosen the extreme bouncing version of the tour. I can therefore verify the presence of steel in the car's upholstery – both of seat and ceiling. I would also recommend that human shielding in the middle back seat of an Indian Ambassador should only be undertaken with portable cushions.

'Where you want to go, Sir?' the driver asked Arnie.

He glanced helplessly at me. Where did we want to go?

I'd read *Shantaram*, so I knew.

'Gateway of India, Taj Hotel, VT Station, Colaba…'

'Okay, okay, Madam. I take you.'

We sallied south, taking in the buzzing mass of Mumbai outside our little green runabout, noting the swirl that sixteen- or seventeen-million people create when creating – businesses, movies, designs and whatever else they choose to contribute here. With the brashness of New York and the glamour of Hollywood, this city is no Washington or government-tinged Delhi. Eclectic, electric and liberally dosed with chaos, it flings itself along to a Bollywood beat, exuberant, extemporary and exhausting

Of Palm Trees and Pigs

all at once.

With this being an impromptu tour with a valiant taxi driver for a guide, the specifics were a touch sketchy. We got the picture anyway. You can't help it in Mumbai. A city belonging to the species *metropolis colossus*, it's also India's financial centre, its fashion hub and the home of Bollywood, sprawled on the west coast of the country under a permanent cloud of carbon, like a dirty curtain drawn over what was probably once a city that sparkled by the sea.

Formerly seven separate islands ruled, in turn, by Hindus, Muslims and Portuguese and called Bombay, Mumbai fell into British hands in the seventeenth century and began to flourish as a centre of commerce. While the population burgeoned, a gargantuan land reclamation project saw the islands unified into one solid mass before the century was out. Mumbai boomed as it bloomed into the chief supplier of cotton to the British during the American Civil war in the 1860s, giving free reign to their colonial impulse to impose their culture in grand style on the city's landscape. Hence the majestic architectural landmarks that still thrust their blackened turrets and buttresses into the hazy sky.

Of course, the British rule of India ended in 1947 – but not easily. It took Mahatma Gandhi to get the ball of independence rolling, which he did with his Quit India campaign. Matching Mumbai's audacity perfectly, it could not have been launched at a more suitable site than this city.

In the 1990s its chronic edginess sharpened, with tensions between Hindus and Muslims flashing, then clashing amid riots and bombings where lives were lost along with trust and goodwill between the groups.

The November 2008 bombings of multiple city landmarks carried the theme into the new century with devastating effects, changing the free and easy face of Mumbai into one more cautious, sandbagged and filled with men in peaked caps and scanners searching eyes, bodies and bags for clues of destructive intent.

With our visit there having predated these events by almost two years, it was with light hearts that we strolled the paving from the Ambassador to the Gateway of India. This impressive triumphal arch in the Islamic style, flanked by four turrets and featuring intricate lattice work, was built in 1911 to commemorate the visit of King George V and Queen

Way out in India

Mary to India. Being so weighty and elaborate, though, it was only completed thirteen years later. Built on Wellington Pier with its outward façade towards Mumbai's harbour, it was intended to serve as a potent symbol of welcome to this powerful city. It was with sad irony, then, that the last British regimental parade took place there at the handover of India to the Indians just after Independence in 1947.

On the ocean side of the gate, pretty boats depart for Mandwa and Elephanta Island, while, on the inland side, a vast plaza plays host as a vivid rendezvous for hawkers and holy men, touts and tourists, beggars and balloon vendors all plying the paving stones, all seeking something.

One such sadhu doing a roaring trade in blessings approached us with his pot of kumkum powder at the ready, his red rakhi threads dangling from his hand and his little brass flower basket all a-flourish. As sadhus go, ours was a distinctly upmarket representative, combed and clean-shaven in a long white kurta. More usually frightening to the foreigner, sadhus are shaggy men in ragged robes or – more disconcertingly – no robes besides loincloths draped over their dangly bits. Devoted to seeking moksha or liberation from the suffering of life and the protracted cycle of death and rebirth, they wander through it with beards, matted hair and sometimes face or body paint, begging for alms and dispensing benedictions in return.

Happy to have traded this way with our sane-looking sadhu under the blazing Mumbai sun, we turned our dotted foreheads to the Taj Hotel across the road, red threads hanging from our wrists as we pointed to its historic magnificence. Officially known as the Taj Mahal Palace Hotel, it was built in 1903 by the wealthy industrialist, JN Tata, who, according to legend, created it after being refused entry to a European hotel because he was Indian. A grand seaside structure of impressive proportions, its architecture blends Italianate, Moorish and oriental influences into a mixture precariously perched between elegance and vulgarity.

We ventured through its fabled portals where royalty, world leaders and celebrities had swanned before us, probably in less rumpled and red-faced shape than our own. The object of the exercise was to explore the place, breathe its history, to sit on its plush chairs looking out to sea and to drink a cool and expensive drink to make memories for the family memory chest. This we did, attended by waiters ignoring our scruffiness with aplomb, while we sipped miserly sips and gulped in the various artworks and antiques around the room. Afterwards we tiptoed as far as we could go, which was not far, on the carpets of handwoven silk. Staring at the grand staircase and onyx columns, we marvelled at the crystal chandeliers and the sense of the elite in more gracious times treading those floors.

'Imagine how they felt using the first steam elevator in India!' I gushed. 'Imagine what it was like to stay in the first hotel in the country to use electricity! And just think about everyone who used this place as a hospital during World War One!'

Noticing their evident glazing over, not everyone in my family found these conceptions as thrilling as I did, so I kept my musings to myself about those swanky gentlemen at the opening of The Taj's Harbour Bar. Just for the record, the year was 1933 and the bar was the first ever licensed in Bombay. While peering into the elevator and fondling the bannister of the staircase, I transported myself to that room full of fine whisky and cigar smoke, while my family stayed firmly in the present, baying for food – and getting fractious about it.

I whispered a prayer of thanks for the hornets' nest around the corner, more commonly known as Sahakar Bandar Pure Veg. Restaurant, where waiters dashed along the narrow aisles between tables, delivering heaps of hot food at high speed to office workers on lunch hour. Curries skimming momentously to a halt threatened to leap from their bowls. Drinks splashed a few tears on to tables. The place buzzed with volumes of diners chewing and chatting, while Michael sat in apparent catatonia until his biryani arrived, only to announce then that, according to his calculations, the exact same lime-soda as the one on the table before him had cost twenty times more at the legendary Taj around the corner.

Every inch its architectural and historical peer, the Victoria Terminus Station soon loomed up before us on that whirlwind tour of Mumbai. A World Heritage Site renamed Chhatrapati Shivaji Terminus in 1998 as part of India's effort to reclaim its identity from its colonial past, this elaborate complex dwarfing everything around it, is still nevertheless known to one and all as "VT".

Built during the latter part of the Victorian era, it flaunts its overcooked Gothic excess with the panache that precedes hubris.

Way out in India

Domes and buttresses, spires and turrets all vie for the eye, eclipsed now and then by a twinkle of sunlight on a stained-glass window. While gratuitous twiddles creep along its gables and domes like a regiment of snails seeking the shells that the architect omitted, it stands proudly amid its palm trees and cypresses, topped with its Statue of Progress holding her torch in her right hand and her wheel in her left, leaving one wondering if the progress in evidence at street level is what the British had in mind. Progress it is nevertheless, attested to in part by VT's boast of more bustle than any other train station in Asia.

Colaba, the district nearby, is a jumble of vibrancy and vintage architecture in steady decline, magnetic shops and little stalls, restaurants and travellers gawking in a state of sensory overload amid the eternal cacophony of the city traffic. In a bookshop tightly packed with both customers and stock, we rooted out some bargains, realising again why that Statue of Progress still perches so relevantly at the pinnacle of the VT Station. The locals love to learn. They love literacy, with this busy bookshop attesting to the phenomenon.

All three places mentioned above were among those that survived the 2008 Mumbai bombings, thereby leaving streets permanently closed around them and the enhanced security changing their vibe to vigilance for the foreseeable future.

Puffed to saturation point with the tumult of the streets, we retreated to the Ambassador for the northwards trek back to the hotel. Talking to the taxi driver on the way, we asked him where he lived.

'Do you want to see, Sir?' He turned his thin and twinkly face towards Arnie.

Sir did. So did the rest of us who'd flopped into the Ambassador, which began to feel more like a fish tank with every metre covered in that vast and sprawling slum adjacent to the airport.

A grey shock at first glance, its tumbledown shanties hustling in the dust and garbage for survival, it evolves into colour with an order of its own after a while. Not order as we know it, but order nevertheless. India's order and systems generally bear no resemblance to our own. They are there, though, slow sometimes, slightly screwball to us, but there. In a narrow lane of shacks, for instance, it's difficult to discern where one dwelling ends and the next begins. The residents know though. They built them after all, supplementing their corrugated bones with skins of blue plastic and rough doorway curtains where necessary.

The tour with scant commentary from the taxi driver left just a whirl of impressions, overwhelming olfactory ones in the absence of any sanitation services, and delightful auditory ones, too, in the high, crystal voices of the boys flying kites from the rooftops. Most, though, were as visual as our image was to the locals. And what an image it must have been: of sleepless white sardines with mouths agape inside the Ambassador's confines.

As we trundled by, a table laden with bright green cabbages came into view, the vendor waving and flashing his perfect teeth. Further along, four young men bathed from a black plastic drum at the roadside, pouring water over their heads from little jugs in primary colours. A solid man with a pot on his head to match and a cane chair slung over his shoulder plodded past a line hung with white washing fluttering triumphantly, while an old woman watched a toddler waddle along their short front step before landing, surprised, at the feet of a dog needing nourishment.

A bicycle leaned wearily against a crumbling wall. A band of neat schoolgirls strode along chatting. A home-made curtain, delicately pink, flapped from a glassless window, its shiny fabric proclaiming all its hope the same way the white washing did and the green cabbages and the backpacked schoolgirls and the young men bothering to keep bathing amid all that cul-de-sac filth.

Flying far above India that night at the reluctant end of this unexpected detour to Mumbai I couldn't settle for the return of my malady – the magnet of the country already pulling me back. Above all the wonders of the place, I glanced through the windows. Outside was only darkness. Pierced by the defiant flicker of fires.

3
Of Waterways and Warblings

A TAD TESTY WITH each other on our first morning in God's Own Country after a long-haul disaster of a flight, we exercised restraint – until one of us just couldn't anymore.

The immediate issue was, well, my husband. He knew how to tour. He unfolded the map, pulled on his cap, looped his camera strap round his neck and slapped on the sunblock.

Oh, dear. Why didn't he realise that that wouldn't work here?

'Why not?' he sort of snapped, his sunglasses slipping on white lashings of lotion.

My attempted sweet voice slid into a whine. 'Because there are no street signs here. And if there were, they'd be in a foreign script. And if you look down at the map you'll be liable to miss someone hell-bent on hitting you because you're walking in the street because there's no pavement and…'

'Okay.' He held up a traffic cop hand. 'Okay, I get it.'

But he didn't and still insisted on at least *trying* to walk to our destination.

'What for? Do you think *trying* will keep us safe from people who drive worse than my mother?'

'So that we don't miss anything.'

I rolled my eyes under my cap, catching the sparkle in the breeze of the tinsel tassels strung up in the alleyway outside Rosa Villa in honour of Christmas.

Within five minutes an engaging sight stopped us in our tracks: an Indian driving test in progress. Oh, yes? Okay, he was right. We would have missed this oxymoronic experience on wheels.

The setting: a dusty field with a big tree. The equipment: a small table, two plastic chairs and a fan of paper folders. The players: two khaki-clad authorities, with ropes through their epaulettes, sitting on the chairs under the tree, shuffling the folders; plus a few hopeful boys – and some girls! The procedure: get into the practice Jeep. Turn on the ignition. Mosey round the field. Brake. Reverse. Mosey towards the table. Brake. Turn the ignition off. Bingo! A driver's licence when the dust settled.

That was it.

On the bright side, as of 2012, there are moves afoot by the traffic authorities to include mandatory gradient and parking components in the testing procedure. Good stuff.

We zigzagged along from the field, Arnie turning the map at every corner in a futile search for street signs, with the mid-morning sun starting to liquefy the patience of one of us. Until a scooter whizzed by, almost hitting a dog and swerving towards our pedestrian selves, as conspicuous and sticky as two vanilla cones.

'Dammit!' I exploded. 'What are we risking our lives for here?'

'Where you want to go, Sir?'

Aha! The inevitable tuk-tuk angel shuffled to a halt in the red sand at the side of the road.

'Probably a rip-off artist,' Arnie mumbled.

'Damn right!' I shot back, leaping in and banking on the flimsy metal shell as our survival tool in the circumstances.

'Princess Street,' I huffed.

This street, the main tourist street in Fort Kochi, is a sweet and manageable blend of colour and usefulness all housed in colonial buildings wearing down gracefully. It's a modest place, charming and productive, expressing the State of Kerala's essence in these ways. This south-western state's natural beauty, its beaches and its backwaters make it an easy destination of choice, especially since a certain book lists it as one of a thousand places to see before the Grim Reaper shows up.

And then in the city of Kochi there's the bluntly named Jew Town, or what's left of it: the last remnants of a once-thriving and powerful Jewish community with a lively history.

"God's Own Country" announces the Kerala Tourism Authority's sign leading to the area, with "Jew Street" capped by an arrow and footed by a flapping pile of garbage. To be honest, the narrow old roads there

Way out in India

produce little evidence to warrant the signage. Only the old synagogue, reached after a short walk, gives any clue of the community's existence.

Essential to this enclave and extant, this Pardesi Synagogue, built in the sixteenth century around its communal courtyard, remains defiantly operational with its community of fewer than ten members attending services there. Quite a wonder this is, since the Portuguese in a fit of Catholic fervour tried to raze it through a few volleys of cannon fire nearly a century after its establishment. They almost succeeded, but thanks to the Dutch restoration while *they* were in power in Kochi, it stands resplendent today.

And so it was that we found ourselves in this airy, old building with its antique windows wide open as they always have been in the dry season, letting its community's prayers float out to mingle with the city's aromas. In the prosperous bustle of centuries past, these were the fragrances of spices.

In line with Indian tradition, we left our shoes in the courtyard outside under instruction from a stern man who waved us into the treasure chest inside. Our soles cooled by the willow-pattern tiles underfoot, we gazed around in wonderment.

'They're from the eighteenth century,' said a little man sitting in a pew. 'Chinese. Handmade.' Rising in his fez-style skullcap, his head wobbled slightly. I'd never met a fellow Jew who wobbled his head. I'd never walked barefoot on antique Chinese handmade floor tiles and savoured the intense sense of presence in the moment that is one of travel's most underrated gifts.

The synagogue, its dimensions not designed to intimidate or impress despite the former wealth of the community, was of a modest and amenable size, but filled with riches, historical, spiritual and material. The impression was one of surprising beauty and light, the sun streaming in and glinting off the Belgian chandeliers from the nineteenth century and the lamps of coloured glass.

What set the Indian Jewish community apart from those in the rest of the world through the ages was the unique cordiality they always enjoyed with the rulers of the country. From most others they'd had to flee persecution over millennia, but in India their rights were enshrined by the Hindu king almost two-thousand years ago on engraved copper plates, still in the synagogue's possession. These stated their entitlement to live freely, build synagogues and own property "as long as the moon and stars endure". The maharajas, the Dutch and the British all realised the benefits to themselves of maintaining good relationships with the Jews and all parties prospered for centuries. When the British left after Independence in 1947, however, the Jewish community of India, fearing an uncertain future, emigrated en masse to Israel and other countries, leaving only the remnants of their vibrant culture behind.

'But where did they come from?' I asked a shopkeeper in Jew Street. He folded a traditional embroidered yarmulke and a handmade lace tablecloth and sighed. Then he looped his tape measure round his neck, pressing his palms into his counter. 'It's a long story.'

Some of India's Jews who'd come to the country and particularly to Kochi, claimed they'd been there since biblical times after fleeing the Romans after the fall of the Second Temple. They were known as Black Jews because of their relatively dark skin.

Most of the others arrived there similarly traumatised, but in the sixteenth century from Spain and its Inquisition. These were the White Jews who spoke Spanish and their own language, Ladino, as well as the local language, Mayalam, after a few years in Kochi. Perfectly suited to thrive as traders and trading agents between European clients and the local merchants dealing in textiles and spices mainly, the White Jews flourished magnificently, causing tensions, jealousies and rivalries to simmer between the two groups. Finally splitting completely, they lived separate community lives in Kochi and elsewhere and forbade their children to marry.

'This whole street used to be full of Jewish spice traders,' the shopkeeper smiled, unfolding yet more delicate lace for our perusal. He knew. He'd lived in the area all his life as the son of a cook for a prominent Jewish family. 'All these shops were Jewish shops in those days. Now only antiques and tourist shops. There are some spice shops around here that you can see, but not like before.'

The spice shop we smelled before we saw it presented a cameo of the area in former times. Beyond its wooden doors, merchants sifted powders into tasting bowls, weighing rice and spice on old-fashioned scales while delicious aromas reached out to strollers, drawing us

Way out in India

towards its ancient enchantment.

There was modern enchantment, too, of the quirky kind, in the area. Where else would you find a chic little set-up with starry paper lanterns leading you down a passage to a place called Café Jew Town?

WITHOUT THE PORT of Kochi nearby, there would have been no spices, or anything else to trade in the region. Should you dawdle along to see it, you'll be met by a remarkable sight: the area's iconic Chinese fishing nets that stretch their strange and spindly limbs over the sea as they have done for centuries. Exactly who brought their design to Kochi remains one of its mysteries. Some say the Chinese. Some say the Portuguese – all the way from Macau. Whoever it was added something unique to the ocean's edge here, since nets like these are found hardly anywhere else in the world.

Permanently installed on land, they stand along the shore like bony sea monsters, their woody limbs creaking up and down, raising and lowering the nets in predatory slow motion. Mechanical and immense, they rise at least ten metres high, nets swinging horizontally out over the ocean in poetic gauziness when viewed from afar. Measuring about twenty metres across and attached to a cantilever by ropes bound to radiating spokes, they are raised and lowered by the counterweight of a series of rocks tied to a long and sturdy length of rope.

Four to six stringy fishermen work the rope, one of them treading the central beam way up off the ground to adjust the weight distribution, which, when increased on the ocean side, lowers the net. Some minutes later it is hoisted up again by the rest of the fishermen pulling on the rock-laden rope. A small flurry ensues as the net is emptied and the fish sold on the spot to waiting buyers.

From a distance, especially at sunrise or sunset, the sight of these installations silhouetted against the sky lends romance to the old trading seaport. Close up, however, the picture is very different. The work is crippling, with the fishermen sweating through the whole arc of the sun for the meagre catches the sea offers. Sadly, for tradition, there are few young ones among them.

The whole system is disappearing under the light weight of the catch,

Of Waterways and Warblings

the heavy weight of collapsing fishing nets and the absence of any help from the government for maintaining or repairing them – however enticing a tourist attraction they may be. With all the occupational hazards involved in the work, no insurance is available to the fishermen, whose existence is a garbage-strewn shoreline, the stink of fish and the racket of gulls cawing and wheeling for the same reason that they themselves hoist ropes and rocks all day long.

Should you stroll the paved promenade away from the garbage and gulls, be prepared for the sights. Not being the usual or expected sights, they are the kinds of encounters that make India, well, India. You may, for example, find a goat on your meander. Seriously. We did. He posed on some rocks beyond the public garbage bin shaped like a friendly lion, its smiling maw saying "Use Me" in red letters. He chomped on a banana peel. He followed us past the band of handsome young locals licking ice lollies. He led us to his fellow goat.

Sharing a promenade bench face-to-face with a fat man cross-legged and barefoot chatting on his cellphone, the fellow goat's forepaw lay lovingly along the man's foot. Was he the one who'd tied a bandana of pale blue around his bench mate's furry neck? Was he his pet? His milk producer? A casual acquaintance? And what of the other goat? Where did he fit in? We never did find out, since the fat man chatted on, unperturbed, as we smiled at each other, shaking our heads and murmuring: 'Only in India.'

And perhaps only in India would you chance upon the kind of common construction site that she hosts in many states – to her shame. In Western terms such a site means invariably a place of men and machines. Not so in India. Hence the jarring sight of women in dusty saris bearing wok-like pans on their heads filled with rocks, rubble or cement, traipsing the repetitive routes of building sites for the price of a daily meal, sometimes trailing their bony children behind them. Open-mouthed, one watches this parade, wondering how they do it. How do those graceful necks bear that burden? How do those lives and with what consequences?

The topic of poor versus rich lives in the area allowed me to introduce to my husband – very cautiously – a more formal proposed sight.

'A palace!'

Way out in India

Palaces rate up there in the church stratosphere on his not-to-do travel list.

'Oh, come on,' I sighed. The weather was hot and the palace would be cool – I hoped. 'We're right there.'

As it turned out, it was a good thing we did get to Matancherry Palace – for sheer entertainment value. Not that the place looked so inviting from the outside. Rising damp had encroached up its walls and the general impression was an education in ruin production. Around India there are many such palaces, often imposing compounds, but on much smaller scales than say Buckingham or Versailles and without the maintenance crews to keep up their sparkle. And so we approached the Matancherry abode with its red tiled roof and arched wooden shutters warily, taking in its dusty pathways and unprepossessing grounds.

'So what's this place supposed to be about?' Arnie muttered as we followed the crowds up its wooden staircase outside.

I had no idea but could never pass up a palace.

'It's also called the Dutch Palace,' the brochure told me and I told Arnie in the airless panelled entrance hall that had filled claustrophobically with a school group on a field trip.

'Although it wasn't Dutch at all! It was given to the Raja of Kochi by the Portuguese in 1555.'

'Probably as a bribe for trading rights or something,' he sighed, turning his head to avoid a gust of garlic breath from a sweaty local man pushing up against him, as though he was transparent.

'The Dutch only renovated it in 1663.'

'They should never have left. They're good with damp problems.'

Then the garlic man blasted a full flurry into his face, yelling and waving to his family above the heads of the crowd.

'Just remind me again what we're doing here?'

I flapped a hand extravagantly. 'It's fabulous inside. It's full of Hindu temple art that's brilliantly preserved!'

'Temple art? In a palace?' He flapped his cap off to rub his hand over his head. 'What more could a man wish for?'

'But this is *special* temple art,' I insisted – weakly.

And it was, but not for official reasons.

The kinds of murals on display at Matancherry Palace are typical

Of Waterways and Warblings

examples recounting tales from ancient Hindu texts and legends. They're masterful and magnificent and lots of other adjectives that belong to travel marketing. But there's something else about them, too.

At first they strike the Western eye as the usual blue faces that can get on one's nerves, the multiple arms waving about and the symbols that habitually accompany them.

But *their* gods and *their* nature are different – happier than most others and, on closer inspection, positively ecstatic – romping about as they do with unholy abandon. The king's bedchamber features Lord Vishnu, he of skin as blue as a cardiac warning, although in these murals his heart seems just fine, allowing him an intense bout of frolicking that's lasted for centuries. And this in the midst of conservative India where couples on park benches in places are still policed by men on bicycles. In the Matancherry murals Lord Vishnu in the king's bedchamber, blessed with six hands plus two feet, employs all of his limbs and digits for a session of simultaneous fondling involving no less than eight euphoric milkmaids, known in the Sanskrit legends as *gopis*.

'What the hell's this?' Arnie scratched his head. 'Didn't you say this was temple art?'

But more was to come – forgive the pun – in panels twenty-seven to twenty-nine where nature surrenders to what the palace's caption calls "merry enjoyment". Frisking, gambolling and capering, a jumble of birds and animals cavort in feverish fornication and memorable, manifold penetration.

'Merry enjoyment – huh!' Arnie gusted as we retraced our steps along the galleries lined with portraits of noble maharajas splendidly attired and far too solemn for the kind of décor we'd just witnessed.

'I reckon everyone would go to their temples more often if they were more like this place,' my husband grinned. And with that he flipped on his cap again as we tripped down the wooden staircase and out into the dusty sunlight.

SHOULD YOU NEED a break from such earthly pleasures and all that dust, you may opt for water in the form of a government ferry to Ernakulam a short distance away. As Kochi's twin town, Ernakulam is

Way out in India

the major commercial and financial centre of Kerala.

The ferry station was none too encouraging on our approach. Its paint had deserted it a while before and a rough little wooden board had been slapped on to the opening at the ticket booth where there'd once been a window. Plastered to the booth were posters in Mayalam and English, some for art exhibitions whose galleries were converted spice warehouses. Two weird hand-painted signs above the ticket window said "Ladies" and "Gents". There being none of these outside the ticket window but a ticket seller within opposite the gents' side, I planted myself there with a deliberate 'Good morning'.

But the man didn't answer. He perused a dog-eared exercise book, counting the figures in its columns quite frantically. Then he counted a pile of ticket stubs. A mass of coins and dirty notes in an old wooden drawer compartmentalised for the purpose was next, while unnoticed by me a line of men was forming behind me in dhotis, dress shirts and plastic sandals. Photographic evidence of the scene reveals that they all folded their arms and stared grimly over my shoulders. Slowly it began to dawn on me that a line of women was forming beside me, but being at the front of the constipated queue, I was not going to give up my place – gents or no gents.

The man inside the office began a furious debate with his colleague the minute he arrived, the two of them in a lather complete with desperate gestures, raucous voices and knotted brows over the now clearly missing money.

And all I wanted was two ferry tickets before the ferry arrived and left again.

But as usually happens in India, things did work out – albeit slowly and chaotically. I did get the tickets eventually, as did the locals – but not at the same price – as happens also, so often in India. That was probably how the missing money was made up, but I didn't care by that point and sank down on the hard bench in the old government tub, enjoying the breeze as it swished freshly and freely. It wasn't a bad old boat, this commuter ferry. And it carried a beautiful girl or two with long shiny hair, who kept Arnie and his camera occupied while I watched the mesmerising waterside scenery.

Ernakulam was a place you needn't go. It was too ugly and busy and hot for a couple of weary, hungry travellers such as us. But it did have Hotel New Colombo – "Traditional Taste for the New Generation!" – thank God. Such "hotels" are often just restaurants of local character – perfect for us. We dove in and ordered a feast of thali – rice and chapatti with little pots of sauce into which to dip them. A dirty fan on a yellow wall above our heads waved the worst of the heat away as we tucked in, watched by three eagle-eyed matrons in saris who seldom saw Westerners, it was clear.

In an effort to blend in – what a joke! – I decided to eat the way they did, since I'd had some practice with thali in Pune. The trick is to use the right hand only, for tearing the bread or bunching the rice, then to scoop up the sauce with the starchy stuff and ferry it to one's mouth without messing. The Indians do it so naturally. And so ensued a non-verbal lesson from the lady in red on each step of proceedings, punctuated with finger licking, smiles and nods with every mouthful of this squelchy comfort food I got right.

IF IT'S THIS kind of smiling local hospitality you're after in India, you'd do well to choose a "home stay" as your accommodation option.

In a moment of experimentation online we chose Rosa Villa in Kochi, named after the lady of the house. It was a beloved home down an alley, approached by us in a state of unspeakable exhaustion after some serial thumping in the plane's underbelly two days before, soon after take-off from Cape Town. A bumpy landing back home had followed before delays that had made tedious feel appealing; while a stopover in the overschmaltzed Emirate of Dubai had been tinged with slight paranoia.

It had offered an airport clerk in a sparkling white keffiyeh with a black rope around his head perusing the Israeli stamps in our passports, tugging his moustache, sucking on his teeth and sliding his computer mouse around until we wondered if it was chasing its tail, before handing over some papers with the passports.

'Hotel vouchers,' he announced with an inscrutable gaze and a pointed finger. 'Check in at desk.'

Way out in India

STAGGERING FINALLY INTO the villa at dawn, we found sweet-faced Mrs Rosa – as she was called by her husband Stephen – looking as rumpled and shell-shocked as anyone would, who'd been up all night tossing and waiting to welcome a couple of drooping strangers called guests into one's home. Mr Rosa, or rather Winston, with his long lungi down to his ankles, masked his fatigue with calm grace and sent us upstairs after his wife.

Up we trudged, laden with luggage, past the tasselled pelmets and the plastic pot plants to our room. Spotless, sweltering, airless and boxy it was, with a tiny, shiny bathroom to match. Not that we were complaining. As a traveller you don't expect The Ritz when booking lodgings featuring a twenty-four-hour hot-water facility and homely atmosphere. We nodded mechanically as Mrs Rosa handed over our key, promising her that we'd report for her famous breakfast at nine after a welcome shower and a nap under the precious fan.

An urgent knocking in our dreams yanked us into upright disorientation. Okay – pant, pant! So it wasn't the banging of plane parts smacking each other to bits. What was it then? Where was I? Sari-ing myself roughly in my floral sheet-cum-blanket, I lurched for the door.

It was Mrs Rosa, still looking shell-shocked, but this time because her fried breakfast puris were in danger of wilting irreversibly in our absence.

Humblest apologies assured and accepted, we scrambled, swearing, down the stairs to arrive at her morning table laden with a Keralan breakfast feast. Mrs Rosa settled her ample self at her big kitchen table, beaming prettily with every second helping accepted, until in marched the high-intensity architect from Mumbai, tapping his rolled newspaper on his thigh.

'Morning,' we all greeted each other.

He was a dapper chap, the young architect, with a shirt pressed as crisply as his enunciation. His bearing confident, his handshake brisk, he proceeded to regale us with the history and functioning of his beloved home state of Kerala, to which he returned intermittently on family and other business.

'It really is God's own country, although it has its issues,' he assured us, unfolding his serviette precisely. 'And there are multiple reasons for this.' From the way he set aside his newspaper and settled a triangular platform of slanted forearms and interlaced fingers on the table top, Arnie realised the wisdom of requesting a second cup of caffeine.

'Kerala, first,' began the young architect, 'is abundantly blessed by nature.'

It turned out that while its western border is the Arabian Sea – 'a bounteous asset if ever there was one' – to the east flows a watery network of rivers, lagoons and lakes, known to many locals as the backwaters. Still further inland to the east rise the Western Ghats, a cool and beautiful mountain range of such rich and diverse flora and fauna that UNESCO has proclaimed it a World Heritage Site.

The architect poised his spoon in mid-air to nod, before tapping it on his puri to break the pastry shell of this hollow delight.

'The natural gifts of the state have often determined its history also,' he said, spooning a potato mixture into the hollow. 'You see, the shady slopes of the Western Ghats are ideal for growing spices, especially black pepper. The damp conditions are perfect there, so it was very lucrative in the past when pepper was so much in demand.'

With that he tilted the puri mouthwards and plonked it in for a good chomp. Mrs Rosa glowed.

I dredged up a memory in sleepy slow motion from a *National Geographic* show deep in my past.

'Oh, yes, wasn't black pepper the currency or something back then?'

'It was indeed,' he said, dabbing his mouth deliberately, his eyes wide. 'The seeds in past centuries were a currency more valuable than gold. And the waterways of Kerala, also full of fish, proved ideal for transporting them. Tea also is a Keralan crop, by the way, at the higher altitudes. Very lucrative, too. At our lower altitudes we grow cassava, yams. And rice, of course.'

Breaking off a piece of idli, a rice dumpling, with an elegant twist of his right hand, he dipped it in red and spicy sambhar before popping it into his mouth.

'For five-thousand years, different rulers feasted on the wealth of the region,' he told us. 'It was not always called Kerala. Babylonians, Assyrians, Egyptians, Phoenicians, Romans, Arabs and Chinese all had a chance until the Middle Ages when the Kingdom of Cheras ruled here.

But the competition for power in the area kept the kingdom unstable – other kingdoms and fiefdoms were always determined to conquer it.

'But then came the Europeans,' he said, his sparkling eyes a signal for me to join the caffeine fest. By the time the Portuguese and their hero Vasco da Gama had led the parade to prominence in the region in 1498 and the Dutch and British had followed each other, I was buzzingly conscious of their multiple rivalries besides their mutual ones. Last in line of the Europeans, and just in time for my last sip, came the British who ruled the area until Indian Independence in 1947.

The young architect continued: 'It took another nine years, though, before Kerala was created by the merging of the states of Tranvancore, Kochi and Malabar – as well as the Kasaragod area.' I'd begun to hope for the narrative's grand finale, while Arnie appeared either rapt or catatonic – I couldn't decide which. 'But, you know, inheriting this paradise involved a huge responsibility for the new administration. It's always that way with sudden good fortune, is it not?'

We nodded.

'You know in those days the Western Ghats teemed with animals that are now endangered – or threatened. The place was full of tigers then, elephants, civets, macaques...'

'They're the very intelligent ones, aren't they?' Arnie interjected, suddenly alive at the entrance of wildlife into the conversation.

The young architect bit into a hard-boiled egg coated in curry sauce. 'That is what makes this a tragedy. All the natural resources have diminished here. Even our enormous Lake Vembanad. It was once four times its current size; and the Kochi Port is precisely at its outlet to the Arabian Sea. This is a matter of absolute gravity.'

He waggled his head for emphasis, then seemed to forget the breakfast steaming in front of him, leaving Mrs Rosa frowning distractedly at his plate and Arnie and I disappointed at the sudden deflation of God's Own Country.

'So what's caused all this?' Arnie asked.

'The same things that cause problems everywhere: industrial effluent, poorly planned construction, excessive agriculture. Even the numbers of birds and fish are down.'

'Well, I pray that God will look after this place,' I ventured, ready to leap up and leave. But the young architect was having none of it.

'Oh no,' he perked up. 'It's not all bad.'

So I began to peel a plantain, a tiny, sweet green banana the length of my forefinger. 'So where will the solutions come from?'

'The state's human resources – the cream of India's crop with a long tradition of education and culture. Kerala is one of the most advanced states in the country.'

The reason for this, it transpired, was an intriguing one: communism.

'Communism?' That was Arnie. 'In the world's biggest democracy?'

'Indeed,' nodded the young architect. 'You see, as soon as Kerala was formed, the citizens elected a communist state administration. Can you believe that? It was a world-first in 1957 and, of course, a total aberration in a democracy. But time and again over the years, the voters here have elected communist state governments.'

'So how has that led to success?' my husband challenged, lowering his cup.

The young architect raised his eyebrows. 'Well, as a result of the communist outlook, this has always been a more egalitarian state than many others in terms of education, health, income. Land distribution, also.'

'Huh.' I stopped squirming in my chair as Mrs Rosa left hers to clean up.

'It's not that plentiful funding for education was a novelty when the first communists came to power here. It had been a long tradition in Kerala because, among others, the maharajas who ran it as a princely state before Independence, always gave generously of their wealth to educate the population.'

'Hang on,' I said. 'Who exactly were they?'

'They were the traditional rulers of certain areas of India. During the Raj they were partially independent of the British. And don't forget that the missionaries, too, Portuguese, Dutch, British' – he unfurled a hand elegantly and repeatedly – 'they all played their part in developing local education. So over the centuries this has resulted in a better-educated population than most others outside Kerala's borders.'

Perhaps, as a result of this, the infant mortality and life expectancy statistics of Kerala remain among the best in the country. The state's literacy rate tops ninety per cent. The education level among Keralans also enables many of them to find employment in the Persian Gulf, with a good portion of their income flowing into their home state.

'But there is, unfortunately, a shadow side to this positivity as well,' the young architect lamented, folding his serviette into an exact square and laying it on the table. 'With a communist administration often in power here, foreign investment is scant. Job creation is sluggish because of the strong trade unions and the state loses some of its best people to the Gulf countries. Many of them earn enough there for early retirement.'

'That doesn't seem a problem,' Arnie smiled. 'Where does one sign up?'

The young architect puffed half a laugh through his nose before his mouth turned downward again. 'Well, if only it were all good,' he said. 'You see the boredom and frustration of the unemployed youth and the idleness of the early retirees have led Kerala to have the highest alcoholism rate in India. And, very unfortunately, the highest suicide rate, too.'

And this is God's Own Country? I wondered what was next.

The young architect brightened up then to tell us: tourism, which is thriving. But at what cost? Like beautiful places everywhere, Kerala's fragile riches need careful management to keep delivering returns.

IT WAS HARD to leave the warmth and sweetness of that kitchen and of Kochi a few days later. The driver who'd struggled to get out of the alleyway at Rosa Villa on our arrival, repeated the performance at our farewell to the place when we set off on the road to Allepey, sharing the car, this time, with a couple of Brits.

Mr Brit was from the North, which made understanding him a challenge for us, or "ooz" as he told the driver.

'Could ya find ooz a bo'le store soomwhere on d'weh, please?'

The taxi driver glanced panic-stricken into the rear-view mirror.

'Pardon, Sir?'

'A bo'le store. We'd like ta buy a bo'le or two. Y'know!'

The driver clearly didn't.

'A bottle store,' I interjected. 'The gentleman would like to buy some liquor.'

'Hah,' said the driver, which in India always sounds like the second half of 'Aha!' but which really means "yes" in Hindi and Mayalam among other languages. 'Yes, Sir, there's one on the road out of Kochi.'

It was a horrible place, the bottle store – an ugly building painted vomit yellow with a railing outside like that of a bus stop. A line of men queued in the sun on a carpet of paper garbage and left the place with newsprint wrapped parcels.

I never did see the inside of the bottle store, since I'd had enough of queuing among gents – the only customers, it seemed, of these establishments. They're government-owned in Kerala, which is a double-edged sword for the government. Since it derives tax revenues from them and they are the only legal sellers of liquor, it would seem to be in their interests to keep them open for as many hours a day as their custom demands.

The problem is that this is all hours, which doesn't help diminish the state's alcoholism rate. One statistic claimed that Keralans drink sixteen per cent of all alcohol sold in India – mostly rum. And that's the legal stuff. Off all the official graphs are the smuggled goods with a port conveniently at hand for their traders' purpose. Then there are the home-brewed options that also account for the overwhelming headaches of the drinkers, their families and the state.

More positively, though, there have been recent moves by the government to reduce the number of trading hours at these outlets, but, to date, alcoholism remains one of the chief problems of this beautiful state.

We were to have an unexpected taste of Keralan liquor consumption before that day was over, but first we had the sixty-odd kilometres to drive south to Alleppey, translating all the way for the benefit of the bewildered driver.

ALLEPPEY, OR "THE Venice of the East" as it's also known, seemed the sort of romantic place to warrant a splurge. The site selected for this was an establishment known as Tommy's Homestay.

And what a site it was! Sequestered in a lush garden and up a long driveway, away from the roaring road that passes it, it beckoned us

'Plunging into Kunga's for a bowl of steaming momos.' Darjeeling

Indian pavements, 'which traders clog in cross-legged oblivion'. Pune

Relief of BKS Iyengar at Ramamani Iyengar Memorial Yoga Institute, Pune

Painting of Mahatma Gandhi and his wife Kasturba in imprisonment, Aga Khan Palace, Pune

Mulshi Lake, with grand floral arrangement and insistently descending pants, Pune District

Virupaksha Temple and other ruins, Hampi

Beach scene, Palolem

Tightrope girl, Benaulim

After the catch, Benaulim

'A young girl came by with her bundle.' Trinket seller, Benaulim

Paravan coconut plucker, Benaulim

'In Margarida's sunlit garden, enjoying big chunks of watermelon.' Benaulim

'A flash of white tulle whizzed by.' Catholic confirmation, Benaulim

'Precariously perched between elegance and vulgarity.' The Taj Hotel, Mumbai

'Overcooked Gothic excess,' the Victoria Terminus Station, Mumbai

God's Own Country, Kochi

'[They] stretch their strange and spindly limbs over the sea.' Kochi

'Only in India!' Kochi

'Bearing wok-like pans on their heads.' Female construction worker, Kochi

Akhil's canoe, Alleppey

'The scenes were repeated as inverse echoes of the beauty above.' Backwaters, Alleppey

'Brandishing his secret weapon, a disc the size of his palm.' Alleppey

A raptor and a coconut, Alleppey

'An ancient scene it was, harmonious, rhythmic, just right.' Fishermen, Varkala

'Venus herself emerged from the ocean.' Varkala

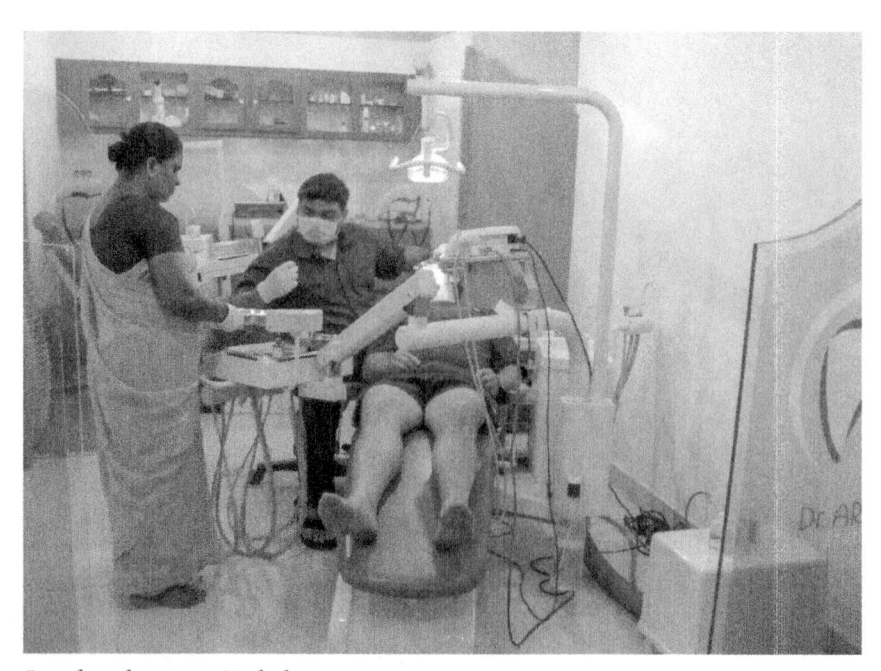

Barefoot dentistry, Varkala

'Hello Auntie!', Ajanta Caves

The trophy Westerner, surrounded, Ajanta Caves

'The Nizam of Hyderbad had a neat pathway built along the curve of the cliff.' Ajanta Caves

The twenty-four foot reclining Buddha in Cave 26, Ajanta Caves

'Inside one massive rock was this object of awesome beauty.' Kailasa Temple, Ellora Caves

The generous gardens, Ellora Caves

Colourful tempera painting, Ellora Caves

Secret caves and rock pools, Ellora

Holy cow and Hotel Broadway, Varanasi

'Dipping a new bicycle in for a blessing.' River Ganges, Varanasi

'Laundrymen whacking their washing on slabs jutting from the Bank.' River Ganges, Varanasi

A vision of Hell, Manikarnika Ghat, Varanasi

'Aarthi puja, a great whacking punch of a religious ceremony or extravaganza.'
Varanasi

'Sturdy, rough-hewn and in tune with the river's rhythms.' Oarsman, Varanasi

A 'soup kitchen', Varanasi

Saris drying beside the Ganges, Varanasi

'The eerie banyan tree, its roots snaking their way down to earth.' Ranthambore National Park

'There were four-hundred eyes searching the shadows for one celebrity beast.' Ranthambore National Park

Arnie's tiger trophy, Ranthambore National Park

So light and lacy, Taj Mahal, Agra

What political correctness? Taj Mahal, Agra

'The gems inlaid in her marble skin.' Taj Mahal, Agra

'But wife no make accident.' Rickshaw cyclist, Delhi

Qutb Minar and the Iron Pillar, symbols of power from two eras, Delhi

Frescoed haveli courtyard, Nawalgargh

Agricultural abundance, Nawalgargh

'A procession of miserable beasts.' Amber Fort, Jaipur

Intricate inlaid mirror work, Victory Hall, Amber Fort, Jaipur

'Pink and flimsy, whimsically windowed.' Palace of the Winds, Jaipur

'Money is literally hung around the neck of the groom.' Wedding Market, Jaipur

'The country women bought only the kind of brilliant colours you'd associate with gypsies.' Market, Jaipur

Only their wares were smiling that day, Market, Jaipur

The glorious Baby Taj

'AC 1 on Indian Railways is a feast!' Radjhani Express, Delhi-New Jalpaiguri

Dorje Ling, the Buddist monastery from which Darjeeling's name was derived, Darjeeling.

'Human donkeys with anaesthetised eyes.' Porters, Darjeeling

Kanchenjunga, the world's third highest peak, Darjeeling

Eccentric tea tour, Darjeeling

Way out in India

towards its white walls, red tiled roof and teak woodwork all set against a background of green.

A little man in a long dhoti marched out smiling to greet us, his beard grey, his voice nasal and his underbite severe.

'Come in, come in!' he exhorted, herding us round the shoulders beyond the magnificent teak entrance to his pillared and arched front veranda. There a table stood with welcome drinks and the paperwork necessary to administer our stay. My eyes roamed the place, drinking in the elegant furnishings and ojects d' art of all kinds.

'Your room is in a separate building,' he added, leading us across the garden, up a flight of wooden stairs into a space as palatial and homely as one could imagine, with its central feature being an antique carved wooden bedstead inlaid with painted tiles, beyond which a balcony invited relaxation.

But not for long. Tommy was the kind of host who liked to arrange his guests' visits. And he fairly insisted that we join him and his wife for dinner that night. Not wanting to offend by counter insisting on our freedom, we accepted and escaped down the driveway to explore Alleppey and hunt for lunch.

THE DINNER AT Tommy's that night was to prove one of the most memorable ever. We'd imagined a quiet and formal affair hosted by our man chewing on interesting subjects, stroking his beard and forward-thrust jaw while his wife scurried about in the kitchen between courses. We'd imagined being happily ensconced in that glorious antique bed before ten.

We were wrong.

On arriving at seven, the front veranda was dressed for a party. Chairs clung to its walls like waiting dance partners. The table hosted a fan of bottles in a basket in the candlelight. We'd clearly not been the only guests invited.

Soon the company trickled in – young couples from the West – until there were eight of us, all residents at the house. Then Tommy appeared in a silver silk shirt and dress pants to match his beard with his wife Mari in an elegant salwaar-kameez.

'Welcome, welcome!' Tommy enthused, descending on the basket of bottles, offering everyone a drink.

We were all to try the traditional Keralan concoction that made me panic slightly, since I don't *do* rum. I'm sure it involved some lime along the way but didn't sip long enough to find out, courtesy of a convenient pot plant which I swear sighed 'Ah!' as the booze bit its roots.

There was gin, too, which might have gone well with some tonic, but that wasn't on offer and the Johnnie Walker Fancy Colours only emerged at the arrival of Tommy's old friends from his youth.

Three jovial gents they were, successful and happy with plump and silent wives also in salwaar-kameez, who disappeared straight into the kitchen. Their husbands accepted the Johnnie Walker gladly. They'd been driven a couple of hours for this and were going to make the most of it. That was clear.

A few snacks began to circulate, fresh from Mari's kitchen – all meaty and off limits to my stomach, herbivorous as it has been for decades. Conversation melted slowly into liquid, more meaty snacks came round, an hour or two passed. My stomach rumbled. Then Tommy's friend began to sing. Some tragic, traditional song it was that held us all enraptured, even those of us who understood not a word of it. Johnnie walked from one of Tommy's old friends to the other and back again at a rapidly quickening pace, while the rest of us made do with rum or pretended to – gulping bubbles of soda water with squeezes of lime as the night wore on.

A lovely young British man next to me had read some of the same books that I had, a blessed road down which to travel conversationally between poetic recitations of opaque eloquence by Tommy's second friend, filmed – skilfully, we were assured – by the third.

Then Tommy extended an invitation to a young Australian guest to sing, which she declined with giggling grace and a ducking head. But one didn't decline invitations from Tommy. So there she stood in the candlelight, croaking out a Beatles number – tunelessly as I recall – with her shoulders drooping and her eyes perusing the veranda's wood-panelled ceiling, while the poetic friend clapped in time, the musical one clicked his fingers and the photographic one – not to intimidate or anything – filmed her from across the table.

Way out in India

All at once a flare of excitement filled the jolly space. An American girl, pretty, strident and utterly charming, strode out of the house into the midst of the gathered company, bearing in her arms a tiny sausage-dog puppy with a giant red bow around his neck. A silence fell as she began to speak in that clear and friendly way Americans often do, breaking everything down into manageable sound bites.

'In case you're all wondering what we came here for tonight, it was for this little boy!' She stroked the puppy, which burrowed into her bosom, followed closely by Tommy's gaze. 'We have a major *task* to perform here tonight and we need your help with it. We need to find a name for Tommy and Mari's newest little darling and I have a proposal for how we can do it.'

The proposal followed, complete with rules for suggesting names, hands up and no interrupting. The voting would be, first and foremost, entirely democratic (what else?) and, after several rounds involving a process of elimination, the little chap would have a name. Between rounds it would be mandatory to drink and entertain each other in an unspecified manner, but in the meantime more snacks from Mari's kitchen would be passed around.

This time they included a spicy mix of peanuts and crispy bits. In I dove, wiping out half the bowl to alleviate the encroaching hypoglycaemia, for the purpose of enhancing my judgement and creativity when it came to naming the canine.

Observing my peckish enthusiasm, the young and literary Brit leaned towards me, his mouth pulled skew and enquired, sotto voce, if I thought dinner might appear at any stage. By then we were three hours in.

'Dunno,' I mumbled through a mouthful of munchies, reaching again for their bowl, 'but I'm taking no chances.'

He grinned wanly and slugged his rum again.

Thus the naming began with suggestions ranging from Snoopy to Simha, the Sanskrit word for lion. The American girl and her partner who were working for an NGO in Tanzania at the time, suggested the African version – Simba – at which I let out an uncharacteristic whoop born of sudden homesickness. Tommy flinched and frowned until Johnnie Walker was also suggested, as was Dimple, with Hans, Fritz and

Schultz adding a Germanic theme, since the pooch was a dachshund – who'd not yet been disciplined. Amid the merry fray he lifted his leg and peed on an antique umbrella stand.

Then it was time to drink and "entertain ourselves" while the votes were counted. I reached for the soda again – the spice was biting – and turned to the Brit for a review of *The Hare with the Amber Eyes*, but alas! No sooner were the words 'Have you read…' out of my mouth, than a smiling Tommy, his bottom teeth on full display, pointed his jaw towards my new buddy with a mellifluous suggestion.

'What about a song from our London representative?'

Oh, dear. Not only was the hapless Brit now unsteady on his feet, but his tune-carrying aptitude made the squawking Aussie girl's a carolling delight. And an ominous pattern was developing. The Aussie sat to the left of the three Indian friends. The Brit sat to the left of the Aussie. You know who sat next to the Brit: the matron who'd whooped at the clarion call of Africa, who'd weathered hunger pangs in refusal of meat chunks on sticks, who'd remained steadfastly sober in a sea of rum.

She who did not obey. She who did not melt with the other matrons into the kitchen. She who would not be called to sing and dance for the company. To the left of her, however, and alas, sat Arnie. Arnie who was brilliant in so many ways but who'd make the baying Brit sound like Frank Sinatra. I wouldn't survive it.

'So just say I'll represent you if he asks, okay?'

Arnie grinning a rum-infused grin was more than happy to oblige, his eyebrows wobbling up to arches of "why not?"

And so it was a very short while later that I found myself on a hot Indian night standing before a motley gathering on a splendid veranda and as clear as a bell belting out my country's national anthem in the jumble of all five of the official languages in which it is written. With feeling. As I hit the high notes I noticed Tommy blink and frown. As I blared the more martial bits left over from the apartheid era he mopped his brow with a handkerchief. By the time I finished, his belligerence thrust his jaw where I'm sure no jaw had ever been before – quite a feat considering the circumstances.

In this way the evening continued, the silent Indian wives having no opinions on the name of the puppy or much else upon attempted engagement, their husbands waxing louder and friendlier with each dose of whisky. The names suggested became more bizarre and I managed to gollop the rest of the spicy goodies between continuous swigs of soda.

Finally, the people had spoken and the name of the hound was announced, American-style by the lovely compère, exhorting us all to *praa*mise to remember the date and this special night as the one on which we all participated in this heart-warming ceremony.

'Christ, I'm hungry,' muttered the Brit, leaning towards me to deliver his update.

With one hand the compère clutched the pup to her bosom again, where Tommy's eyes now rested permanently. With the other she held aloft a cake pierced with one burning candle.

'And the puppy's name is...' She accepted a piece of paper from her partner who'd been tallying votes furiously all evening. 'The puppy's name is...Jack!'

'Christ,' the Brit mumbled again as the company erupted into applause, whistles and whoops – the latter not from me though. I was all whooped out. The Brit set his elbows on his knees, letting his head fall into his hands. 'Christ! After all that! Jack!'

'And what's his surname?' the portly Indian friend called out. 'What's his surname?'

Tommy grinned slyly. It could only be one. 'It begins with a D,' he said – superfluously.

Great stuff, I thought to myself. Now we can all go to bed.

But we could not. Mari had not had her moment yet and here it was. Appearing in the front doorway, she invited everyone inside to serve themselves dinner.

'Christ,' the Brit moaned again. '*Dinner?* It's nearly breakfast time! These people are worse than the Spanish! Are they mad?'

Apparently not. Apparently this is the way celebratory dinners are conducted in India. One just has to be forewarned, keep awake long enough and eat lunch with sundowners.

From the gusto with which the dinner was gobbled, it seemed quite delicious. For me at that hour, though, a few spoons seasoned with zombiehood were enough. And I certainly didn't manage any of that candle-pierced cake for dessert.

BEFORE WE SUCCEEDED finally in making it through all the hugging and handshakes that ended the evening and trudged the stairs to our room, Tommy cornered us in the moonlit garden.

'What are you two doing tomorrow?' he asked.

Tomorrow? What was that?

'If you don't mind the suggestion, I have a wonderful man who can take you around for the day on a canoe trip you'll never forget.'

'Uh… well…' I began but was beaten by Arnie who consented – blearily.

'Done! What time?'

To my utter astonishment, Tommy slipped out his cellphone and dialled the man.

'Does he realise it's 1:00 am?' I whispered to Arnie who didn't seem to register that that might be a problem.

It must have been mine only, since Tommy was smiling at the end of the call and his man fully prepared to collect us six hours hence.

'How quickly do you think we can sleep?' I asked my husband as we flung ourselves into the carved and creaking bed. His answer was a snore.

THE CANOE TRIP was everything Tommy had promised and more – including a bus trip, a ferry trip and a ride into a parallel universe.

In the cool of early morning his man, Akhil, came striding up the driveway in his long green dhoti, the twitter of the birds his entry music. Freshly combed and wearing a sparkling smile, he shook each of our hands with the vigour of an alarm clock at dawn.

'First,' he announced, leading us down the driveway and into the street, 'we take bus.'

Sure. Like two fuzzy sheep we followed him into the early bustle of town and boarded a bus that appeared on a street corner.

Well that was a wake-up call. The bus was a government specimen for commuters. Its most virile days had ended a few decades before, its main feature a floppy gear lever that needed as much persuasion to wake up as we did. Bumping and rumbling past lush rice paddies and palm trees in the brand-new day, it passed flocks of women as bright as sunrise, with no concern for the dust it showered over their saris.

I had no idea where it was going or how long it might take, but at some apparently random point it lurched to a halt where Akhil announced: 'We get off.'

Passing the rice paddies on foot, the smell of earth rose as rich as coffee and the perennial question puzzled as always when an occasional chicken crossed the road.

Soon we stopped at a modest building adjacent to a paddy. Partially painted and punctuated with baby-pink and blue shutters, it wore a corrugated roof and sat in a garden that nature had lavished around it. Banana and coconut palms, herbs and giant-leaved specimens nodded in abundant welcome.

'This is my house. You sit here,' Akhil smiled, pointing out a blue plastic table with two cane chairs covered by towels in a clearing. 'We bring breakfast.'

Oh, thank God! I thought. We hadn't asked about food and I was wondering when it might be polite to pull out my emergency pack of Japanese rice crackers.

They'd never have competed with the breakfast we were about to enjoy, served on banana leaves the size of platters by Akhil and his wife, Babitha. A metal dish holding a pile of hot chapattis was presented along with a boiled egg each and some mildly spiced sauce to pour over it. We were to eat with our hands the traditional way, washing them first with a jug dipped into a bucket of water that stood on an outdoor ledge with a cake of soap and a towel.

Glasses of chai followed, bottles of water were offered and the whole went down with delicious disbelief at the magical setting and experience.

Having fed and watered us – and presumably himself and his wife – Akhil sprang out of the house again, marching towards us.

'Canoe is waiting,' he smiled. 'At front of house.'

The waterway fronted Akhil's house as it did all the others that made up the village, so we had but to walk down a few steps to the canoe. In it two low seats with back rests had been placed, since few Westerners could sit upright for the trip's duration. A toothless, old oarsman sat at the front of the canoe, his voice as stringy as his arms and legs, while Akhil, after folding his dhoti to a manageable length, took up his position at the back, to row us through one of the most beautiful places we'd ever seen.

Going about their business on the water's edge we passed the villagers, Akhil's daughter and her friends in 1950s-style school uniforms waving to us from the shore; before we entered the silent backwaters where the sun rose to shine its full light on the most lush and tranquil paradise imaginable.

In the stillness of the water the scenes were repeated as inverse echoes of the beauty above. Quiet canoes and canopied boats mirrored themselves in the liquid gardens that nature had planted there, her tallest palms reaching down into a fluid blue sky. All manner of birds twittered and flitted above, including the malachite kingfisher – a tiny bird gemmed in so many colours. Dragonflies refracting sunlight danced above the water while every so often a home would appear on the bank. One, a splendid specimen, stood out from the rest.

'What's that all about?' Arnie asked Akhil.

'Husband work in Gulf.'

That was all. No envy, no malice on Akhil's part. Just a fact before his oars dipped and pulled through the magnificence while fish darted about and he offered a pair of incongruous black umbrellas to his pale-faced guests in their sunlit trance.

After a while we began to notice little clumps of hyacinth, which soon thickened along the route, until they almost choked off the possibility of movement.

'Here we walk,' Akhil announced, rowing to the bank and helping us off the boat.

The old man would battle through the most blocked part of the water without the heavy cargo and meet us a little way ahead.

'This is a problem,' Arnie suggested as we walked along the water's edge.

'Yes,' Akhil agreed with as much cheer as he could muster, 'it is problem, but we clear the hyacinth when it's very bad. Everybody helps.'

We nodded and smiled politely and listened to him as he showed us various plants along the path, negotiated with the fisherman delivering our lunch to his wife and chatted with the kiosk owner where we stopped to buy water.

But the truth was that something man-made had changed the ecosystem to allow the water hyacinth to grow in the first place. As always the something had had greed as its motive. It had all started, Tommy explained later at dinner, with the realisation by the rice farmers that they could grow two crops a year if they blocked the sea mouth to keep the salt water out and the fresh water in all year round. They'd never accounted for the role the sea water had played in clearing the area of any matter that might unbalance the ecosystem. By blocking its flow, the rice farmers had ensured that the seeds of the hyacinth problem were sown and had now grown to a density that threatened to obliterate an age-old way of life.

Several efforts have been made to discover which animals or insects might enjoy eating this plant but none have so far been found to do so sustainably. And even if such a solution were found, its introduction might further unbalance an already fragile ecosystem. Besides this problem, the politics involved in the situation has ensured the paralysis that allows the hyacinth to keep growing. The fishing lobby and the rice lobby and several other agencies have failed to work together to solve it, each one only serving its own agenda – a tragedy when one realises all that's at stake.

As the sun rose to its zenith, we returned with Akhil to his home, awed and sobered in equal measure and feeling assured that we were witnessing something fragile, soon to vanish from the Earth for ever. Men like Akhil, which means "complete", are thin on the ground in these parts. The younger men no longer want to scamper up coconut trees and have their wives plant their meals and chase chickens in the back garden.

Strong and fit and in tune with the Earth, Akhil's breed is disappearing, since educated younger people, pulled towards the cities and the Gulf by a "better" life, are no longer content to tend their rice patches as he does, or catch the odd fish, or maintain his canoe, or teach children to swim in the backwaters. Such a pity it is that these vital people radiating health are being bent into soft and sedentary shapes by the promise of something their paradise can't offer them.

With some heaviness in our hearts, then, we ate the generous lunch at the blue plastic table in Akhil's garden, so struck by the breadth of the banana leaf platters and the little fried fish that had been swimming that morning. The rice from the field in front of us, blanketed with sauce, contained herbs from the patch to our right, while the coconut juice in our glasses had been part of the tree to our left.

Replete, we sat back and murmured to each other about the wonder of this, while Akhil and his wife got on with their day with a calm and cheerful vitality, until a sound we couldn't discern initially made him spring up from his weeding.

'The ferry!' he pointed. 'The ferry is coming. We go quickly.'

QUITE WEARY FROM the day's events, we lumbered up the driveway of Tommy's, only to find the little man seeing off some other guests in a taxi.

'So you had a good day with Akhil?' he grinned.

'Oh, yes!' we said.

'So you'll join Mari and me for dinner again tonight?'

'Oh, yes!' Arnie said. I stood dumbstruck, vowing inwardly that neither a sip of rum nor a word of the South African national anthem would pass my lips that night, no matter what, but that a veritable heap of emergency Japanese rice crackers would – as fortification for whatever lay ahead.

'At seven o' clock then,' Tommy smiled.

I didn't, as we plodded upstairs to our room.

AT THE APPOINTED hour the front veranda, thankfully, had shed its party dress of the night before and hosted but a single guest seated at the table: a tall, grey and bespectacled man swirling his whisky in a tumbler, examining the movement of its ice cubes through a most peculiar method. Leaning his left elbow on the table with his head at a tortuous angle resting into his left hand, his fingers hoisted up his right eyebrow, while his left one frowned, intrigued by the contents of the tumbler.

'Good evening,' we greeted quietly, not wanting to alarm him.

'Oh!' He straightened up still clutching his eyebrow, his forearm perched atop his head. 'Good evening.' His right hand shot out to shake ours.

Way out in India

As we sat down he bowed into his former posture, hand suspending eyebrow. It dawned on both of us simultaneously, as transmitted by glances, that without the help of his fingers, not only his eyebrow but his eyelid would collapse and the poor man would be doomed to a Cyclopean fate, though in an undoubtedly more vertical body.

He'd come all the way from chilly Delhi with his wife, he told us, to meet their daughter who worked in Mumbai as a lawyer. Wife and daughter were just dressing for dinner, so he was "taking the air" by himself for a while.

Sure.

After a few light exchanges about the loveliness of Kerala, he revealed himself to be a maths professor who'd studied at Oxford in his youth and who now taught at one of the most illustrious universities in India. Intrigued by how he might lecture with his arm up in the air for an hour at a time, I missed its name, my thoughts spinning around the Indian habit of spilling one's full credentials on to the table within minutes of meeting, especially if they involved academia.

Presently, wife and daughter sauntered on to the veranda, wife as plump and silent as the wives of the previous night and similarly attired. Daughter, though, was a trendy girl with silver hoop earrings and a cascade of curls that bounced and jiggled as she articulated everything with a charming humour and intelligence.

'Akriti,' she smiled, holding out her hand to meet us.

'That's a lovely name,' I said. 'What does it mean?'

She giggled. 'Diagram, if you can believe it.'

Combining her father's brainpower with his lack of inhibition, her mother's legacy was a mystery – a mystery that was, besides that lovely skin and smile. One thing was clear though: in one Indian generation, many girls had advanced from the Western equivalent of the 1950s to the present.

While we got acquainted discussing all manner of topics, from the plane-stopping mist in Delhi's winter to the heat of communism in Kerala, Tommy served drinks and withdrew to help Mari in the kitchen.

Then Arnie had a conversational brainwave that blurted out as a judgement. It had to do with an obstacle he'd observed on India's road to superpower status.

Of Waterways and Warblings

'Can I ask you a question?' he asked the professor.

'That *was* question,' came the retort, with one eyebrow raised manually while the other took care of itself.

Touché.

'But go ahead. Ask another.'

'Right,' Arnie began, twisting his neck to make eye contact with the professor. 'What's the deal with the sanitation system in India? I mean can a country be a superpower if it can't get its own sanitation under control?'

'That was two questions,' the professor tallied, 'but anyway, you're a hundred per cent right. The Indian way of sweeping your rubbish in front of your neighbour's house so that your own path is clear will not do. Our lack of sanitation is a national bloody disgrace. And the government needs to step in boldly and tackle it on a macro basis instead of shilly-shallying about with these various bloody political agendas and all its corruption and theft of funds on the way.'

End of conversation – a good time for Tommy to swing through the doors bearing plates of a traditional Keralan dish: fresh fish wrapped and tied in a banana leaf, its fragrance of ginger, lemon, chilli, turmeric and coconut steaming out when the parcel was opened.

I was wondering how the professor was going to manage the operation without an extra hand to help him, but it turned out he had two.

'Dolly,' he turned to his wife, 'would you please assist me with this?'

Dolly? What kind of a name was that for a woman with a bindi on her forehead, a jewel in one nostril and a filmy dupatta draped across her chest and over her shoulders?

We never did find out much about Dolly, except that she cut fish into cubes with a geometrical precision that seemed to satisfy her husband. And she kept house and nodded nervously when asked if she enjoyed it.

All the while the professor seemed unperturbed by the tasks of suspending his eyelid, conveying his fork to his mouth and regaling us with tales of his youthful Oxford years simultaneously.

'They consisted mostly of bridge and cricket,' he chuckled, 'with a bit of bloody studying thrown in at intervals.'

'Ah, Daddy, you always say that,' giggled his daughter, fluttering a delicate hand to her lips and smacking her juicy fish parcel to her lap

Way out in India

on the way.

With sudden alacrity Tommy sprang up and flew into the kitchen, returning to wipe the mess with great relish from the young lady's lap.

'A-hem!' The maths professor cleared his throat, twisting his head and glaring at Tommy with his droopy eye pulled wide open. 'I'm sure Akriti can manage that herself.'

The little man bit his top lip with his bottom teeth and reversed bowing through the swing doors while Dolly and Mari occupied themselves with a bout of furious blushing.

I, in the meantime, was trying to remember an unfinished thought. It filtered back while oblique whiffs of apology in the British style augmented with waggling heads issued from the men and Akriti joined the women for a rosy flush or two.

The thought was a question which I kept to myself: had it been one of those Oxford cricket balls, in a blink of miscalculation on the professor's part, that had spun off course and cursed him to a lifetime of manual eyelid suspension from the moment of impact?

ESCAPING ANY ASPECT of trip management by Tommy required careful planning and quiet sneaking down the garden path, which, when we did manage it, felt both triumphant and terrifying, like playing truant. Drawn by the aroma of an odd-looking place for lunch, we plonked down at Indian Coffee House down the road, high-fiving and asking each other what a coffee house was doing in India when it's so famous for tea.

There was something vaguely grim in its darkness lit by neon strips with the customary garlanded portrait of the establishment's founder glaring down from above the shrine and manager's desk. But then the colours started to talk to us: cheerful walls of blue and mint green, red plastic chairs and the waiters liveried in white tunics with bibs and cummerbunds trimmed in gold. Best, though, were the fan-like crests on their headdresses and the delicious crispy dosa filled with potatoes. If only we'd known how famous the place was, we would have tried its unblended coffee or perhaps bought some of the powder to take home.

For the Indian Coffee House is no ordinary business. Each of its outlets is part of a society that is owned and managed one-hundred per cent by its employees. The way this came about was that the original Indian Coffee House, established by the Coffee Board during the British Raj, failed to meet expectations. The colonials shut it down and dismissed the workers.

Undaunted by these events, the communist leader of the time, AKG Nambiar – "our beloved Godfather, AKG" to his followers – structured a cooperative society in which every worker would have a stake and the first Indian Coffee House of this kind opened in 1958. Since then outlets have burgeoned all over India, with more than fifty of them serving a loyal public their "caterings", which range from banana fry to veg biryani, with a variety of dishes in between. Along with brands such as McDonald's and the savvy local chain, Coffee Day, Indian Coffee House has been selected by its customers as one of the country's preferred consumer brands.

OUT ON THE street afterwards, a disconcerting dose of communism was waiting to smack us head on. Now if you grew up in the West any time before 1989, your knees would also probably jerk at the sight of a main street festooned with hammers and sickles and a big billboard arrayed with the faces of Che, Mao, Lenin and the Indian Communist Party patriarch, Jyoti Basu.

Scratchy loudhailers on cars, bedecked in red, hammered the imperative of voting for the local candidate. For a moment, one expected the unsettling scene to be snowy and grim with onion-dome buildings and a pale population in ushankas scurrying around. Instead, the scene featured bicycles, motorbikes and a small cavalcade of tuk-tuks all ringing and tooting among the sandaled citizens while the sun burned down. The strangest items amid all that anti-capitalist red, though, were the banners flapping from every street pole emblazoned with one word – Vodafone.

Between the disconcerting coffee house and the bewildering communism amid all the tumult, I was briefly overwhelmed and caught rubbernecking by a mighty statue of Karl Marx – bushy of beard and wild of hair – into which I bashed quite vigorously on a street corner.

Way out in India

Expecting a flash of pain as flesh met granite, I was thoroughly perplexed yet again when Marx began to tumble from his plinth, all two metres of him, whom I caught – quite easily – and restored to the upright. Under his skin-deep granite paint, you see, Comrade Karl was all polystyrene.

It was time to take time out the way one would in Venice, strolling the streets for a sensory overview of the place. In Alleppey, though – or Alappuzha, as it's known officially now – it's never long before a canal crosses one's path. A flotilla of boats, all pretty and varied, lined the banks of the one crossing ours. Among them one boat proved irresistible, its canopy yellow-frilled at the edges and supported by poles of gold.

'You want canal trip, Sir?' a handsome, young man beckoned from under a tree. His eyes were big, beautiful and sad.

'Yes, I want canal trip, please,' I burst before Arnie could even consider the matter. When in Venice… I thought.

How could I not want such a trip when the open-sided boat featured a chaise longue with a bolster, a clean sheet spread over it and two clusters of cane chairs draped with towels? How could I not when bright strings of fake flowers and little lanterns graced the front of the boat's canopy and two painted swans posed on the back of the divan where the boatman would sit for the journey?

'Is this a traditional Kerala boat?' I asked the handsome, young man with the big, sad eyes, casting my sandals off to swing my legs up on to the chaise.

'This boat Kashmiri boat,' he said as his mate fired up the motor and began to edge away from the bank.

Aha. Kashmiri boat. In magnificent Kashmir, far up north, the boats are as famous as down south in Kerala, but for fear of bombs and being caught in the crossfire between India and Pakistan up there, tourists keep away. More than that. We are asked on the Indian visa form to promise to stay out of the region that includes Jammu, too. And those big, sad and beautiful eyes? They're the trademark of Kashmiris all over India who form a Muslim minority in most places they go to trade and who never seem quite to get over the longing for their home.

The boat cruised calmly along the canal and into more open waters, past the government ferry station, past palm trees and little clusters of water hyacinth, past a wooden canoe ferrying ten people and a bicycle, the oarsman standing like a gondolier in a short dhoti while we sank into a reverie of afternoon sunlight sparkling on water.

Young village women on the banks washed their clothes in the river and mothers hitched up their handmade dresses to descend the few steps before their lakeside homes to wash silvery pots and bowls in its waters, while their children toddled on the bank. A slim, young schoolgirl in a neat salwaar-kameez stopped and stooped to sip from cupped palms under the palms, while farther on a grey grandmother poured a pitcher of water over a bowing young woman's hair. Each one was a scene from a dream, shattered suddenly by the blast of officialdom.

It blared from Janani, the party boat flying multiple hammers and sickles and sporting two giant speakers at bow and stern. Two grim party apparatchiks sat atop the boat's canopy, pens in shirt pockets and looking like they'd rather go home.

'Houseboat,' Arnie murmured then, lolling in a cane chair when the communists had passed, pointing into the sunlight and springing me to the upright, since people come to Kerala from all over the world especially to cruise on this type of craft. These fairly large and strange-looking vessels begin with a wooden canoe-shaped hull about thirty metres long and end with a closed canopy of palm-leafed thatch. Known locally as kettuvallams, they originated as rice barges for transporting the harvest from the waterside paddies along the Keralan backwaters.

Over time they transformed into living spaces for royal families, replaced in time by tourists pampered by the staff on board who also cook traditional fare often served on the houseboat's veranda, a shaded area open on all sides for the tranquil views and the breeze.

All kinds of amenities are available on a houseboat, from loungey living areas to Western toilets and generators for the air conditioning. Necessary when the boat stops for meals or for the night along with the breeze created by movement, they're a godsent antidote to mosquitoes whizzing out to annoy. A cruise's route and duration is as variable as the quality of houseboats on offer, making the choice of an expedition an exercise in discernment.

Presently, our boat stopped at a bank where a minuscule restaurant was concealed by the foliage. Its small menu specialised in my old favourite – coconut juice – with the proprietor selecting two specimens

Way out in India

full of it from the pile outside, yanking a machete from the resident tree stump and decapitating the fruit in seconds.

For added excitement, from some hidden branch nearby and with alarming suddenness, he produced a raptor – a *raptor!* – which perched on his arm and glared about.

'Madam want photo with bird?' he suggested, approaching my shoulder with the clawed raptor too swiftly for comfort.

'NO!' I fairly shrieked, ducking and spilling a splash of coconut juice.

I was not in the market for a predatory peck thanks and didn't much fancy a carnivorous drip of raptor shit down my shirt either.

In the end it was Arnie – calm, gracious and nature-loving Arnie – who posed with the raptor on his shoulder and had to pay for the privilege to boot.

The sunlight turned golden as we boarded the boat for home, gilding gliding canoes and palms, water and sky and all was well with the world.

NOT FOR LONG, though. The shaded rumble of the town took over as soon as we docked, whole families on motorbikes vying for space with Suzukis of all shapes and sizes in the tumult of rush hour traffic. Fun fact about India: Indians love Suzukis.

Soon we came to a traffic circle or roundabout as we might call it. The Indians call it a chowk – a word denoting maximum mayhem since no rules seem to apply for how to get around it or how to peel away from it. In every other Indian town I'd visited, I'd pumped enough adrenalin crossing roads at a chowk to walk a tightrope across the Grand Canyon.

Not so in Alleppey where a heroic traffic officer stood in his peaked cap and khakis, a radio strapped to his belt like a weapon and a civil-service pot belly to show who was boss.

'How's he going to manage this lot?' I yelled at Arnie above the din.

But we needn't have worried. Our man in khaki, at a seemingly random moment – stepped forth into the fray brandishing his secret weapon: a disc the size of his palm and strapped neatly to it, saying "STOP" in red and white. Duly equipped, he levered his arm to the horizontal and they did. The Suzukis and bicycles, tuk-tuks and a donkey all spied that little disc in the chaos and obeyed. It was a small Indian miracle.

Of Waterways and Warblings

DESPITE OUR POLITE efforts at independence, our trip southwards to Varkala buckled into a Tommy-managed venture with a Tommy-appointed lunatic at the wheel. As one of the Russian roulette players of the Indian road, he played by the rules. Just so you know, they are: the creation of extra traffic lanes on the opposite side of the highway, overtaking other overtakers, relentless hooting at nothing in particular and often nothing at all, and the main ingredient – top speed accompanied by Top Hits of India blasting their beat in stereo at a volume that wobbles the wheels.

Halfway through the hundred and thirteen kilometres he roared to a halt in the dusty parking area of a roadside mansion.

'What's this?' Arnie enquired – tremulously.

'Palace, Sir. Mr Tommy said take Sir and Madam to palace.'

'Palace!' my husband exclaimed, 'excellent!' and sprang from the thumping vehicle, sprinting faster towards the palace than a ball off Tendulkar's bat.

Besides its salient feature being its location outside our car, this palace had much to offer by way of entertainment, interest and intrigue; the latter surrounding a rumoured secret tunnel running beneath an indoor pond, in case the royal inhabitants of centuries past needed to escape any enemies.

Two to three centuries, to be more precise and just for the record, the name of the palace was the Krishnapuram Palace, built during the reign of Marthanda Varma, "the king of erst while (sic) Travancore", according to the sign on the entrance wall.

If you look for Travancore on a map you won't find it. Until 1858 it had been a Hindu feudal kingdom, but the British transformed it into one of the princely states of India, ruled by the Travancore royal family. As these states went, it was a big one, consisting of most of Kerala and part of the present-day neighbouring state, Tamil Nadu. It was also one of the most successful of the princely states under the British.

For the Interest and Colour Award bestowed by me on the most captivating aspect of British India, nothing beats the subject of the princely states. They were states governed indirectly by the British through titular princes. Also known as maharajas, rajas, diwans, khans, nizams or nawabs, many of their wives and widows were known as maharanis.

Although there were more than five-hundred of these states by the time of Indian Independence, only about twenty of these were considered major and three or four were considered large.

The princely states were, surprisingly, not officially a part of British India. That is to say they'd neither been annexed nor conquered by the colonial superpower, although it was clear to all from the outset that an alliance between both parties would be mutually beneficial. A treaty sealed this arrangement, whereby the princely states would govern their own internal affairs, while external matters would be the business of the British. Although officially this was the case, the British wielded considerable power and influence in all spheres of governance.

For their loyalty to the British Crown, the princes were rewarded with income which, if they ran their states successfully, usually fell into the category of Fabulous Beyond Belief, a major factor in their winning my aforementioned award. Their lifestyles beggared belief, their relationship with the British authorities and culture still fascinates, as do their various approaches to ruling their subjects. In return, the princes provided their colonial allies not only an income stream of taxes, but a safeguard against the radical political groups of the day who might have murmured about Indian nationalism.

The states, varying enormously in size and status, even had a strictly graded system of gun salutes conferred on some of their princes by the British Crown. The highest number of guns for a prince of a state was twenty-one – which the Travancore ruler attained, if only to be saluted this way within his own state.

By 1931 the princely states housed about a quarter of India's population, a substantial portion that could be kept under control if the princes did their jobs properly, according to British requirements..

But such control could not and did not last. The nationalist movement, led by Mahatma Gandhi, rumbled to a roar over the next decade and a half to overwhelm the British imperial lion and gain India her independence in 1947.

It was a time of great turmoil for the princes, for they stood to lose enormous wealth, status and power by having their states absorbed into India. That was inevitable, though, and after much emotional, financial and strategic wrenching to and fro, plus various outbreaks of violence that have never ceased in the cases of Jammu and Kashmir, the princely states were scribbled out of existence by the redrawing of the new Indian map. Some held out longer than others, the Himalayan state of Sikkim only succumbing after a referendum in 1975.

And what of Travancore on which the Keralan sun now shines? The prince of Travancore at the time, known as the diwan, decided that his state would remain independent of the new India. Although he'd contributed much to the legacy of the region, he'd tended towards military dictatorship and a strong-armed approach to opposition, which had cost his opponents hundreds of lives around the time of independence. But after an assassination attempt on him by a socialist leader before 1947 was out, he agreed to Travancore's being merged into India and fled to London where he died almost two decades later, having worked in various fields and travelled to his heart's content.

As for the other princes, many experienced the squabbles, indecision and upheaval that accompany a major change in status, identity and political transformation. They were all pensioned off by the Indian government, finally, to varying degrees of satisfaction. Many of their descendants still carry the pride of their royal heritage in their refinement and bearing – if not always in their financial status.

Back at the Krishnapuram Palace, a small, sweet, bespectacled and entirely unintelligible female guide met us at the entrance and rattled on at some length about the king of "erst while" Travancore. No matter. The grand interior was cooled by an ingenious system of dormer windows – wooden slats effectively – between the roof and low walls of the room to keep them shady and breezy in a manner that modern building techniques have all but obliterated. It was pleasant to be out of that hellish car for a while and to wander unseeing past royal murals of half-humans with bulging eyes and multiple limbs.

Once out in the gardens, consciousness returned to take note of their style, which exemplified a curious phenomenon – the Indian horticultural landscape. Of course, there are exceptions to the rule such as the famous gardens of the Taj Mahal complex in Agra. The Indian garden, generally, is a strange and linear creation whose habitat is above the ground – in pots. The pots and their inhabitants come in various shapes, shades and sizes, but they seem always to have one thing in

Way out in India

common – military formations.

Even if a large gathering of them clusters together in an apparent circle, an eye travelling across the diameter will invariably find a straight line of similar pots marching along it. Pots line up on red carpeted steps to salute dignitaries, pots rest in lines of wall brackets to catch the sun in the chill of Himalayan towns, pots sit atop low walls and the edges of verandas, and pots – believe it or not – comprise the indoor gardens of Delhi's airport, disguised somewhat by rim-high soil, as if slightly shy about their home-grown landscaping.

The gardens at Krishnapuram Palace did provide a lovely display of coloured leaves, from yellow to purple against an array of greens. And there were a few attempts at topiary in the ground's low hedges. Their only function, though, was to frame displays of terracotta specimens standing in the dust in their mandatory linearity. I reckoned our maths professor would have hauled up his eyelid and proclaimed the garden geometrically sound.

We ambled around pretending enthusiasm for a variegated leaf or textured stem until one of us spoke: 'You want to head back to the car now?'

'No. You?'

'Definitely not.'

AND SO IT was a hot and rattled pair that staggered into the soothing afternoon interior of Varkala's Kaiya House after a hundred and twenty white-knuckled kilometres, where the owner's helper, Bapuchi, greeted us quietly and offered us tea.

'I could do with a whisky,' Arnie muttered, peeling his cap off with a trembling hand as she wafted down the passage in her long cotton dress.

It was immediately apparent that Kaiya House in Varkala is no ordinary place. We knew that the moment Bapuchi returned, called the owner, Debra, and put her on the line.

'Did you arrive okay?' an American voice chirped. 'Do you have local currency or do you need Bapuchi to pay your taxi fare?'

What?

She was dead serious.

A former Indian family home of large dimensions in the style of modern mediocrity, Kaiya House has been transformed by Debra's touch into a work of art – quite literally. From her renovations to her interior design, from her furnishings to her artworks all over the building, the whole creation breathes art. The art she understands best, though, is the art of hospitality, which she elevates to extraordinary heights. From the laundry racks placed for guests on an airy balcony to the concept of breakfast at any hour, Debra and her staff of three dedicate themselves to this little enterprise in a way that amazes.

To be honest, I had my doubts about the guest house when we'd booked it online. When the blurb boasts "cool showers" and lacks a sea view in a town on a cliff top with waves roaring below, one might think twice.

But just then it became interesting with a jumble of young Brits and their luggage tumbling through the door, tow-headed and cursing the heat. Bapuchi's eyes widened slightly before she regained her composure.

'We'd like to check in,' one of the young men informed her – and me.

I nodded – in a friendly sort of manner. 'And d'you by any chance know where we can 'ire Enfiewds?'

Me? I needed help understanding the question.

'Enfiewds,' the second young man added helpfully. 'You know' – he gripped a pair of imaginary handlebars – 'bikes.'

I flapped a helpless hand to my chest. 'Henfields? I'm just a guest here.'

'Oh, we fought you was Debra.'

'Yeah, we fought you was Debra.' The young British lass covered her smile, her nail polish gleaming in peeling green cheer at the mistake.

'No, I'm not Debra,' I chuckled. 'She's on her way here.'

'Great!' The first young man folded his arms, rubbing his hands over his tattoos and anticipatory goosebumps and addressing the others. 'She'w probably know where we can get 'em.' Then he turned to Arnie. 'We 'eard you can hire 'em around 'ere. D'you know where?'

'No,' he shook his head. 'I just know they're manufactured in India.'

'Yeah! We can't wait to get our hands on a pair of 'em.'

Clearly.

I'd just whispered 'What's a Henfield?' in Arnie's ear when an

Way out in India

American voice called 'Hi, everybody!' and a petite parcel of energy whooshed through the door, folding a paper parasol and instructing her Labrador retriever to sit.

In a whirlwind of management, Bapuchi was consulted, Royal Enfields assured and a grizzled and silent retainer in a lungi dispatched up the heavenly staircase to escort us roomwards. And what a room it was – its carved four-poster its main feature with a palm tree brushing its window and a breezy balcony outside.

VARKALA, WHOSE VERTICAL cliffs and gushing ocean lull and lure people of all stripes to its shores, provides those thirsting for rest its cliff top, where open-air restaurants serve up sea views with cold beer and wonder. The mood is casual, and the food Indian and Asian with a few Western offerings for the gastronomically tentative. In between these establishments, hotels and ayurvedic massage studios vie for space with bright stalls, most of them qualifying as little clouds of hippy heaven.

As a bonus rather than a defect, the location of Kaiya House away from the beach ensured a vivid route to it via various local sights. One, a temple tank, was a vast square pool with steps leading down into the green and slimy water, where locals purify themselves in happy oblivion. Another was an elephant stable whose resident was only ever evidenced by fresh piles of pungent offerings.

At the beach a puja was in progress, a Hindu ritual for what the Indians routinely refer to as an "expired" relative.

'This is the Indian beach,' a leathery hippy with an age-thinned top knot told us as we paused on the golden sand of that first declining afternoon. 'The Western beach is farther along.' Oblivious to the way that that jarred a pair of South Africans who'd frolicked in childhood ignorance on segregated beaches, the hippy man greeted the locals with a namaskar, a traditional Indian form of greeting in which someone joins his or her palms before the chest or face, often with an accompanying bow.

Viewing the Varkala beach scene, it became clear that the Indian side was sacred to Hindu worshippers while the Western side was sacred to sun worshippers. And there was no problem with either variety strolling across the territory of the other. Beautiful.

Stopping to watch the puja proceeding, we were enchanted by the trio setting off from under the jolly prayer umbrella, bound in white lungis and carrying small parcels wrapped in cloth towards the sea. It was only later that we understood the contents of those parcels being discharged into the foamy brine in which we'd be swimming: expired relatives in powder form, set adrift to join the Westerners for a romp in the waves if the currents decreed so.

On closer investigation, it seemed that people journeyed to this site in large family groups that included the precious parcel. On arrival the procedure was to choose a priest for the ceremony among those for hire under the primary-coloured umbrellas. A small industry of hotels, restaurants and other establishments for these travellers is part of the Varkala beach scene, where the family might make a kind of holiday of the event, all dressed up in the equivalent of their Sunday best for some light-hearted play after the ceremony.

At a Nepalese restaurant we stared out over the flaxen beach while prayer flags flapped in the breeze and the bubbles rose and popped in our sundowners. Down below our hippy friend meandered along the sand where yogis bent and twisted. There security men gazed about under their peaked caps, while the sun flashed and glittered on the sequinned trim of the Indian ladies' hems.

In the twilight we strolled the road shouldered by red dust, passing the bright buildings, the palm trees as thin and high as Mahatma Gandhi's voice and the little boy with too-short pants chanting 'pen, pen!' to passing Westerners who might, if he was lucky that day, part with a precious bit of plastic-and-ink. Past the smarter homes we ambled, with their little signs declaring the owners' names – such as KS Jain, Senior Government Pleader. Past the general dealer we wandered, whose name should have blighted it long before: Margin Free Market.

Then drifting towards Kaiya House, a sight of some splendour stopped us in our tracks: two Royal Enfields parked outside, their chrome mirroring the afternoon sun, their black enamel shining, their gold trim winking retro cool.

These bikes have a long and interesting history in India, having begun their lives there forty years after their birth in England in 1909.

Way out in India

The Worcestershire company that made them manufactured weapons, too, and sold the bikes under the macho motto "Made Like a Gun" reinforced with a cannon logo.

In 1955, the Indian government decided on the Bullet model for its police and army to use and purchased eight-hundred units, a huge order at the time. To manufacture these, the Worcestershire company partnered with Madras Motors, which over the decades gradually took over the complete manufacturing process of these bikes. While British production stopped in 1970, India has continued to manufacture Royal Enfields and to market them as a status symbol and a key to an exclusive community. In various parts of India, Royal Enfield clubs have flourished, uniting people with a passion for speed, style and skill at dodging potholes, maniacs and livestock of various species.

As obvious aspirants of this club, their translucent flesh now fried a bright red, the happy British lads flip-flopped from the front door, their vests hanging loose over their shorts.

'Got y'fags? Got y'wallets? Let's go!' giggled their little blonde companion in denim shorts as she swung on behind her man and away they all roared.

'I wonder what time they'll be back,' Debra smiled, leaning against the door frame, folding her arms.

'Late, probably,' I replied. 'They're here to party. But they've got a key to get in, haven't they?'

'Yeah,' she said, 'but I always wait up until the last one's in.'

That was what it took to win hospitality awards in Varkala.

ALTHOUGH OUR VARKALA was viewed mainly from the vantage point of two ancient but sturdy sunbeds under a series of umbrellas all afflicted with the same arthritis, it was hardly a hardship. In the way of most old things in India, they were repaired unto a long postponed death, held together with string, or tape or a nail or two knocked in to delay the inevitable. The disposable era has not reached the majority of Indians yet, and where it has, sadly, they dispose for the most part heartily and indiscriminately with few systems in place to contain the practice.

A sparkling innovation in Varkala, though, was the beach cleaning scheme – a breakthrough by all accounts. It involved little bands of women in blue saris, white headscarves and short-sleeved jackets trudging along the burning beaches collecting garbage and proclaiming "Kerala", via the print on their backs, "A Clean Destination".

Another official contribution to Keralan tourism were the lifeguards on the beach: three guys in traffic cop outfits of blue shorts and epauletted shirts, sitting on plastic chairs shaded by one umbrella. Their presence, flimsily reassuring to begin with, dwindled after a dip in the Arabian Sea churned into a series of flip turns with added saltwater sinuses and a question about how those epaulettes would withstand the currents.

That evening Debra had a suggestion for us.

'Do yourselves a favour,' she said, 'take a walk on the wild side.'

SHE WAS UP in the dark to see us into a taxi driven by "her" driver, Rajesh. She'd hardly slept. The Enfields had come roaring back in the wee hours with their jolly cargo crashing in none too silently.

But all was silence as we were driven to the farthest point of the coastal walk, which would take us through some local fishing villages as the catch came in.

Slowly the sun dispelled the dawn grey to reveal the coast with its fishing villages rustling to another day of simplicity amid the abundant greenery. Off the main tourist route, it was a privilege to be on that path to watch the daily local drama.

A canoe nearing the shore approached, rowed by a dozen strong men with oars of wood and heads bound in white cloth. An ancient scene it was, harmonious, rhythmic, just right. From nowhere though and suddenly, Venus herself emerged from the ocean in front of us.

Who? What was *she* doing there? What was she doing in our ancient scene all shapely and blonde, lounging in her own private centrefold on the beach?

The dozen fishermen who rowed their canoe of planks sewn together and smeared with sardine oil and eggs, among other things, didn't seem to notice her. But we did. She was a nakedly jarring note. While they wore formerly-white or checkered lungis folded above the knee with

Way out in India

shirts stained and torn, she sported a tiny green bikini, staring at them as they leaped to shore yelling, their rough voices mingling with the caws of the gulls while sweat salt and sea salt crusted their bulky limbs.

After hauling in the nets and settling into a circle, one or two of them lit bidis before dividing the catch. One, the obvious simple son of the village with teeth like a bunch of bananas, watched dull-eyed from the circle's edge while an old uncle – right in his line of vision – sneaked an extra handful of silvery specimens from those flapping on the fringes and tucked them gently into a fold at the waist of his lungi.

Clearly it paid to move stealthily amid the bellowing men, the flapping gulls and the flipping fish with the waves crashing and foaming so constantly in the background. And with Venus displaying her hip bones nearby, clicking her camera in studied oblivion to the spectacle of herself in this time-worn setting.

It was hard to say when the voices and heat had risen to the point of antipathy. But suddenly thick fishermen's fingers pointed, palms opened to throw out questions about quotas, voices rose to raucousness and finally fists flew, with Venus so close to the action it was surprising she survived intact. It was an ugly display of frustration with poverty to shatter the romantic Western notion of the simple life. It was a wake-up call that ended only with the intervention of a few burly men calming down the combatants and sending them off, two to a heavy basket of silver, their clothes smeared with mud and their faces weary and damp.

We turned away, then, to walk the cliff path and to discover along it some discreet and simple lodges, until at last we were back in Varkala where the sun was high enough to summon its worshippers to the beach and prompt the shop owners to open, among them a tailor who addressed his customers via a sign on his door.

"*Dear Customers*", it said, "*We are happy to offer you customised clothes or make exat* [sic] *copies of dearest pieces of clothing. Everything else you find in our shop it slso* [sic] *for sale.*"

IT WASN'T THE fault of the beaches that my husband began to bristle and nit-pick a day or two later, but rather of a dental niggle building to insistence. And the fault of his resistance to addressing it on foreign soil.

Yes, I understood. And understood. And understood. Until the Disprin Extra Strength and I could no longer hang on and one of us exploded in a fit of temper.

It was time for Debra's dentist.

Reached by tuk-tuk down a midtown alleyway featuring rubble, dust and attendant apprehension, the office's gaudy entrance framed a glass door and a welcome mat on which a few pairs of shoes lined up. Inside, it inclined steeply and suddenly upmarket with an air conditioner, bright lights, sparkling tiles and a TV set in the waiting room. A barefoot nurse in a blue sari beckoned us into the consulting room where the affable Dr Arun was waiting to greet us.

'South Africa!' he beamed, 'Kings of Cricket and all!'

Then he went to work on Arnie's holey molar with a thoroughness and deftness that left me wondering if we'd really traversed a rubble-strewn alleyway to get there.

Arnie had never sat barefoot in a dentist's chair before, talking cricket and Indian politics with cheeks full of cotton wool. I'd never photographed such a scene before and might never do again. It made me laugh and glad to travel. It gave me blurry pictures and Arnie a souvenir filling that's still holding its own a few years down the line. Most of all, it obliterated the testiness between us as we shook Dr Arun's hand at the door.

'Come back to visit us again,' the good doctor smiled. 'Kerala has its troubles, but it's God's own country and all.'

4
Of Caves and Crystals

TO EXPLORE THE AJANTA Caves near Aurangabad is to plunge into a fairy-tale world of jungles and hidden treasures, royalty and mystery, heroes and villains, that twines *The Sleeping Beauty* with *The Tale of Aladdin*. Discovered by a tiger-hunting British officer in 1819 gazing out from his elephant howdah on a cliff top overlooking the Waghora River, he spied an ancient stone stairway climbing the side of the gorge.

'I say,' this officer might have said, without an iota of dash or flash to his name – John Smith, to be perfectly anticlimactic.

'I say,' the gorge may have echoed a tad, 'what *is* that?'

Without further ado he proceeded down the pathway to find himself a short while later fighting dense heat and foliage to chop his way up the ancient stone stairway to his next surprise: the magnificent arched entrance of the first cave.

'Good Lord!' he may have exclaimed, lighting his lamp, pulling up his nose and stepping on a heap of bat shit, 'What have we here?'

Hearing his heart thumping in the silence as though he'd shot a tiger, he found himself in a majestic hall, hollowed out by human hands, with a vaulted ceiling like a cathedral's above him and multiple carved columns towering along its sides, while beyond them ran a cloister. At the hall's far end the strange structure of a Buddhist stupa loomed, while from the walls and ceiling several pairs of hooded eyes regarded him in silence. Painted in gemstone pigments, they belonged to all kinds of figures, including the Buddha, all revealing their magnificence reluctantly in the flickering light of his lantern.

Deeply astonished and weighing his limited options for his next move, our officer of the 28th Cavalry chose vandalism. "John Smith, 28th of April, 1819" he carved into one of the cave's walls for posterity, before puffing his way back into the sunshine.

Although he may not have realised it then, he had made an exceptional find – the first of about thirty Buddhist monastery-caves carved on the site into a volcanic basalt cliff face. On the southern side of the gorge that curves in a horseshoe shape along the Waghora River, they are unique in their age and scale, in the astounding quality of their art and architecture, in their glorious riverside setting and in their sacred energy.

Little could our officer have understood then that he'd stumbled on a treasure two-thousand years old: that first cave, the oldest in the series, where a community of hundreds had once lived and which had been concealed for almost a thousand years. Little could he have known either that the Ajanta Caves were about to begin their renaissance as a subject of serious study and an attraction to millions of people who have visited since then.

LIKE MOST OTHER tourists in the district, our base was the thriving nearby city of Aurangabad, from where we'd elected to hire a car and driver for the hundred-or-so-kilometre trip to the caves. He was a striking looker, the driver, too tall, dark and handsome to be squashed up in his little Tata with its artificial turf for carpeting. And he was enterprising.

'You want see caves from viewpoint?'

'Sure.' Who wouldn't when the other option was caves from parking lot?

'This is going to turn out expensively,' Arnie predicted – not that one needed a crystal ball.

On cue, the viewpoint suddenly entailed a friend who spoke good English and who assured us of our luck in finding ourselves at the exact spot where officer John Smith had first spied the caves. He was a chivalrous chap, the friend, bearing our water bottles all the way down the leafy path on the gorge's north side. Chatting all the way about the Indian economy and his real field – the crystals and gemstones with which this area of Maharashtra State is abundantly blessed – he mentioned oh so casually that he had a shop nearby selling the sparklies.

'Oh, joy,' I smiled at Arnie, 'exit through gift shop again. What's the bet?'

At the bottom of the gorge I held a question out to our friend, which translated from the gracious was this: 'Talk straight please. What is your fee for this jaunt?'

But as so often happens in India, there wasn't one. The fee is commonly the value that the client attaches to a service. It's inevitably too little and invariably elicits a bitter face, either slappable or guilt-inducing, depending on how hardened a traveller one is.

'But there will be,' Arnie assured me. The guide assured him that he was just helping his friend the taxi driver while a third man would be helping us through the caves soon. His title was Helping Man.

'He's over there.' The guide pointed vaguely towards the basalt cliffs looming above us with brightly dressed visitors streaming past them on the path as we sat on a low brick wall on the riverbank. Helping Man's job description was a little vague, but turned out to be varied. He was to jump the ticket queue, buy our tickets, guard our shoes outside the caves, direct us through any further queue jumping en route and generally bow and scrape his way through the tour for an unnamed fee.

Then there he was, Helping Man, solemn and lugubrious with his three brown teeth and ragged clothes, bobbing and ducking, conveying our water bottles from cave to cave and balling our socks ferociously in his fists outside each one. Short of shodding us himself on each exit from the splendid monasteries, he served his heart out, negotiating with the whispering illicit guides who creep up in the dimness to offer something small and unique to those not too hurried, suspicious or oblivious to take advantage of their services.

Perhaps an official guard has spotted some symbol in a painting or sculpture and will share it for a tip. Perhaps some unemployed local knows which paintings bear the remnants of a mother of pearl necklace or some obscure feature. Clearly lower on the food chain than these shadowy figures, our Helping Man would nevertheless share the bounty of our presence in these spectacular caves.

'This had better be worth it,' Arnie grumbled while Helping Man bought the tickets. 'So far we're paying three people plus the Indian government to see a whole lot of caves that are not even caves. What's

Of Caves and Crystals

the matter with us?'

He was right. The Ajanta Caves and the spectacular Ellora Caves in the district are not caves at all but exceptional examples of rock-cut sacred sites, Ajanta's being exclusively Buddhist, while Ellora's are religiously diverse and include Buddhist, Hindu and Jain caves side by side.

Ajanta's caves are older, the first having been created in the second century BCE and the last about halfway through the first century CE. Whatever the precise dates of their creation, the inconceivable manual labour required to carve them, the staggering skill involved, the consummate finesse of their murals and the stupendous sums paid for their construction by the patrons who ruled the area, all make such details almost irrelevant to those simply seeking awe.

Everything about the caves inspires it, from the idea that hundreds of masters and students could live, study and worship in each one, to the wealth, exquisite quality and rarity of their murals and sculptures.

Constructed in two broad types, the first are the *chaityas* or worshipping halls like the one John Smith discovered, with their stupas at their far ends. The others are *viharas* or monasteries, which include an assembly hall with a large statue of the Buddha carved – unbelievably – from the same rock as the hall and a series of dark little cells, with or without stone beds.

The paintings in both types of caves burst with all sorts of lively figures and symbols, from country folk to the Buddha represented as a king in royal settings lavish with contemporary decoration and style. These paintings, commonly called frescoes but technically temperas since they were painted on dry surfaces, are sealed with the binding agents of cow dung, jute and rice glue. For their pigments the area's profusion of minerals was used, with only the lapis lazuli having been imported from Persia to create the dark-blue hues. Wandering through some of the unfinished caves, a mysterious assortment of crater-like hollows in the floors catches the eye, raising one's curiosity. What could they be? The painters' palettes, it turns out.

As dark and mysterious as the caves are inside, the scene outside bustles and hums with locals dressed up and wound up to a day-tripping pitch. With the site being perhaps a bit remote and a bit esoteric, the

Way out in India

percentage of Western visitors there among the hundreds of thousands annually is minimal. Hence we become objects of even greater interest than the caves to some families and high-school groups who, in return, may shine as works of art to the Western eye.

Brimming with life, these crowds of young people, dressed in their best, brighten the site with their smiles and curiosity.

'Hello, Madam,' greets one student at the front of the line, which echoes in each voice as the Westerner passes by, lapping up the dose of intense colours of the girls' tunics-over-trousers and the sharp tailoring of the boys' shirts and even suits.

Then one daring voice will call 'photo, auntie!' and the whole orderly line will dissolve into a cluster around the Western auntie – or uncle – coaxed into the mood by the infectious spirit of youth. Multiple cellphones appear, their owners popping out of the cluster for a picture or two, holding auntie and uncle hostage until a smiling firmness is required to break away. At the next cave the whole scene is repeated, differing only if it's a family group that stands stiffly around the trophy Westerner, sometimes with a bewildered little child pressed into the closest possible proximity to those prized legs from far across the sea.

For anyone who gets to Ajanta the trip is an adventure, but minus some of the daring required in days of yore. Back then ladders or staircases, like the one John Smith first discovered, led up from the river to the cave entrances. Ranging in height from one metre to more than thirty, they led to narrow ledges, visited sometimes by wild animals and sharp arrows shot by the fierce Bhil locals who'd inhabited the area for centuries.

John Smith, back on his elephant and mercifully unharmed by any of the above, discharged his duty of reporting his find. Soon the news reached the Nizam of Hyderabad, in whose territory it lay. The nizam, sovereign of the largest and richest of all the princely states in India, was a man of untold wealth who received the news with glee.

Dispensing money and dispatching teams with gusto to clear the jungle and accumulated rubble from the site, it didn't take that long before teams of archaeologists and historians were climbing those ladders and dodging those arrows to establish the extent of the treasure. On realising its pricelessness, the nizam had a neat pathway built along

Of Caves and Crystals

the curve of the cliff – no doubt so that he himself could visit his new treasure, probably in an elaborate palanquin hoisted on to the shoulders of his bearers.

Amazingly enough you, too, can traverse the selfsame pathway borne aloft today, although in a chair lashed and bracketed to a couple of poles, with your bearers wearing orange vests saying "Porter" on their backs, courtesy of the Archaeological Survey of India. Only in this country would the disabled access challenge have been solved this way: using practicality and charm not only to cater to the infirm and to those with a taste for tradition, but to create employment, too.

The Nizam of Hyderabad, meantime, surely itching to show off his latest prize, could probably never have imagined that the hordes of visitors two centuries hence would be posing a threat to its existence. The increase in heat and humidity caused by the crowds in the caves when they're open draw destructive insects to the site, while the drop in temperature when the caves close causes cracks in the precious paintings.

The current authorities, alarmed by their rate of deterioration, are planning to begin displaying them through replicas in a new extension to the visitors' centre, whose other aim is to show these works in full light since the dimness of the caves masks much of their beauty.

Strangely enough the same idea took root at the time of British Raj, when copies of the paintings were made by various artists. One of them, the hapless Major Robert Gill, had eighteen years' worth of his replicas burn to ashes in London's Crystal Palace blaze. Then seriously jinxed, he had another batch of his work go up in flames in a later fire at one of the forerunners of the Victoria and Albert Museum. Undaunted by all this, though, and having come to identify himself completely with his work, he continued painting and eventually photographing the Ajanta paintings until the end of his days in 1879.

The value of these treasures was so obvious to the nizam and the British that early on they tried various ways to preserve them. One of these was to call in the Italians, presumed to be masters at sealing masterpieces. Slathering varnish and shellac over the Ajanta paintings, they did them more harm than good, sadly, while subsequent efforts at cleaning the paintings damaged them even further.

One couldn't blame the British and the nizam for trying, though. The impact of the paintings at first glance is intense, but the more the caves were explored, the more priceless its riches revealed themselves to be. All kinds of religious figures grace these works, often lavishly bejewelled with the region's gems and accompanied by figures from folklore, natural motifs and abundant symbols. Some of the caves' ceilings are also painted with pastoral people, or life at court where the Buddha reigns. In between dance a variety of designs, especially on some of the ceilings.

And then there are the sculptures, on walls, on archways, on plinths. All are intriguing, many intact and some literally breathtaking. One of these, a twenty-four-foot reclining Buddha in Cave 26, sleeps smiling slightly on his side, his head resting in the palm of his hand that lies on a tassled bolster. Viewed in pieces between the columns of a cloister, it's difficult to discern him as a whole. And then comes the gasp at his scale, his smoothness, his tranquillity through two-thousand years. He could be said to be The Sleeping Beauty of Ajanta.

He could also be said to reflect the Ajanta era, when the Deccan region covering most of southern India was largely peaceful and prosperous, providing good conditions for trade to flourish and art and culture with it.

During this time Ajanta became the wellspring for the unique and indigenous Indian classicism which was to influence Buddhist art the same way that the Parthenon sculptures influenced Western art. Its style became known as the Ajanta style and, with the region so rich in gemstones and the artisans so skilled as to exploit their beauty to the full, it became famous for its jewellery whose designs can still be seen in the Ajanta paintings today.

With the beauty of the caves providing such a visual feast, some of its less obvious riches may go unnoticed. The acoustics in certain caves, for example, are positively haunting. With the porous basalt rock in them carved into arched nave-like ceilings, the chant of even one voice carries a resonance that vibrates to one's bones. In one uplifting moment we were to enter an empty cave just as a man stood in its centre and began to chant a prayer. The vibration was riveting. So to imagine multiple voices chanting in unison all those centuries ago is to conjure a state of spiritual transportation probably only few ever experience.

And amid all the fine art and architecture of the caves, their purpose may be forgotten somewhat. As far from archetypal cavemen as possible, whose rocky homes provided but survival and safety, the Ajanta dwellers created their caves for the highest evolutionary purposes: for meditation, for intellectual development, for spiritual evolution and, ultimately, for enlightenment.

On moving from the heat and harsh light outside into the relative cool of the caves, this can be difficult to remember. In all the racket of sightseeing groups bouncing back off the walls and all the staring eyes examining one's every move, the dense tranquillity that must have buzzed there once might escape one. The shrieking whistles of schoolmasters trying to control their charges and the sharp smell of urine from some shadowy cloisters can obliterate the mood and concentration. Throw in dim lights quite hard to see by and watermarks creeping through the basalt to flush the paintings away and you have a situation that might challenge even the most serene Buddhists.

Standing there in all the tumult, I wondered what they would have thought of the scene. If fully immersed in their belief in transience, they may simply have shrugged. I wondered if the last of them accepted with grace the eighth-century decline of Buddhism in the region to make way for Hinduism. I wondered, too, about the emotional state in which the diminished Ajanta community had left the caves to the jungle that their forebears had conquered to create them so many centuries before.

Our visit to Ajanta ended – as predicted – in another kind of cave, our guide's glittering Crystal Cave in the market at the exit of Ajanta. There a host of sparkling geodes and glasses of sweet chai waited for us on a table, the field of battle for the hard sell that ensued. The band of brothers who owned the shop did well out of us there, as did the taxi driver no doubt. Were they the fairy-tale's villains? It was hard to tell, especially when the paradoxical policeman pitched up on cue as the money changed hands, to loom over proceedings, jingling the change in his pockets.

A PARADOX LIES at the core of the Ellora Caves near Aurangabad, too, a paradox of creating by destroying. With the community's stonemasons

Way out in India

having chiselled away at a hillside for more than a century, they revealed a glorious version of its essence, a Hindu temple complex so astounding as to require a moment to make sense of it.

Besides the rock the stonemasons had to carve through, they had to conquer perhaps their own resistance, wavering motivation, internal politics, technical challenges and all the other obstacles that inevitably attend a complex building project. And there must have been plenty of those at Ellora and particularly at the site of the Kailasa, this temple complex that so dominates the site.

Entering its huge domain, which, just for comparison, is double the size of the Parthenon and gazing up at its multiple storeys and massive elephants carved into its base, a sense overwhelms one of the astonishing audacity displayed by its eighth-century creators who were convinced that inside one massive rock was this object of awesome beauty just waiting to be chiselled into its form. So certain were five generations of the same end that they handed the idea and will to each other until the work was complete.

Approaching the Kailasa it's difficult to imagine that it was carved from one piece of rock. It is the world's biggest monolithic temple. Although now in a state of ruin, its multiple storeys open to the sky are carved everywhere with expansive panels housing deities – some erotically posed – while the central temple, almost thirty metres high, rests on a base held by sixteen chunky pillars. With masterful sculptures everywhere telling the tales that informed and infused the community, the site is a satisfying feast. And with vertical rock faces surrounding the temple on three sides, one wanders through it – unbelievably – inside what was once one of the Charanandri Hills.

The conviction a community has to have to create such a masterpiece is unfathomable, the strength to relinquish any chance of savouring its completion in one's own lifetime laudable. Being such a spiritual community, though, faith must have been the food that nourished the project to completion.

And faith is still expressed here by the multitudes of worshippers who come to pay their respects to the deity Shiva, to whom the Kailasa temple, appropriately, is dedicated. Through the towering entrance they go, encountering the shrine of Nandi the Bull who served as Shiva's

Of Caves and Crystals

gatekeeper and mount, according to tradition. Through the assembly hall they wander towards the temple's inner sanctum with its Shiva lingam.

To the Western eye this seems a strange object, a simple stone cylinder with a rounded top, mounted on a plinth. Surrounded at its base with money, flower and incense offerings from the faithful and wet with their milk offerings, it's a phallic Hindu symbol representing the male god, Shiva. The lipped plate that forms the base and holds the offerings represents the goddess, Shakti. Together they represent the unity of the sexes to create completeness.

Although completeness, spiritual or otherwise, was always the goal at Ellora, it was sometimes not attained in the construction – or perhaps deconstruction – of the other caves there. Thirty-four in number, they are more suited to the description for being roofed by rock, but are still not caves in the true sense, having been cut by humans into the cliff face of the hills about thirty kilometres from Aurangabad. The incomplete examples with their chisel marks, their half-carved pillars and intimidating rock masses still intact, make the contrast of the finished ones all the more remarkable.

Not as old as the Ajanta Caves and never hidden the way they were, the Ellora Caves were created between the fifth and tenth centuries by members of three separate religions: Buddhism, Hinduism and Jainism. A remarkable feature of the site that provides such a useful example to humanity is that as each new religion rose and cut its temples or monasteries into the hillside, the others continued on their paths without territorial or spiritual wars between the groups. The site, ultimately, accommodated them all simultaneously.

Like Ajanta's Caves, Ellora's could accommodate thousands of people for praying and studying, sleeping and eating amid their splendid sculpture and paintings, with nature abounding just outside each cave's entrance.

Under the Archaeological Survey of India, the Ajanta and Ellora sites are managed in a typically low-key, slightly chaotic fashion. With their dusty parking lots full of shunting vehicles and their questionable toilets so inconveniently placed that visitors relieve themselves in the temples at times, the survey does itself proud with the vast and pretty gardens

Way out in India

on the approach to the Ellora Caves. These, lowly fenced, declare the authority of this authority through little signs in no uncertain terms.

"*Entry inside the lawns,*' they proclaim, '*playing, jumping, garbaging and plucking flowers and leaves are prohibited.*"

At Ajanta, the survey's warning includes the consequences of breaking its rules: "*Shouting, teasing, clicking photos of any individual without consent is strictly prohibited and offenders will be prosecuted.*"

As happens at Ajanta, the local visitors flock towards the foreign ones, which can prove overwhelming at times. One lone, young Asian man, who'd settled against a stone pillar of the Kailasa to sketch the magnificent carvings before him, found himself slowly surrounded by a host of bright schoolgirls. Floating down from the storey above like a bubble of balloons that hovered and bobbed about him, he closed his sketch pad, folded it across his chest and looked up as they drew closer. Then squeezed eventually by their sequins and questions, he panicked, fleeing the area with sketch pad a-flap, the bolder balloons in persistent pursuit behind him.

We were also about to exit the site, though more decorously, when a thin, young security guard intercepted us on the pathway that runs along the caves' entrances. After some initial pleasantries, he cut to the chase: 'You want see secret queue?'

No thanks. I didn't want to see any queue, secret or otherwise.

But he was insistent, young Madhu.

'Secret queue very good, Madam. Very good, Sir.'

It took me a while to tune in, to remember that the "V" sound in India is often pronounced as "W" or "B" or a cross between the two. Right. That took us to "kyoove", which translated after several repetitions by Madhu to "cave".

Well. We weren't sure. Where might this young man lead us? There was a whole unknown hillside above the caves. Maybe he'd lead us into an ambush. Maybe we'd be mugged. For all we knew we might disappear without trace by following him to this desolate area.

Finally communicating our consent to adventure through mutual glances, we set off up the hill in the blazing sunshine to be met by another realm there. A lovely stream ran through it, interrupted by rock pools large and small, their smooth, circular shapes obviously caused by erosion over millennia and their flow from one to another creating gently trickling waterfalls.

Along the water's edge smaller vertical rock faces than those of the main caves rose, with several little temples carved into them. Their condition varied greatly, with some collapsed and half submerged in the water, while others revealed frescoes so detailed and colourful, that they rivalled many open to the public in the caves below. All the paintings at Ajanta and Ellora bear signs of wear in their peelings, pockmarks, graffiti and wilful destruction by Emperor Aurangzeb's men.

Being the same ruler who killed his brothers and imprisoned his father in the seventeenth century and being militantly Muslim, he had no qualms about destroying other religions' art. Viewing it in its various states of decline only magnifies the sense of privilege and unreality in viewing it at all. And its setting enhances it, a paradise for spiritual pursuits, silent and evidently deserted until one cave's Ganesh idol doused in fresh orange paint as an offering, indicated otherwise the quiet presence of a few devotees.

This fascinating area must once have been open to the public we concluded, since multiple metal railings wobbling to the rickety, line the water's edge. But probably as time passed the visitor volumes threatened to overwhelm the fragile site, now returned to its former stillness as the caves erode and nature asserts itself gradually again.

Sensing our delight and willingness to crawl through hollowed rocks and climb over tricky ones, young Madhu unveiled for us more and more of his secret stash of treasures by the waterside until replete, we all reclined in some scant shade together in the precious silence up on the hillside, chatting quietly, creating a sweet connection and hearing a goat or two bleating in the middle distance.

Leading us to a ledge that appeared, he invited us to look down over it. A stunning view met our gaze, of the hillside carved to rooflessness along a temple's passage. There, far down below, little doll visitors wandered between its sheer, high walls.

Inviting us to descend by ourselves to this most marvellous cave temple, he left us – all of us warmed and inspired by our meeting – to wander this mammoth temple with its massive columns and sculptures soaring like inspiration.

Way out in India

It dawned on me later, rolling along in our driver's little Tata with my feet firmly placed on its astroturf, that we'd created something too that day, an experience memorable and valuable, but only by destroying fear and suspicion first.

5
Of Rot and Religion

IF MEN WITH RED teeth don't disturb you or goats wearing T-shirts, visit Varanasi. If urchins shitting in alleyways and cows' heads or corpses floating and bloating beside your boat don't bother you, head for this sacred city on the Ganges where a horde of sham shamans will lighten the load of your sins – and your wallet.

It's the City of Temples, Varanasi, the most colourful conjuror's trick in India, its heart of darkness hiding in its devotional dazzle, its rot permeating the air heavy with the smoke of cremation pyres and twisted piety. As part of the far north-eastern Indian state of Uttar Pradesh – the most populous in India and the most notorious for illiteracy, poverty and disease, not to mention communal violence, corruption, casteism and crime – the city swings between Dickens's London and *Death in Venice*.

With its leathery boatmen, its august buildings porous and powdering into the Ganges, its religion as theatre or business, and its grey-skinned children selling flower offerings, it radiates what may be called a low vibration. And here the food chain feeds in public. Cows feed on marigolds strewn ceremonially over corpses ready for cremation, goats feed on garbage and locals feed on outsiders by whatever swindling tricks they can. These are the less extreme locals. There are others who feed on corpses – literally – but more about that later.

Varanasi is an auspicious place to die if you're Hindu, an easy one, too, amid all that cavalier filth – and on what it calls its roads. Just patches of tar between pot craters, they goad its drivers to meet head on, which they do gladly, at speeds that make the afterlife seem the destination of choice.

Approaching this city in the south-eastern corner of Uttar Pradesh,

Way out in India

one of the oldest in the world to be continuously inhabited, you may spy a car or a van with an odd-looking load rocking around on its roof rack. Wrapped in cloths of orange and gold which flap merrily as it passes, it's likely to be a loved one en route to Varanasi's famous funeral pyres on the banks of the Ganges. Anyone cremated there according to tradition is instantly released from the endless cycle of death and rebirth and catapulted up the spiritual ladder.

An unsettling sight, this cargo is but an appropriate introduction to Varanasi, so notorious for disturbing the visitor, agitating him in nameless ways until he rushes away to places more sane and predictable. The most baffling aspect of the city is that the source of this discomfort changes shape, leaving just a sense of shaky ground on the river's edge where the outsider is unsure of whom to trust about anything, if anyone at all. Can his own eyes even be trusted? Can they really be witnessing the sights all about him?

At the core of all this is a paradox. It begins with the city's appearance of living and dying with ruthless transparency. For here the faithful pray in the sacred river, cupping her waters in raised palms joined while wading in, paying homage to their gods and ancestors. Here, two metres from the worshippers on the steps of a ghat, a barber shaves a squatting man while a fisherman baits his line.

Here a man dunks his cows in the river while another dips his new bicycle in for her blessing, only a stone's throw from the laundrymen whacking their washing on slabs jutting diagonally from the bank strewn with and stinking of garbage. Here a dog digs for morsels in the mud below a priest all bearded and robed in saffron, dispensing teachings and blessings for a fee, while against the wall of a perishing maharajah's palace on the bank, a man pisses steamily, oblivious to the ashes of a corpse being shaken into the water just behind him, or a gaudy god peering down from a niche, or a dying beggar pleading thinly to no one in particular, a band of urchins skipping past hardly noticing her as they rush the strolling foreigner with pleas to buy their postcards.

Here the old guest-house owner sleeps in his bedroom separated only by window bars from the public passage, in full view of guests, watched over by a silent employee. And here lives are lived on the rooftops, the higher ones viewing the lower ones washing themselves, hanging their laundry, chasing monkeys away from their children, reading their newspapers, and smoking.

To the foreigner, accustomed to bathing and eliminating, shopping and praying, ailing and dying with delicacy in privacy, Varanasi's unabashed whirl is shocking. In its nakedness, in its matted beards and faces painted with kumkum powder, in its raucousness and rough displays of living and dying he is confronted with the primitive in us all – with that simple, open being having nothing to hide and so hiding nothing. At once an appealing and an appalling aspect of our own humanity, he is both drawn to and repulsed by it in equal measure.

But then the paradox arises – over and over in Varanasi, the most devious city in India where everyone seems focused on a single game: fleecing the foreigner. For this the competition is tough, necessitating the honing of cunning by the locals, whom any visitor will tell you are among the most creative manipulators ever encountered. And so the paradox is this: with so much of life lived so transparently here, the trickery presented as healing or holiness, business or hospitality, strikes a discordant note. When repeated at every turn it turns the city's tenor up to a screeching frequency at once deafening and inaudible. It's a most bewildering experience.

And beneath the fragrance of all the temple incense lurks the stench of danger and decay. It's a dog-eat-dog city. Or dog-eat-corpse if one or part thereof happens to wash up on the banks. Not to mention a man-eat-man city in more ways than one. And not only the dying are dying in Varanasi. The city itself feels over-encumbered, crumbling, pieces of it heeding the river's siren song, so that a temple spire pokes above its surface at the foot of a ghat, a wobbly brick wall mourns its plaster that's cracked and powdered down to the depths, while a railing bends and bows towards the water as if accepting its inevitable rusty fate down there.

The Ganges herself, revered as a goddess by Hindus who aspire to spiritual elevation by immersion in her waters, seems superficially to flow along as gracefully as she has done for millennia. Especially at sunrise or sunset, mirroring a poetic pink sky, one can almost believe in her purity. The vast flood plain on the opposite bank, stippled with little boats, hovers on the edge of inspiring a verse. Beneath the surface, however, the waters of Mother Ganges are troubled – deeply troubled. Contaminated to the point of inclusion among the world's ten most polluted rivers, she struggles to support even the few fish, birds, river dolphins and amphibians that once thrived in and on her glorious waters.

Now call me pernickety, but it strikes me as a tad hypocritical both to worship a river and to pump a burgeoning population's untreated sewage into her daily. It strikes me as a little duplicitous to ban alcohol and meat consumption on her waters and banks and then to release industrial waste into her at a rate that has turned her so toxic that cancer has become more likely to afflict riverside dwellers than anyone else in India. It also strikes me as a touch feeble that an action plan, begun a few years ago to clean up the river, foundered on the rocks of corruption and misappropriation of funds, while the Ganges is left to dwindle, rot and cause diseases like diarrhoea, dysentery, typhoid and cholera that rob citizens of their lives amid all those deafening proclamations of reverence for her.

And here's another Varanasi paradox: the rituals that express the worshippers' veneration of the river contribute to her afflictions and their own. This is not a simple matter to resolve. To understand it, one must consider a deep-rooted belief in a river as a mother-goddess with the power to elevate the soul, soothe the spirit, annul a karmic debt and bless a petitioner with good fortune. One must understand the profound yearning passed between generations for thousands of years to immerse oneself in her watery womb, to drink from her bosom, to have her receive one's most precious possessions into her fluid embrace and finally to return to her in death; to this potent, silent and ancient mother whose font of purity and blessings is believed infinite and who is available to all.

With this longing so ingrained in the Hindu psyche it would be a difficult and delicate matter for any authority – particularly one with similar collective beliefs – to stop the traditional rites of immersion in the Ganges by the millions of Hindus who bathe there annually – many of them combining their spiritual cleansing with soap, toothpaste and scrubbing brushes.

It would be difficult to stop their dipping their cows in for a wash or setting thousands of little foil bowls afloat every day filled with flower-and-candle offerings to the river. It would also probably be almost impossible to curtail the tradition of pouring the ashes of loved ones in. Just as unthinkable would be the banning of burning bodies on the banks not only to clear the smoke drifting over the water, but also the body parts left over when the wood runs out and the families can't afford more. In various stages of decomposition they drift by regularly or wash up on the riverside, these being only some of the remains of the daily cremations at Varanasi, which number between eighty and two-hundred, depending on whom one believes.

Even more alarming are the categories of Hindu corpses committed to the river who, according to Hindu tradition, are forbidden cremation. The children, the priests, the pregnant women, the snakebite victims, the lepers, the suicides and the paupers are all consigned to the Ganges in death. How this is done and the ultimate end of these bodies, however, is unclear.

As some sources would have it, they are bound to a rock, rowed to the middle of the river and buried there. According to others, though, they are floated downstream on bamboo stretchers, to be welcomed there by a sect of sadhus or holy men who – wait for it – eat them. The Aghori babas, in their quest to overcome the fear of death, tuck into the flesh of these corpses full of venom or leprosy, nicely marinated in sewage and chromium and, by so doing, tick the bravery box as far as this fear is concerned.

So when cannibals are drinking from crania and laundrymen's sheets are stewed in E.coli, what hope is there for the Ganges?

'SOUNDS LIKE A disease,' Arnie had said when I'd first introduced the subject of Varanasi to him.

'It *is*. Well, virtually.' I'd not been willing to euphemise the place. He'd needed to know where my wanderlust would take him if he would but agree to go.

And for my sins I was punched in the solar plexus by the city. Arnie was punched in the lungs, standing beside rather than smoking the Ganga. That is the river's Hindi name. He was, however, literally

Way out in India

smoking something probably far less wholesome than ganga.

The occasion was our unplanned visit to Varanasi's main burning ghat, Manikarnika, during an exploratory stroll on arrival in the city.

The ghats of Varanasi are Varanasi Central in reality. By definition, a chain of wide steps leading down to an expanse of water, they are where life is lived on the riverside. With each ghat having its own character, function and significance, the walk of about seven kilometres along these ghats provides a raffish and fascinating obstacle course. Through young boys flying kites and swinging cricket bats, through cows offloading everywhere, through boatmen, everymen, hawkers and holy men the riverside meanders. With some ghats having alternate steps painted in contrasting colours, the view from the river is a stunning striped optical feast smelling of fried food, incense, dung and garbage – punctuated with people or their laundry spread out to dry.

It's easy, then, not to notice the scout perched on a railing, waiting to pounce as you approach Manikarnika Ghat.

'You going burning ghat?' His teenage voice is casual, but his sudden leap off the railing is not. 'Come, I take you burning ghat.'

At which point you smell the kind of smoke produced by the backyard braai or barbecue at home.

'Burning ghat?'

'Yesss,' hisses the priest so softly under his dirty orange turban as he receives you from the scout. 'It'sss where we burn the bodiesss. Thisss way pleassse.'

By then you're halfway into the place already, the priest looking ssso sssolemn and asssking you not to take photographsss.

'Ressspect,' he almost whispers. 'Thisss is very important. 'Ssso no photo. No photo.'

No shit.

I'm telling you all this in case you, too, get hypnotised by the smoke and the fascination with the taboo and you, too, get drawn in to witness a vision of hell before you reach the hereafter. I'm telling you all this, too, in case you get fleeced the way we were, by the priest and his tale of woe.

And hell the place is. Whatever classical or other paintings you may have seen depicting it as a place of chaos, filth, death and smoke, they might have had Manikarnika Ghat sit as a subject. Vile with the detritus of cremations, their discarded outer shrouds of orange and gold trampled underfoot, their muddied straw and splinters of wood garnished with plastic bags, it burns bodies twenty-four hours a day.

This was what the priest told us, sidling close and muttering about how the cremations take place, while we watched, sweating and horrified as three or four bodies on their pyres sizzled and crackled, melted and popped, surrounded by the men of their families. Hindu women do not attend cremations according to tradition. Some say it's because they might cry, thereby drawing the soul back to earthly life while it should be journeying on. Some say because tears, like all bodily fluids, are impure and should not be shed at the cremation ground.

Breathing the smoke that bore particles of the dead into our lungs, we stood transfixed, scarves pressed to faces, paralysed by the spectacle, by the Doms, the untouchable caste, going about their jobs-for-life, carrying the bodies on their bamboo stretchers, building the pyres, scratching through the ashes for a gold tooth, a silver ring perhaps. It would be theirs if they found it since higher castes may not touch anything that has touched a corpse. Barefoot, these smoke-blackened men with matted hair would gather the ashes in a sack and pour them into the river.

Unbelievably, a cow wandered amid the smoke and fires, grazing the fresh marigolds adorning the bodies – and nobody blinked an eye. Unbelievably, beneath the remains of a bamboo stretcher turned on its side, a litter of puppies yapped and yelped, their mother a tottering skeleton with glittering eyes, searching for a charred finger perhaps, a nice barbecued toe for the little ones. Why else would she have chosen that site to birth her babies?

And on the priest pattered about the kindly hospice looming, ashen and shaky above us, and his role in trying so hard to maintain it. Yeah, right. If anyone had put even a few rupees into it, it wouldn't look like that from the outside. Dickens would probably have felt at home within.

'And then the eldest son lights the sheaf of grass from the eternal flame inside this building. And then he circles the body five times to represent the five elements – earth, water, air, fire and ether. And then he lights the pyre with the burning sheaf. It is very expensive, the wood.'

We nodded, tying our scarves more tightly around our faces,

Way out in India

squinting in the smoke.

'And then the family watches the fire burn, two to three hours it takes to burn the body. Family needs good-quality wood. Deodar or sandalwood. Very expensive, the wood.'

'Exit through gift shop,' I mumbled to Arnie through my scarf.

'What?' His eyes were tearing up. 'I can't hear you.'

'Exit through you-know-what,' I repeated.

He grunted in response, rolling his eyes.

'Look, Sir, the ashes of the body are then given to the Ganga.' The priest was pointing at one of the Doms pouring his load carefully so as not to miss a possible glint. 'But if the family doesn't have enough money, then they have to throw the body parts in. The wood is very expensive.'

Of course the wood was expensive – about three-hundred times the price for foreigners expected to support either the practices unfolding before us, or more probably just the priest and all those who fed off his slimy operation.

He wasn't grateful for our contribution, the priest. Of course, it was too small. But greed kept his charm flowing with a despicable bonus offered at the end of the visit. It kicked my solar plexus into overwhelming rolls of nausea: an exclusive, secret viewpoint from which photos, amazingly and suddenly, could be taken.

'No, thanks,' Arnie said, backing away, then unleashed a fit of coughing that carried him to bed for the next few days. It had all been that toxic.

SO BY THE time the turbaned man stepped into my path at Dasaswamedh Ghat two days later, I'd had enough of the city's so-called culture.

'But, Madam,' he smiled, 'I just want to talk to you.'

'No.'

'Why not? Madam!'

I spun to face him, feet apart, arms akimbo and stared at his weathered face with its thick, grey beard.

'I'll tell you why not. Because everyone in this city lies and cheats and claims that it's a holy place. But it's not. It's a disgusting place, rotten to the depths of its river.'

For a second his eyes registered something like shock, like offence, before they cracked at the corners as if around a bullet hole and he twinkled a grin. What a wound-up, hysterical woman, his chuckle said, stamping her feet virtually and baring her teeth over nothing at all.

'But, Madam,' he cajoled.

'No.' I pushed out a palm and strode away, huffing and muttering to myself, reflecting on the guest-house owner in his family's imposing home now transformed into a fleecing factory, where he'd assure all his guests that they were his family – for an extortionist rate. An oily, old man hunched and wrapped up behind his desk in the cavernous entrance hall of the house, he'd accost all of us as we entered or left, first with an obsequious 'namaste.'

The invariable question-as-imperative would follow after that: 'What can I do for you?' On offer was a litany of delights: yoga, boat trip, massage, large and crappy room for a ridiculous rate complete with stinking bathroom and an absence of bedside tables or lamps, minimal food kept tasteless at his command, taxi, silk garments – finest quality...'

All of these involving a merchant delivered a double whammy for him – a ripping off of both merchant and guest in one transaction. It was an elegant model but an obvious one, which was why the Swedes they were a-sprinting up and down the thumping staircase, their long, strong legs carrying them beyond the reach of that wheedling voice. It was why the Dutch they were a-ducking into the alleyway outside, gasping at their good fortune, having escaped the owner one more time. It was why the Americans aimed three storeys high in as few strides as possible to meet us breathlessly at the balcony on the rooftop.

'He's quite intense,' they'd say, then sink into the plastic chairs up there to order a soda from one of the owner's "boys" – young men, really, at his relentless beck and call.

Sparing his spices on instruction from him, they'd cook up the kind of bland and sloshy fare he enjoyed, called "softs" in old-age homes – not exactly the aromatic local dishes sought by his clientele.

Because of this, we'd wandered away from the riverside and into the warren of alleys there in search of decent food. Known locally as

Way out in India

galis, they twist and wind their way along with their people on foot, on incongruous and reverberating motorbikes and high on paan, which they use to festoon the ground here with red splashes of spit. Otherwise embellished with rotting piles of garbage by the resident adults and by shit by the resident animals and children, they carry on regardless, their shutters open for business and life.

From dull doorways bright things beckon – rows of little brass pots, silks and cottons hanging in multihued layers, garlands of jasmine twining their fragrance with incense and spices and sewage, little religious figurines dancing on their perches and merchants beckoning, 'Come see my shop' as you pass by.

Shrines and temples, vegetable stalls and laundries line the alleyways, some of these standing their ironing tables outside when space constraints or the heat of the charcoal irons get too stifling to use them indoors. In the path of rushing motorbikes, the laundrymen risk life and limb here, or at least a squirt of red besmirching their clothes or their customers'.

The locals' fondness for paan or betel leaves in Varanasi is as famous as silk here. Mixed with tobacco, some grated coconut perhaps and dried dates or lime all rolled into a pretty leaf package, it's chewed then spat out, having delivered its payload of carcinogens along with its kick of euphorics.

As an offering to a deity or a little gift to wedding guests, paan is spun by its marketers as an appetite suppressant, a breath freshener and a dental aid. In reality, it can be lethal, especially through the various oral cancers it may cause. And, at the very least, it makes one ugly, like a horror-movie character with a blood-sticky smile.

IT SEEMED EXPRESSIVE of this city that even in the restaurants the food lacked something: taste, texture or warmth, a phenomenon unusual in India where even the humblest street food is often just delectable. It also seemed expressive of the city that the restaurant owner could find a tailor for us in the blink of an eye and lead us personally through the maze to get to him.

Once handed over to him, we embarked on the business – common in India – of having a favourite garment copied.

To do this, you sit on a cushion on a carpet with the tailor. You talk cricket, you touch on politics. You drink a cup of intensely sugared chai. You apologise to your pancreas, which flares in protest. Finally, you get down to business, which is absolutely simple: 'I'd like to have these pants copied, please.'

But, before you know it, there are jackets on offer, 'silk, hand-embroidered, very elegant, Madam', reams of fabrics unfurled before your eyes, 'saris for that special occasion and, for the gents, shirts, trousers, waistcoats and the finest-quality suits, Sir. Bespoke and all.'

'But I'd just like these plain cotton pants copied. That's all,' you plead.

More fabric unrolls, samples appear, shawls and blouses in every shade and shape. But at last you insist, knowing the result: that face sinking towards sulking, mortally insulted, the price of the cotton pants soaring towards the stratosphere, the transactional net closing – which is probably why you see so many tourists on the smelly ghats in the fullest possible local kit: silky tunics and scarves, puffy pants and jackets jaunty with Indian pizzazz.

Meantime, you plan the grab in your mind. Amid all that grave offence that you've managed somehow to cause, how will you get your favourite pants out from under that mountain of fabric and get the hell out of there? It's an art form assuredly, which you may choose to practise if you're not adrenalin averse. The alternative, I'm afraid, is high-intensity haggling.

Getting out of the alleyways or trying to, the crowds about us swelled. They bulged and bloated, squashing and pushing, some forwards, some backwards like cells multiplying in a confined bodily sac. Stuck to the walls lining these passages policemen watched – lots of policemen – with hooded eyes and truncheons.

'What's going on here?' I asked one of them.

'Golden Temple. Festival going.'

Ah, the famous Golden Temple, up there on the bucket list.

'Why are so many policemen here?'

He sucked his teeth irritably. 'High security. Hindu temple. Mosque next door.'

High security? And how did these policemen propose any movement

Way out in India

to quell whatever might erupt?

'Can we go to the Golden Temple?'

'No. Foreigner no allowed inside. Outside only. But leave bags at shop. Camera at shop.'

Was he *nuts*? In *this* place?

'Ah, no thanks,' I smiled sweetly. He didn't. And in a flash the Golden Temple of Varanasi was booted off the bucket list.

'OKAY, SO NOW we're officially lost,' I declared as we landed up panting slightly somewhere between here and there.

'What are you looking, Madam?' a man in a doorway asked us.

'River. *Ghats.*'

'Ah, Ganga. Follow me.'

What choice did we have?

His route, inevitably, involved an undisclosed detour to his cotton shop where we ditched him unceremoniously, but not before he'd flashed a russet grimace and an outstretched palm to make his point: 'But I help you, Sir. I help you, Madam!'

Huh?

Stopping in at a pharmacy for an urgent supply of headache pills along the way (surprise, surprise), we asked the pharmacist where we might buy a cap for Arnie. A lot of complex directions followed, involving several kilometres and a tuk-tuk, which he would – amazingly – organise for us.

'No, thanks.'

Just as well since right next door we discovered on our exit a men's clothing store, its doors flung wide, its array of sporty caps displayed in the window. Talk about brazen.

SO IF YOU were approached, then, on the riverfront the day after all that by a turbaned older man offering conversation, would you not have felt inclined to invite him to talk to the hand?

'Madam!' He startled me, twinkling in my path again on my way back along the riverside.

'What?' My tone was sharp.

'Madam, why are you so angry all the time?'

'I told you,' I snapped as a kid tapped on my leg, offering small packs of tissues for sale, 'everyone in this place wants money. Lies and cheats to get it.'

'Yes, many people here want money,' he beamed benevolently, 'but I don't need money.'

And with that he fished a whopping wad of rupees from his grimy waistcoat pocket.

'See I have many money. I even buy gift for you.'

To my astonishment he flapped a note at the garland wallah standing a metre away, who promptly handed me a string of pink flowers.

'There,' said the turbaned man. 'Go make offering in temple.'

I could smell something fishy, but what was it exactly? If I left my battered shoes outside and went into the temple four steps away, what might happen? Not much, I reckoned, so I did. Once inside I waved off the priest who offered me a blessing, no doubt with the perk of a rip-off. I dumped the garland at the foot of an idol and swept back out into the sunshine where my turbaned sparring partner stood with the garland wallah, who'd probably refunded him half the price of the garland, to align it with the market rate.

'You like temple, Madam?'

I was tempted to say I did not. I did not like temple. I did not like priest approaching me for an inevitable fee or being manipulated into going there. But I nodded and began to walk on.

'But, Madam,' the bearded one called after me.

'What now?'

'Can I talk to you? Just talk?'

I gave him ten out of ten for persistence and allowed my curiosity turn me around.

'About what?'

'You see, Madam, I am most excellent palm reader. I want to read your palm. As a gift.'

'Why?'

'Because I want to show you that even if ninety-nine people in Varanasi are cheaters, there is one person who is true. I am the true person.'

Pull the other one, I almost blurted.

'Come sit on the steps and I will read your palm.'

'As a gift, right?'

'A gift,' he nodded, his money-chomping rabbit well secured under that grimy turban, I was sure.

We sat there in the rowdy traffic of bathers and beggars, gawkers and hawkers, while he read my palm. Vaguely enlightening, moderately interesting, his reading rolled round to my three children. Two were to have bright futures ahead of them – spectacular futures – my son in an office and my daughter in a good marriage where their aspirations and mine clearly belonged. But for the third child there was a wavering, a skirting of the subject interspersed with a little patter on life's obstacles – particularly if they included twenty-three souls to support, which amazingly enough, my palm reader's did.

'I get it,' I said, getting it loud and clear and already tacking mentally back to the hotel and Arnie recovering from his respiratory ailments, 'but can you please finish the reading? I need to go now.'

He sniffed the air solemnly. He gazed sombrely into my eyes. 'Your third child,' he intoned, 'will have some great difficulty in life.'

'And?' I had to stop myself from tapping my foot.

'And it will make big problems for him and your whole family.'

'So what do you propose then?'

'I can help you.'

Here it comes, I sighed to myself. 'With what, a mantra?'

'No, Madam. With a very special talisman, which I can get for you. It will be one-thousand rupees, but for you I will give special price because you are beautiful.'

Aha. A talisman. For a special price. Lucky he didn't think me ugly.

'Yes, Madam. It is very powerful. Your child must use it, otherwise very hardship things will happen. Very bad things.'

So I'd managed to get myself a free palm reading with a bonus curse thrown in. Fancy that.

'I tell you what,' I said, opening my handbag. 'I've decided on a little gift for you. Not for your palm reading, but for your time. You've given me a lot of your time.' I handed him a moderate rupee note and rose to leave.

'But, Madam, what about the talisman?'

'No,' I said simply.

'Then there will be many problem for your child.'

'I'll deal with that.'

He blinked rapidly, his mental cogs clanking violently. 'What about another gift for me?' he pleaded, frowning as though at an insult. It was a reflex in these parts.

'What other gift? What precisely do you have in mind?'

He pointed to my gold wedding band.

'Uh, 'fraid not,' I said, 'not this week anyway.' Then I scratched in my handbag for one of the plastic pens I carry for enthusiastic children. 'But I tell you what, you can have that.'

The pen seemed to puncture him and he deflated, drooping and disgusted as I strode away with a 'bye!' and a spring in my step. Until a cool, young local in sunglasses marched up and kept pace with me.

'Where you from, Madam?' he grinned.

I glared at him, hard eyed and rancorous. 'A parallel universe. Would you believe it?'

Then I broke into a trot.

AND YET, WHEN you least expect it, some bit of beauty appears in Varanasi, some sweetness.

I least expected it at the Ganga *aarthi* puja, a great whacking punch of a religious ceremony or extravaganza – depending on your perspective – on Dasaswamedh Ghat. It happens every evening, drawing thousands of ordinary people and the priests and politicians who sit on white chairs in the front row where they belong together. Everyone else finds a place on the steps of the ghat, on little stone platforms there or on one of the hundreds of wooden boats clustered near the bank for the spectacle.

Building up around each sunset, it's a dramatic Hindu ceremony beginning with a long row of about ten low, wooden platforms placed towards the water's edge. Each holds its aarthi plate, an impressive bronze ceremonial tray along with the requisite utensils for the performance. Tall, decorative archways frame the platforms and above each hangs a

Way out in India

cluster of fairy lights in the shape of an umbrella.

About ten young pandits robed in red and gold step up and, synchronising with each other, begin various rites with the sacred objects. They blow conch shells, and they wave huge incense sticks to weave matching smoky patterns in the air, which tranquillise the audience with their fragrance. They cup downturned palms over the flames of their bulky brass lamps, then turn them up to touch their foreheads. Wheeling these lamps through the night air above their heads, they chant sacred songs while cymbals clash, the whole heady combination designed to transport one towards religious rapture.

Still reeling from the scene at the cremation ghat, we encountered the crowds gathering for the Ganga aarthi puja, our curiosity and the cooling outdoor air bidding us to stay. Amid the buzz of expectation we found a little spot atop a sacred stone platform, perching with about ten others along its edge while our shoes nestled just below. While sitting there absorbing the scene, a bespectacled young man approached us with an eager manner and an interesting arrangement of teeth.

'Where are you from, Sir?' he asked Arnie.

I wilted. I just couldn't cope with another of these, so Arnie replied, his words as perfunctory as his posture was defensive. I listened in to all the usual questions, wondering which would herald the commercial punchline. But the more I listened, the more I realised how earnest they were, how probing and incisive and how this now evidently young man was still a schoolboy and a spectacularly successful one at that.

He was a font of information on the politics of his country, on his City of Temples and on the recent visit of the CM to inspect it and to drum up support for his party.

'What's a CM?' I asked in a haze of exhaustion and overload, suddenly irritated with the Indian penchant for abbreviations.

'Chief Minister, Ma'am. He was here very recently.'

A little girl of about ten came wandering up to him and stood with her back against him, barely able to look at us.

'This is my little sister,' he said. 'She's very shy but very naughty, too, and she still needs to learn English.'

The little girl tugged on his windbreaker and murmured something in his ear as he stooped to listen.

'Ah,' he said, straightening up, 'my parents invite you share our bench over there for a better view of the puja.'

So there we sat warmly ensconced with the family who spoke no English, just below the performing pandits, or more correctly pandit directly in our line of vision. A campy and delicate one he was, pouting and twirling his incense holder with a flaccid wrist above our heads, struggling under the weight of his splendid lamp with its flickering flames.

Hungry for connection with the world beyond Varanasi, our new friend Dipesh chatted to me through the entire performance, earnestly, searchingly until his final question at the end of the evening.

'Are you on FB, Ma'am?'

'FB?'

'Facebook.' With a grin that revealed his teeth crowding each other as tightly as the audience pushing to exit the ghat, he nodded, clearly thrilled at the idea.

'I'll send you a friend request!'

'Sure.' I smiled a warm and tired smile as the family departed in party mode and the boatmen rowed away to their mooring points.

THERE'S A beauty to these men, too, sturdy, rough hewn and in tune with the river's rhythms.

'Boat going?' they ask as you pass them by on the ghats. 'Boat going?' is the simple question sans the bull. Yes or no? A to B. A price is fixed and it's oars to water to earn their keep by the sweat of a brow as it has been for centuries on this river.

But what happens to those who fall through all the fragile, cracked systems here, to those who haven't the shoulders or the shrewdness to make it?

'They probably end up eating garbage like every other hungry creature in town,' Arnie ventured.

Yet at least some of them don't. Or don't need to. They eat at what we would call a soup kitchen, two long rows of people sitting cross-legged on a cold ghat landing, each with his shoes on a step behind him and a dented metal plate in front. At the head of the rows on a raised tiled platform two ancient gents manage huge pots of rice, of curry and dhal, while a third, barefoot in a dhoti, walks down the rows ladling food out to be eaten with the fingers. Whoever runs this operation we never did find out, but the aroma of those humble meals just beyond the stench of the burning ghat sent a glimmer of warmth from us towards the city.

AND THEN THERE were the guest house "boys" – the kitchen boy, the cleaning boy, the maintenance boy and one dear quiet, young man, Mr Fixit, willing to fix anything from drinks to electrical sockets that resisted the intrusion of foreign plugs. There was a trick to it that he showed me, involving a hidden spring in the socket and a screwdriver to coax it into place.

'But don't tell, Sir,' he murmured. 'He no like this.'

I got the distinct feeling that Sir was the headmaster there and all these boys merely that to him, scurrying about serving until all hours of the night, terrified to be called to his desk and just grateful to have their jobs.

One of them, the kitchen boy, was watering a plant beside a pillar behind Sir's desk while we sat in front of it, being harassed to buy the finest something-or-other that Varanasi could provide. I caught the glint of the water, then the kitchen boy's eye. Instantly he raised a finger to his lips, his brows jumping in apprehension. Was this how it worked here?

It was. You could tell by the sweet relief of gratitude on these young faces if you but gave them a greeting and a smile. Mr Fixit, particularly, rewarded us for that, by opening the curtain on his life for a few moments on the rooftop terrace after doing battle with our intransigent bathroom smells. Here, three storeys up, Sir – on his septuagenarian legs – couldn't easily reach him. Here, he pointed out the monkeys leaping about the walls and neighbouring rooftops, the eternal card game on the steps of the ghat and a little spat between a dog and a goat down below.

Then, in answer to my questions about his family, he pointed out his wretched pair of rooms across a ground-floor courtyard, where his wife lay ill and where his son was retrieving his kite from a hiding place behind a stepped stand of pot plants.

'That is my boy,' he beamed, as his son ran off towards the other

Of Rot and Religion

boys on the ghat, their kites whizzing and rustling until sunset. 'I have another one also, so I must get up very early to make the chapattis for them to eat before I come to work.' His smile was wan, depleted.

One day he came to me gingerly as I sat on that rooftop amid the red pots that he'd painted and their identical plants in a row. He wanted to ask me a favour. My chest contracted. I shouldn't have been so friendly. He was holding out a piece of paper and a pen. That could only mean one thing. The question was just how much.

But it didn't. Mr Fixit, his eyes glowing in his thin face, was taking a small initiative to improve the guest house. He wanted to make a sign – correctly spelt – for the toilet door on the rooftop. The favour was this: would I please write the word TOILET for him in capital letters?

From his blissful face you'd have thought I'd written him a winning lottery ticket.

On our departure he returned the favour with an invitation from the heart.

'Madam, Sir. Next time you visit India I want you please to come to stay at my village, my home.'

Probably because this deathly dazzling place is so ugly, the blossoms of grace that do appear flourish into a sense of redemption that – even if fleetingly – make all seem well with the world.

Take those goats wearing T-shirts. At first hilariously zany, in retrospect they came to represent hope for the city. Shuffling past us in an alleyway, stinking and bleating and beating the cold in those cast-offs, they paraded the compassion of some kindly soul who'd thought to clothe them against it.

Now don't get me wrong. I never did convert to starry-eyed hippiedom, falling in love with Varanasi and its colourful crust of illusion. The place had so rattled me that my mental faculties melted to mud there, resulting in a missed flight out of the place. Only realising this on our trip to the airport, I wailed our fate to the taxi driver.

Once again, then, Varanasi produced a gem – a decent old chap willing to help us however he could – speeding us off to an ATM to pay for new air tickets in cash, since the airline's credit-card machine – inevitably – was not working and the next flight would be leaving shortly.

Way out in India

'May I ask you a question, Madam?' He peered at me in his rear-view mirror, drawing towards the airport's drop-off zone at the end of this adventure.

'Sure.'

'With respect, Madam, why didn't you check your time of departure yesterday?'

How could I explain that yesterday my equilibrium was a see-saw rocking between the men with red teeth and goats wearing T-shirts? So I shrugged.

'It was a bit stupid, I know.'

He smiled at me like a father forgiving a childish mistake. And his teeth were white.

6
Of Tigers and Tall Tales

COMBINE AN AFRICAN MAN'S wildlife passion with the rare Bengal tiger and, BINGO, you have a quest! Throw in his beloveds – camera and wife – and the dust begins to churn.

Camera was definitely the favourite here, since she didn't equivocate about the matter. With no apprehension she'd focus at any moment, adjust and shoot, even though she was the new girl and I the safari veteran – but on my own African turf, thanks very much.

The setting would be Ranthambore National Park, a few hours south-east of Jaipur by road. Famous in India for its tigers, its appeal is also its romance. Once a vast hunting ground of maharajas in their heyday, it's also home to a tenth-century fort that hovers above the park like a legendary castle. Here and there ruins from bygone times appear amid the foliage, which includes the eerie banyan tree en masse, its roots snaking their way down to earth. Reaching out in some cases to strangle a decomposing building, in others changing direction to link limbs with its brethren's across the road, these trees twine into structures fit to make designers of movie sets tingle.

But at Ranthambore the tigers, alone, hold currency, their golden stripes piled like coins that visitors boast about seeing. Lesser residents of the bush also qualify as entertainment, but how can the ubiquitous sambar, even so splendidly horned, compare with that drama on pads? How can the uglies, the wild boars and crocs, even with the latter's talent for snapping and snoozing undetected? Of course there's amusement in a monkey troop's picnic in the ruins or amazement in an owl's arboreal camouflage, but it's always the tiger that burns bright in the forest of Ranthambore, which was transformed into a reserve originally to protect the feline and encourage its breeding.

Way out in India

Fully prepared to rough it near Ranthambore, I rocked back in my hiking boots as a rose garden flourished into view at Tiger Den's entrance.

'A what?'

'Yes, just in front of that lawn over there,' Arnie pointed, 'with those little clipped hedges all around. There, where those people are playing cricket – oh, and badminton – in front of the bungalows.'

'Oh, I do beg your pardon, my dear.' That was me. 'See anyone having a spot of tea on the veranda?'

It really was that kind of place, but with nary a "Britisher" in sight. Rather the upwardly mobile of India were frolicking in the countryside en famille, interspersed with a busload of unhappy Germans in their latter years. Emerging from lunch bitter-faced with spicy fragrances for company, they clutched at lower backs bemoaning the dearth of "tikers" for their troubles this far from home on bumpy roads.

They couldn't complain about the service at the resort, though, where the room boy had sprinted – sandals a-flap – to address a supposed Indian emergency on our arrival: the lack of succession plan for our room's lone toilet roll noticed by me. With great care and delicacy later his manager enquired at the reception desk: 'I trust Madam is feeling better now?'

Tiger Den Resort, an island of order, stilled some of the butterflies flapping inside me towards the unknown, as did a poster outside the dining room which enumerated bush etiquette in reassuringly familiar terms.

Bottom line? It said blend into the bush. Don't impose your sounds, your colours or your litter on nature. And keep safe via a low profile. It wasn't rocket science and it concurred with our custom of crawling around game reserves at home in South Africa, eyes peeled and watering with dust and concentration. At a sighting everyone froze, whispering in awe, then rolled away to allow other visitors a view. That was the way of the bush as we understood it.

Not so at Ranthambore where a beast on wheels called a "canter" roared up, complete with Naturalist ('I am Jameel. I will be your Naturalist today.') and twenty mouldering seats. Mysteriously stretched along with our patience, twenty-five of the most diverse bods I've ever snuggled up to set off finally on our "safari excursion". Our cocky, little Naturalist stood on the seat beside the driver, undoubtedly to tackle concerns striped and feline, but in his hands matters turned instantly administrative.

'Fill up the form.'

The form? With what? On what surface? And how would my family history in triplicate qualify me for a tiger hunt?

You fill up the form, I wanted to blurt. *You* find enough elbow room between a bony young German and a portly Sikh for the procedure. And *you* try to bump along the potholes without *your* pen poking holes in this paper-serviette form. It was Indian bureaucracy at its best.

As we took off through the bush past various flora and fauna, it occurred to me that maybe the form was the document they used to identify the bodies after these jaunts. This one began with a bruised coccyx, but at the rate we were going, where would it end?

I thanked every deity I could for the respite when an alleged tiger appeared in the distant dust. As happens everywhere else in India, hordes descended from nowhere, all rumbling into view in vehicles like ours until there were four-hundred eyes searching the shadows for one celebrity beast – probably wearing sunglasses against the glitter of sequins on sunlit saris.

The viewing spot was Stereotype City, with the women in bright burkas following the pointing fingers of their men, bearded and fezzed, all jostling with the Chinese in their surgical masks. My Sikh gent with his safari hat perched atop his turban stood up, obscuring the view of everyone else except my tall young German in khaki who announced that he'd spotted 'ze tiker – o, ja!'

'Where?' I enquired.

He pointed to a spot in the distance. 'Exactly sree-quarters of a metre from ze big tree on ze left.'

That was Arnie's signal to unleash a flood of adrenalin for his push through the UN towards the Naturalist for guidance on matters stripey. The photographic result of his efforts was a tiger in the abstract, blending so astoundingly with the surrounding foliage, as to be entirely invisible. I'm still wondering why.

The German and his matching girlfriend, however, not delighted

Way out in India

with the afternoon's haul on our low flight homewards, waxed suddenly animated at the sight of – wait for it – a *wild boar!*

'Eine kleine *schwein!*' they both exclaimed, hoisting their cameras as we bumped back home in the dusk.

I couldn't see what the fuss was. Maybe they'd just had one vegetarian curry too many.

Our intrepid Arnie, though, not satisfied with that, suited up for the next day's excursion in the morning freeze, accompanied by his darling camera, his reluctant wife, her beanie, gloves, scarf, bruises and recently amplified dread. Very soon the bush presented its offerings of antlered deer and peacocks, abundant dust and vigorous flingings of inmates around the battered vehicle. A crocodile vegetating beside a riverine plastic bag in camouflage seemed to perk up the Naturalist having a bad day at the office – but there was nary a damned tiger in sight.

Our sight that was. The previous day's Germans had taken a different route that morning and bounded away from the lunch table towards us.

'Ve saw ze tiker! Ve saw ze tiker!' Flashing their photos of the creature at Arnie, they may have missed his startled greenness. But clearly only some of the party had been so lucky – those not snapping images of ze tikers on ze dining room valls.

Having retired from spinal injury provocation, I sent Arnie off to represent me on the third jaunt and stretched out on the lawn in the sun, a little like a tiger myself, with a fabulous Indian autobiography, which you might enjoy – *A Princess Remembers* by Maharani Gayatri Devi. There was no dust, no bouncing, only a few Sikhs on cane chairs enjoying cool drinks and a giggle plus a few older Germans complaining to the manager about 'das kalte douche' in their room.

The peace was broken by the roar of an engine and the accompanying flags of dust that could only herald heroism. My husband appeared, leaping from the vehicle, cradling his camera. Flushed, ecstatic, he'd encountered and captured his quarry repeatedly, artfully and at close range – its golden stripes filling his quest pockets to popping point.

7
Of Palaces and Protests

IT WAS A DENSE-aired trip on the road to Agra. Outside the car the fog rolled over the mustard fields in yellow bloom. Inside the farts rolled from the front seat to the back where we exhaled desperately and opened windows with discretion.

Although there's not much shame in India about such matters. The view in this country is that if the body needs to shed something, then shed it must – solid, liquid or gaseous. Hence the hawking and spitting in the streets so commonly associated with India; hence the unbridled burping even in upmarket restaurants.

Rahul seemed to feel no disgrace about the gusts. He shed away, airing his views on the vile city of Agra between percussive bouts from his behind. While we checked Agra on Google, confirming that it did indeed fail on almost every measure of a city's civilisation, he approached the drive with gusto, propelling us with as much gasoline and methane as possible in an effort to get us to a site called Fatehpur Sikri before our next guide gave up on us and left.

Our shredded arrival after that kind of drive was a red-flagged reminder never to travel this way again. Such monuments are momentous and deserve a savouring and a wandering rather than the kind of marathon whizz already in progress.

The guide, having been at the site for four hours already, was in a froth. A flappy-wristed man, fretful, lisping and beautifully dressed in a sports jacket and dress shirt, he whisked us through this World Heritage Site that was built by the Mughal Emperor, Akbar the Great, as his capital about half a millennium ago, before his second and third capitals at Agra and Delhi.

Well preserved and superbly designed, this complex of palaces,

Way out in India

mosques and public buildings became a prototype for Indian town planning for centuries to come.

Racing after the guide through its sandstone marvels, my eyes became more mesmerised by the multicoloured gems on his bracelet with every flourish of his arm in the direction of a frieze or column.

'They're fake,' he responded to my compliment on his jewellery. 'Tour guideth can't afford real oneth. Can't even afford to marry. That ith why I am thtill thingle.'

Hmmm. The comment hit my solar plexus as he flapped, 'Let'th hurry along,' which I did wondering about this talented man who'd probably live as a bachelor for the rest of his life in denial, in his traditional family home, in this conservative country where there are few safe or open places for him.

On we chased through ancient edifices whose door frames included a raised stone ridge for keeping water out or tourists tripping centuries hence, so that by the time the astounding porticoed audience hall rolled around with the afternoon fog, my head, steaming with saturation, was ready to burst. My internal pen was meanwhile noting in bold upper case that NEVER would be too soon for the sight of another royal building.

'IT'S A PALACE!' Arnie confirmed as I collapsed backwards on the bed of our Agra hotel, my cap still squeezing my head.

I groaned, having forgotten that we'd booked an overwhelming faux palace all those months ago, and rubbed my temples to remember why.

'Because of the Taj,' he intoned soberly, gazing at the hotel's reception buildings in the distance beyond the gardens as we clinked our welcome glasses.

The idea, any guidebook will tell you, is to get to the Taj Mahal at dawn and watch its marble change from pink to white in the sunrise. There's only one way to do this in the Agra traffic: stay close by. A good theory but be warned, my friend: between October and March there is *no* sunrise. On almost every winter day the fog clears in the late morning, if at all, and the temperature can drop to two degrees Celsius. These conditions are still preferable to summer, though, when the heat cranks itself up to forty-five degrees. The third choice is the steamy-and-wet one from June to October.

So we'd spent a lot of money to sleep downhearted in an upmarket bed and have people bow and scrape and hang around for sizeable tips amid the spritzing fountains. But an error in the law of averages found our guide the next morning hopping from foot to foot and twisting the gems of his bracelet breathlessly.

'The thun is shining!' he beamed. 'Let'th go!'

Whatever you've heard about the Taj is true. She – there's no disputing that – reveals herself gradually from her grand gateway like a woman so beloved that she glows far beyond her space and time. Pale and perfect she hovers, like a spectre in the splendour of her gardens, her sovereignty enticing the visitor closer. Astonished by the gems inlaid in her marble skin, he is drawn ever nearer to the screen of lace in carved stone veiling her inner sanctum, her symbolic tombs. But deeper still her mystery goes where very few ever will. Her essential treasure twisted with tragedy lies in the remains of the royal couple whose story she tells, in a crypt far below the floor's cool surface.

On shuffling around the Taj's tombs with the goggle-eyed throng, one can only guess at the level of grief the Emperor Shah Jahan suffered on the death of his wife over three centuries ago – a grief so deep that it bound him in seclusion for a year from which he emerged stooped, ashen and determined to build the most magnificent memorial to her that the world would ever see.

Mumtaz Mahal was no ordinary wife among Shah Jahan's three. Lover, advisor and confidante to the potent Mughal emperor, she accompanied him wherever he went, even on military campaigns – and even while pregnant. She'd so proven her loyalty to him that he'd entrusted her with the seal of state.

Not all was bliss for the royal couple, though. Of the thirteen children she bore him, only six survived, but the greatest loss for the emperor was still to come when, after four years of their reign, Mumtaz Mahal died giving birth to their fourteenth child.

The emperor's sorrows were far from over, though. His sons began to battle for supremacy and, although he'd chosen Dara Shukoh as his successor, another proved more powerful in battle. He was Aurangzeb, who killed his remaining brothers, deposed his ailing father and

Way out in India

imprisoned him in the mighty Agra Fort that Shah Jahan had built. One concession granted him in imprisonment was the view from the fort of the Taj Mahal, at which he gazed, it's been said, in desperate sorrow for the rest of his days.

Now just to get things straight, you have to work hard for all that poetry. And pay up – roughly the equivalent of thirteen American dollars. Unless you're an Indian citizen. Then you pay up the equivalent of about thirty American cents.

Then there's the business of shoving your way on to an electric car from outside the complex to near its gate, since ordinary vehicles are banned within a polluting radius of the monument. Once you've alighted from the car, you run the gauntlet of the souvenir hawkers who get my Most Persistent Worldwide award, bestowed on the basis of the need to sprint from their grasp. When you reach the gate you join a gender-specific queue to be frisked. You merge then finally into the company of "high-value ticket holders" – no kidding – which affords you a short cut or two around the complex, while the twenty-rupee troopers have a longer trek in parts.

You'll also be offered surgical slippers to be worn over your shoes if you keep them on, my recommended option for a long stroll on either icy or smelly marble, depending on the season. Once inside, do ignore the odd prod or bump from the public. It's really not worth wasting precious marvelling time on this minor contact sport at the Taj.

A FAR MORE serious kind of strife was afoot up north in Delhi at the time of our visit. It had been our point of entry to India on that trip and, at first glance, had fitted the general idea of a national capital, displaying more or less the level of order, cleanliness, wealth and dignity one would expect of such a place. Of course, some poverty was visible, along with generous swathes of modesty in the tiny stalls that served as citizens' livelihoods. But it soon became apparent that all hell had broken loose.

A young woman had been gang-raped in the city on a private bus less than a week before. She was fighting for her life in hospital and the populace was out in force to vent its rage against its national and city governments. Both had failed to protect this woman and all women, the citizens were baying – pumping thousands of fists to demand redress for this state of affairs.

Roads were closed and traffic officers were blowing frenzied whistles and waving their arms. Motorists glowered, hooting and pushing against the jam. In our "fine air-conditioned car" as promised and supplied by our tour company, its representative squirmed, at pains to point out the uniqueness of the case that threatened to blacken the rainbow of joys blurted in the marketing media of Incredible India.

With the required grace of a guest in a foreign land I challenged him as gently as possible, since the matter begged to be challenged.

'Surely this is relatively common in such a patriarchal society as India's? Many cases may even go unreported because of a woman's fear.'

But as the colour of his shirt collar deepened with the seepage from under his haircut, I felt it best to drop the matter – unlike the citizens of Delhi who used their vote to oust the sitting Congress Party from power in local elections the following year.

Throughout the journey Rahul the driver kept peering at us in the rear-view mirror with his sparkly eyes, sizing us up and steering us towards Connaught Place and our hotel. There we Filled up Forms plentiful enough to cramp the fingers. Then, having warned us against roaming too far through the city's streets outside the hotel, the representative prepared to leave.

'But this is Connaught Place!' I protested, having read about this famous commercial and financial centre of Delhi life. 'All the way from the airport you've been telling us that Delhi is safe!'

'Okay,' he conceded, his haircut leaking again. 'But stay inside the inner circle of Connaught. Don't go wandering outside.'

So much for Delhi's squeaky clean image. As it happened there was nothing for us to fear at Connaught Place, into which we lurched after a hot shower and a superb lunch at the hotel restaurant.

Named after the Duke of Connaught, this financial and commercial hub is the epicentre of New Delhi, so called for being purpose-built by the British in 1911 when they relocated their capital from Kolkata (then Calcutta). There'd been several old Delhis north of the British site for centuries, but the colonials had wanted a planned showcase of a capital in India, and Connaught Place with its grand Georgian architecture provided the site.

CP, as it's known locally despite official and more Indian name changes to its sections, is a collection of colonnaded two-storey buildings designed in two concentric circles, segmented by radiating roads, some of which are broad enough to be boulevards and one of which – the Imperial Mall – leads to the magnificent India Gate where the crowds were presently bellowing their fury. At the centre of the buildings lies a vast green park, adjacent to which an underground bazaar buzzes and hums with life.

Into the fray of shops, travel agencies, banks, touts and cafes we ploughed, with that blend of exhaustion and exhilaration peculiar to the first day of a trip abroad. In this instance – we could not pretend otherwise – it was tinged with an emotional queasiness. Being a Saturday and sunny in the midst of a fog-laden winter, everyone who was not protesting was out eating ice cream, which seemed a tad bizarre, given the cloud darkening Delhi at the time.

Our queasiness came from the ice creams, we decided; each one a little mirror held up to us, the way travel holds up mirrors in unexpected guises. In these leisurely cones licked while a girl was dying of brutality, we had to admit that we saw ourselves. How many times had our own country burned while we'd fiddled the dials that regulate our comfort?

In the comfort level surrounding us at Connaught Place was the upwardly mobile and rapidly Westernising India we'd heard about: the families with bulging shopping bags, the designer goods for sale, the flabby children, the torrent of private cars on roads designed for a trickle and the young couples in the park holding hands and cuddling, so unlike those I'd seen in a Pune park a few years before. There a policeman on a bicycle had patrolled the avenue between the benches where they'd sat in platonic wariness of the pendulum wheeling back and forth until closing time.

We'd chosen Delhi as the first stop on our classic Golden Triangle trip, so named for both its historical treasures and its geometry. This route, commonly the first or only taken by travellers to India, incorporates three cities located in an approximate geographical triangle at roughly two-hundred-kilometre intervals.

However famous it may be, the Golden Triangle tour is not everyone's cuppa chai. One reason is that not everyone enjoys gorging on banquets of extreme architecture built by the shapers of Indian history. Not everyone enjoys the sensory overload involved, the factual saturation and the hollow exhaustion that ensue, all amid the buzz and shove of big cities.

Another reason is logistical. Whatever the means of transport used, crowds, delays and scary moments inevitably attend the journey.

The final reason is time. The historical and architectural jewels explored on this trip are stupendous and deserve time to be savoured and digested, whereas the majority of visitors rush or are rushed through them in a mere few days – the Russians deserving their appellation according to our driver Rahul, with the Japanese in frantic pursuit close behind them.

Should you opt for this adventure, consider your plan of action carefully and, for lower stress, see less. Then plan to pack lightly, do your research and prepare to be astonished. Our delvings into the reality of the route shot us upmarket in fright, into the arms of a reputable Indian tour company offering a private car and protective shepherding for the trip's duration. Aware though we were that the undoubted convenience of travelling this way is negated somewhat by the sense of being bubble-wrapped and anaesthetised, time constraints tipped the balance towards the wussy copout option.

But even that presented a dread: the roads. Even in the hands of one so spectacular as our driver-to-be Rahul, Indian roads can be terrifying, producing adrenalin by the bucket and leaving one thoroughly sapped by day's end.

A semblance of reassurance began to arrive in our inbox with a flurry of flowery emails from the tour company.

"For your entire journey we are providing you a fine air-conditioned car. The car will substantially add to your travelling comfort where the top-quality suspension will not let you feel any discomfort.

"Besides the car, your driver would be special. He would be your Man Friday, your most invaluable friend, a very nice human being with a pleasing personality for whom nothing would be trouble."

Nodding our accord to each other, we clicked "book".

Way out in India

FOR THE FIRST-TIME visitor to India any entry point is a shock, but if you don't mind the risk of fog delays in winter and you have someone waiting to receive you, Delhi's probably a more decorous choice than say, Mumbai – the way Washington is to New York. The tour company had sent our squirming representative for us, along with our Man Friday for the trip's duration, the irrepressible Rahul in his smart navy suit.

THE SAME WAY the British had built their splendid New Delhi, Emperor Shah Jahan had built Old Delhi – only about three-hundred years before in the early seventeenth century. He began with ambitious building projects that would epitomise the new city – Shahanabad. Unfortunately, though, his capital never did move from Agra and neither did he, after his dethronement by his son and imprisonment at Agra Fort for the rest of his days.

We, however, had the good fortune to experience the last of his building projects completed prior to his imprisonment in the mid-seventeenth century. Our guide, slight, timid and bespectacled, shivered in his thin sweater outside the Jama Mosque, a remarkable structure of red sandstone and white marble. Built to accommodate twenty-five-thousand worshippers, it remains the largest mosque in India after all these years.

Conjure a misty vision in pink, of Persian arches and domes, fountains, minarets and spires with a courtyard built to envelop a city's populace at once. Conjure, too, a couple of tourists shivering their butts off outside, their guide's voice trembling in the morning chill, instructing them to 'remove the shoes'.

Seriously? A history lesson at seven degrees Celsius on bare sandstone in thin socks was not a prospect to relish, but there was a possibility of extra insulation for those inclined to share serially and publically borrowed clothes. Supplied by the mosque to those in a "semi-clad state", the notice at the front gate also explained that "for this purpose the gatekeeper will provide you the gowns".

For an extra fee, it also offered splendid views from "atop the tower", informing "interested persons" that they could "procure the ticket".

The only thing I wanted to procure was a pair of sheepskin slippers and something to cover my numbing skull, besides the dubious headscarves proffered for the purpose. At last I threw vanity to the winds and my emergency sweater over my head with its sleeves under my chin and around my throat – scarf fashion – to the quizzical stares of locals and tourists alike. Looking none too chic themselves in the mosque's gaudy dressing gowns, they joined me in ridiculous violations of style protocol as we all shuffled shivering around the sacred complex, praying for a ray or two of sunshine.

The guide, lacking any such outlandish protection, chattered out his commentary to me in a state of deepening blueness. Arnie meanwhile, having paid the hefty camera fee and oblivious to the cold, the history and everything else extraneous to that astounding Mughal combination of red sandstone and white marble swathed in mist, snapped away blissfully, catching a flock of pigeons in flight from the courtyard where the sweeper had fed them half a sack of crumbs.

In one of those typical Indian contrasts, a staircase from the mosque leads directly into a market. But this is no ordinary market. This is Chandni Chowk or Moonlight Square, a rambling bazaar district in the Moslem Quarter of Old Delhi, dating from the time of Shah Jahan and probably very beautiful then. Legend has it that the Emperor's daughter was responsible for designing this area, where a reflecting pool graced the central square and where canals ran along the tree-bordered streets, lending mirrored luminescence to the name Moonlight Square.

Today, though, the place is a warren of narrow alleys canopied with webbed electrical wires, where trade is brisk and colourful, and where cows and rickshaws, motorbikes and vendors vie for space and custom.

Tempered by the cold of Sunday, it presented a mellower face to us along with a lugubrious rickshaw wallah who was hired by our guide to cycle us in traditional fashion around the neighbourhood. Hopping on to his tricycle's passenger seat behind him, I noticed the fatigue in his face, the resignation to his relatively fortunate fate of cycling human beings around his misty, polluted city.

I noticed how carefully he handled the vehicle, his entire livelihood bound up in those three wheels joined with steel piping and finished with flimsy upholstery. I noticed the flicker of apprehension in his eyes when we stopped at a little roadside shrine, where the priest sat reading the newspaper with his incense smoke and idols in their glass cabinets for company, until the lid of the donation box rattled as we pushed in a few rupees. Recompense for both men assured, the wallah's face relaxed, the priest folded his newspaper and we left with yellow powder dots on our foreheads and his blessings for us and for 'Nirbhaya', the girl at the centre of Delhi's drama.

The garland wallah, standing ready at the roadside to share the tourist spoils with the rickshaw wallah, waited for him to sing the praises of the soft, pink flowers rather than the cheapo marigolds. Satisfied with the price for these beauties, both men nodded and the deal was done, its bonus being an offer to Arnie of the saddle for a doddle around the potholes.

'It's hard work!' my fit and healthy husband announced, disembarking after a mere few blocks with his wife his only load.

'Could I have a try?' I beamed at the rickshaw man.

He frowned but agreed anyway.

'But wife no make accident,' he frowned at Arnie, stealing a glance at the white woman of a certain age with a sweater over her head and a garland round her neck, to whom he was entrusting the tool of his trade.

'No accident!' I chirped and was off. But riding a rickshaw is not for flimsy limbed women. Strength, skill, sharp reflexes, iron lungs and focus are the profession's minimum requirements. The rickshaw wallah ran alongside the tricycle for a block or two before his nerve gave out and he signalled me to return it to him – forthwith.

IT WAS TIME to leave Old Delhi, our guide murmured, hugging himself in the rickshaw parking lot.

'Without seeing the Red Fort?' Gazing towards its mammoth walls and wondering what treasures lay behind them, I felt a tad cheated. The Red Fort was the epicentre of the Shahanabad that Shah Jahan had built and we were but to glimpse it from the outside.

'Restoration project,' the guide shivered. 'It was in a terrible state and the project is a long one. It will take years, so hopefully you'll see it on your next visit...'

Of Palaces and Protests

ON THE DELHI banks of the same Yamuna River that slithers past the Taj Mahal to the south-east in Agra, lies another place of death and beauty, though this one couldn't be starker. In a peaceful green park here at Raj Ghat is the site of Mahatma Gandhi's cremation. Marking it, a black marble plinth engraved only with the two words "Hai Ram" expresses both the strength and austerity of the Great Soul. On being shot in 1948, he is said to have uttered these words, which mean "Oh, God" before he fell.

In soft contrast to the marble, five white garlands grace the plinth along with an eternal flame and a clutch of joss sticks burning at its foot. It is a tranquil place and a fitting memorial to a man so devoted to harmony. It was also the perfect setting in which to offer a prayer for 'Nirbhaya', the anonymous rape victim called 'Fearless' by the people. Also within the park are the memorials of other Indian leaders, such as Prime Minister Nehru, his daughter, Indira Gandhi, and her sons, Rajiv and Sanjay Gandhi.

AS AN AESTHETIC warm-up for the Taj Mahal in Agra and a sensation way up on the Wow Scale, a magnificent monument stands on the Ring Road south of Raj Ghat.

This is Humayun's Tomb, though "tomb" is a word way too tame for a complex like this one. Its beauty, extravagance and sheer dimensions attest to the power of the Mughal Empire, whose wealth and political reach are difficult to comprehend as a modern Westerner armed with a camera, gazing at its regal buildings from inside its royal gardens and watching a middle-aged guard puff across the lawn blowing his whistle to interrupt a pair of lovers cuddling against an ancient pink wall.

To explore the Golden Triangle, it is necessary to understand at least a little about the Mughals, from whom our word for an influential or important person – mogul – derives. Descended from two lines of ferocious warrior-leaders, they galloped down from Central Asia, bringing the name Mughal from Mongolia in its Persian translation.

Their first emperor, Babur, fleeing succession battles at home, slashed his way south-west to conquer northern India in 1526 and begin a three-century dynasty. Defeating all the locals in his path, except the

Way out in India

equally bellicose Rajputs, Babur and his men looted and pillaged like all good warriors, then knelt on their prayer mats at sunset facing Mecca to practise a light form of Islam that precluded neither the raising of a cup nor the passing of a hashish pipe.

Succeeding Babur was his son, Humayun, who, despite his astonishing tomb, was more mildly blessed than his father. He ascended the throne at just twenty-three. Fourteen years into his dynasty, he lost the whole empire to the Pashtuns from Afghanistan. But steely and resourceful under that moderate exterior, he won it back again – even if it took him fifteen years and even if he had to marry a Persian and enlist the help of her people in his quest.

His ultimate triumph was his expansion of the empire to span almost a million square kilometres by the time he met his sudden end – at the foot of his library stairs, down which he is said to have tumbled by tripping on his robe. With his alliance strengthened by his marriage to his Persian wife, Haji Begum, who'd eventually build his tomb, Humayun was instrumental in colouring the culture and architecture of his time with the delicate Persian features so expressive of the Mughal dynasty. He and his wife also bore a son, Akbar, who became one of its greatest stars.

After losing his father so unexpectedly, this thirteen-year-old boy-emperor had a torrid future ahead of him. There were Pashtuns to vanquish again and an empire to expand by subduing the Hindu areas before tackling the ferocious Rajputs. All these he did splendidly, although the Rajput warrior clans presented a particular challenge to him. Having learned patience and strategy from his father, he opted for a peaceful war with them, winning his victory with the weapons of weddings that sealed alliances and the kind of deft diplomacy that turns enemies into friends.

A prodigiously intelligent and strategic man and an observant Muslim, Akbar the Great, as he became known, was renowned for his liberal thinking and tolerance of diversity. This extended to his cultural patronage and to his respect for different religions whose clergy he'd consult on various matters. No wonder, then, that his dynasty was marked by such a flourishing of art, architecture, literature and science.

Leaving his son Jahangir to rule his enormous empire in abundance and amity after his death, Akbar the Great passed his genes to his grandson, perhaps the most famous and tragic Mughal of all, Shah Jahan, who was in the process of building his new capital Shahanabad at Delhi when his son deposed and imprisoned him.

If Humayun's widow could have known in the mid-sixteenth century what her progeny was to achieve in the decades and centuries to come, would her grief still have compelled her to mark her husband's fatal roll down the stairs with the extravagant tomb that she built for him? Would the devout Persian lady who'd accompanied her husband through the loss of his empire, years of exile in Persia, her kidnapping by the enemy in Afghanistan and more than a decade of struggle to regain the throne, still have felt moved to plan, manage and pay for the magnificent mausoleum that now houses his remains?

All these centuries later we can only guess at the emotions behind this innovation, the "garden tomb" that set a trend for Mughal tombs from then onwards and culminated in the Taj Mahal. The gardens at Humayun's tomb are no lush bit of lawn but rather twelve hectares of parkland that serve as a paradise on Earth for his departed soul and a fitting setting for the monument that pays tribute to him.

Incorporating all kinds of Persian features from arched niches to geometric stone inlay work, the tomb nonetheless came to express the grand Mughal style with its local combination of pink sandstone and white marble. Domes, minarets and marble lattice screens are used repeatedly in Mughal architecture, but one feature of Humayun's tomb surprised us – a Star of David motif repeated on the building's exterior.

'It was regarded as a cosmic symbol by the Mughals,' our guide explained, strolling with us towards the other tombs in the complex – one of which belongs to Haji Begum, lying eternally beside her husband, the emperor.

On the drive southwards beyond New Delhi with the guide silent and Rahul asking Arnie a thousand questions about life in the West – 'Sir, what kind of car do you drive in your country? Sir, what kind of car is Subaru?' – I escaped into my own mental maze, a paradox concerning the nature of power.

At its centre was the overwhelming tomb of Emperor Humayun which, however splendidly it commemorated his life, was still the

Way out in India

monument to his death. And she who built it, the noble Haji Begum, lay in inevitably bony remains beside him.

I puzzled over the human desire to cling to life, to status, to power, to money even, beyond the grave when we all know from the nursery rhyme that life is but a dream. And all our clinging, all our wills and all our monuments cannot negate its flimsy transience.

As inevitably as individual lives must end, so must those of dynasties and empires, which always seem somehow diminished by their best monuments to themselves, as if these commemorate not their achievements so much as their hubris.

A FEW KILOMETRES south of New Delhi is another of these, from a dynasty that ruled much earlier than the Mughals. The site was the famous Qutb Minar, ostensibly a victory tower established by Sultan Qutb-ud-din, but to my mind a giant collective phallus bursting with his arrogance and that of all the dead sultans who succeeded him.

Standing at the base of this edifice, which rises more than seventy metres high, I found it intriguing that although it begins with a diameter of more than fourteen metres, this diminishes over five storeys to two and a half metres. Is this the way empires work? When does the rot set in? When do they diminish? Are they smallest at their pinnacles, when arrogance perhaps overrules reason?

Sultan Qutb-ud-din was a man not to be messed with. A former slave of an Afghan sultan and the first Muslim ruler in India, he conquered the Hindu kingdom of Delhi in 1193 and decreed that from then on, Islam would be northern India's sole religion. To remove any doubt about his intentions, he built a mosque to accompany his victory tower, founded it on the site of a destroyed Hindu temple and constructed it with its predecessor's materials and those of other temples. These being of richly carved sandstone, their decorations remain among the Koranic verses on the mosque's walls, except those symbols offensive to Muslims, such as Hindu deities in human form. To this day the careful filing by the sultan's sweaty artisans remains, leaving blank interruptions in the carvings' rhythm and beauty.

For all his strivings, Qutb-ud-din never completed his victory

Of Palaces and Protests

tower or his mosque. Less than twenty years after crowning himself in Delhi, his fate dictated death by impaling – on the pommel of his polo saddle to be precise – in the middle of a match in Lahore. Like Emperor Humayun about three centuries later, his was a sudden and scary end, leaving questions about karma and other imponderables that nevertheless provide the traveller with ample food for thought.

The unfortunate sultan's successors all got to work in turn, adding to the victory tower's fluted storeys, each with its balcony projecting like a ballet tutu, until the minar reached five storeys. Some added marble and one a cupola. Nature added drama with a lightning bolt and an earthquake along the way, but the remaining sultan in the fourteenth century and the British in the nineteenth, seeing the site's value, restored it to its former stature that earned it UNESCO World Heritage Site status in the twentieth century.

Among the lawns and the weekend crowd in their Sunday best and the little green parakeets fluttering about the complex, other monuments intrigue the visitor; perhaps none more so than the mysterious Iron Pillar. Rising seven metres high outside the mosque, it dates from a much earlier era and temple complex, its purpose having been to commemorate the Hindu ruler, Chandragupta II, who died in 413. The unfathomable thing about this pure-iron pillar is not that it has not rusted in sixteen-hundred years, but how it was made in the first place. No academic, however well qualified, has ever managed to explain this puzzle, which leaves the traveller scratching her rapidly brimming head.

Curling back to the theme of hubris that began this visit, two more sites among the many in the Qutb Minar complex illustrate its inevitability. One, an attempted competitor to the minar begun by Sultan Ala-ud-din Kalji, was supposed to have risen twice as high as its brother. The good sultan, however, died after building the first twenty-seven metres of it. With no one interested in continuing his project, it fell into ruin, squatting all these centuries later as a rubble-pile monument to his exaggerated ambition.

The other site is an empty space full of poignancy, kept available for the grave of the last Mughal emperor in the nineteenth century. He and his dynasty ended not only shamefully, but outside India much more with a whimper than a bang. Exiled by the British to Burma for treason,

Way out in India

he died there, leaving but a blank space at one of the capital's most historic sites – a far far cry from his ancestor Humayun's tomb.

TWO THINGS TO know when travelling by road in India: (a) the sights beyond the window dull the nervous wreckage somewhat if you stay focused on them and (b) it's a bad idea to calculate the time a journey will take by the distance it covers. So how long will it take? You hope much longer than expected. That will mean you have a sane driver because you will certainly not – unless you are seriously suicidal – be driving yourself.

The road south-west of Delhi may lead one to a district with the irresistible name of Jhunjhunu and the small agricultural town of Nawalgargh. Alone on the road for the first of many hours with our guardian angel Rahul in his sacred Suzuki, we set off with his questions firing away in the direction of Sir, as usual, leaving me to watch the motorbikes laden with tin water pots in the mist, one a tricycle attached to a flatbed piled with boxes towering high above the rider's head and extending as wide. As the city melted into the countryside, tractors with hay loads the size of trucks trundled by amid the faint smell of farmland and diesel until we came to a stop.

Abruptly. As was Rahul's custom. And every stop that we came to from then onwards was the same – a roadside tourist oasis camouflaged among its peers. If Sanitised India is the tour for you, these are your kind of stops. Each one in the many hundreds of kilometres we travelled provided a hermetically sealed escape from India in the raw, with a relatively upmarket restaurant, a shop full of snacks and souvenirs, and toilets that would pass for clean.

The most real and absorbing features of these were the poor wretches who attended them. Usually it was a lowly looking woman in a sari, or even a gentleman outside the door in some places. Whoever it was, his or her best chance of a tip was to flourish out either a ribbon of toilet paper, a crisp paper serviette or both accompanied by the standard commentary: 'Papers.'

Then suddenly there was a camel on the road and we were in Rajasthan.

'A what?'

'A *camel!*' Arnie pointed. Rahul laughed. And sure enough, there was the camel trotting alongside our traffic-jammed car, two teenagers waving at us from its trailer laden with wood.

'This Rajasthan is desert,' Rahul assured us as we passed eternally unfolding green fields, tended by bowed women wearing bright cloth bags strapped around their foreheads and hanging over their backs.

'It doesn't look like a desert,' I answered – helpfully.

But it is. Rajasthan, sprawling in the far north-west on the Pakistani border as India's largest state, is an arid place, among whose wonders are its vast and varied crops, wrested from the soil by the sweat of most of its citizens and sold wherever there are buyers.

Our little town of Nawalgargh was one such place, which for a while seemed intent on eluding us. There were various bellowed conferences involving Rahul and the locals on donkeys, bicycles and motorbikes, with a stop at a roadside shop, where Rahul parked the car. This event produced, magically, a fresh, young farm girl who propositioned him on the spot – for the heartbreaking fee of twenty rupees, equating to forty American cents.

When he declined, scurrying across the dirt road to ask directions at the shop, she took to pressing her face to our windows, knocking persistently at them and holding out her hand whenever we glanced her way.

'No!' I shouted finally in the stuffy car, throwing my jacket over my head in a fit of squirming unease; then asking myself in my suffocating tent whether I was hiding from her or hiding her pitiful life from myself.

Jouncing through the narrow streets of Nawalgargh, our Suzuki turned heads, as well it might with its Tourist Car markings and Rahul in his suit among the men wrapped in dust-coloured shawls. How could we not provide a spectacle amid the cows, bicycles and roadside tailors pressing their treadles, while the fresh-produce wallahs called their wares to passing women pulling the film of their scarves over their heads and faces?

Leaving dust clouds like gossip in our wake, we wound about until we found it: the road to Roop Niwas Kothi. A short road it was, to the outskirts of town, but a world away from the reality of the locals.

Way out in India

An impressive property built by the son of a former Jaipur prime minister in 1737 as a country house, Roop Niwas Kothi sits in all its Anglo-Indian splendour enthroned atop its staircase on a hundred and fifty acres purchased originally for the family's string of thoroughbred horses. Renovated in Victorian times by an illustrious heir, it became the family's permanent home – until its upkeep redefined permanent decades later and a subsequent heir turned it into a hotel.

There's a pathos to the property where the ghosts of the nobles roam the passages and cheap cotton curtains hang in antique windows. Our accommodation, probably the hotel's best, was a vast suite combining a spectral lounge full of carved antiques, where dust motes floated and family photographs faded in the shuttered light. It led into a bedroom where the present impinged on the regal scene in the form of a plastic kettle and a heater blowing lukewarm whispers into the cavernous chill.

'Bit creepy,' Arnie mumbled, opening a shutter in the vain hope of a sunray.

Downstairs in the reception area we met a travel-flustered Indian family who'd just arrived.

'Good afternoon,' the matron greeted. 'Welcome to our family home.'

Family home? Of Mr and Mrs Middle-Class India and their relatives? It was a stunning moment of realisation. All that glory, all that opulence among the princely Indian elite of the Raj had wound down to a gracious lady in a rumpled sari presenting the remnants of her heritage to us.

Strolling the grounds that night after our dinner, we came upon the clan warming themselves at a traditional brazier on the veranda, the patriarch in white cotton and shawl, the waiting staff jumping like the coals in the fire. Uncrossing his feet in their curl-tipped *juttis*, he beckoned us to join them.

With the warmth of fine whisky settling us among our noble hosts, we complimented them on the property's grandeur.

'A beautiful place,' smiled the patriarch, 'although it has a tremendous appetite for money.'

His son-in-law, more loquacious, elaborated: 'Properties like these, before Independence, were much easier for our forebears to maintain. They were well compensated for their services in those days.'

'What kind of services?' That was me, abandoned by my tact.

He sipped his whisky thoughtfully. 'Public services. They served the princes of their states in various capacities. The British had agreements with the princes in those days. They would govern their states' internal affairs and keep order among the subjects in return for lands, taxes, that sort of thing. They were on very good terms with the British, you know.'

No wonder, I thought to myself as a skittish waiter offered snacks from the tandoor.

'In some ways they were quite British themselves,' added the patriarch, arcing a samosa expressively. 'They loved cricket, polo, horses. We still have a very good stable on the property, you know. You can see the horses in the morning. In fact, we've brought our granddaughter here from Jodhpur for her first few lessons.'

'Jodhpur?' I smiled at the little girl. She giggled, shrugging a shoulder. 'Have you brought your jodhpurs with you?'

She shook her head.

'Yes, Jodhpur's a few hours south-west of here,' said the son-in-law. 'My wife and I run a hotel there that was once my family's ancestral home. We're related to the Maharajah of Jodhpur.'

'Wait a moment,' I said, a touch breathlessly, 'Do you still have maharajahs today?'

'Not officially, no. But de facto, yes. The royal lines continue.'

'So what do they do these days – I mean in the absence of official titles?'

The son-in-law swirled his drink. 'Many are in politics, in government. Some are in business and, like us, several run hotels that were once their homes. If you're ever in Jodhpur, you'd be very welcome to visit us.'

Just then the head waiter tiptoed towards the silent matriarch to whisper, judging by the aromas wafting from the house, that dinner was ready. With the utmost restraint I kept my knees from jerking, since it was 10:30 pm. Then we thanked the nobles with whom we'd shared such an unexpected happy hour and ambled back to our spooky suite.

But what, you may ask, were we doing among the spooks and nobles this far off the beaten track anyway? The answer was the havelis – the old merchants' homes from a century or two ago whose coatings had piqued our interest, intensely and delicately frescoed as they were, literally wall-to-wall.

Way out in India

'They lived in ja-int families,' Rahul had told us on the way into Nawalgargh the previous day.

'Giant?' Arnie had whispered. I'd shrugged.

'Joint families,' the noble son-in-law had explained around the family brazier later. 'The whole clan shared the house, as was the case with this house.' He waved his hand over the palatial dwelling. 'Many families in India still live that way.'

'So how does one go about seeing these havelis?' I'd enquired, since we had no plan for that.

The patriarch had sniffed the smoky air. 'Just arrive at the first one and a guide will approach you.'

Simple enough. And we had Rahul in his casual clothes to meet us for the occasion, all spruce and ready for a day out in the country.

The guide, as it turned out, was a lanky youth with a sweet tooth, whose name was Moosa. Just seventeen and quietly amiable, he led us around the havelis like a young colt, bounding up staircases, lounging on mattresses for a hookah-smoking demonstration with a turban on his head, leaning his elbow on an antique four-poster, pulling the curtain taut. He not only felt compelled to demonstrate the operation of a grindstone at one haveli, but to repeat the exercise with an ancient gramophone at another, scratching the needle across the record for the purpose and exposing his sugar-browned teeth with a twinkling grin.

Magical homes these, two storeys high, they were built around central courtyards for their "joint families" who frolicked among the frescoes. With the same abandon as Moosa's, the painters chose their subjects. A circle of wide-skirted Rajasthanis danced around a ceiling in bright red. Hindu gods and goddesses made music on a pillar, while a procession of flowers rambled up an archway. Among the warriors and elephants even a few colonial Brits put in an appearance – one in khakis and pith helmet, complete with cane, pipe and fob watch; one in pearls and a neckline of delicate tulle.

But aside from one of these dwellings beautifully restored and maintained by the original family, the rest are declining fast, their frescoes fading from lack of funding, lending the experience of seeing these unlikely homes in this far off town a sense of unusual privilege.

Of Palaces and Protests

Their presence here may puzzle the visitor who doesn't know how much trade passed through little towns like Nawalgargh in this region between the early nineteenth and early twentieth centuries. From the port of Gujarat south-west of it, the trading caravans would carry their spices and textiles, stopping at such towns where brisk business made merchants who could afford wall-to-wall frescoes, especially when the cost was shared among the clan.

Standing in the middle of a colourful courtyard, one could imagine the noise and the voices of the household: fountains and children playing in the sunshine, servants scurrying, incense drifting among the aromas of lunch; and at night the punka wallah or fan puller, half asleep outside the merchant's bedroom, from which a rope led through a hole above the door into the wallah's hand. Tugging it rhythmically all night long, he'd keep the curtained contraption waving back and forth over the merchant's bed as he snored, dreaming perhaps of sacks of gold or a modest-eyed maiden like the one on the wall beside him.

In another family courtyard we found ourselves lunching with Rahul and Moosa on one of the most delicious meals we'd ever enjoyed in India. Steaming home-made curries kept arriving via the husband, while the cheery, chubby wife stirred the pots and wiped her hands on a cloth.

'You enjoy?' she asked.

We made strange table mates, the four of us, but we laughed, passing the chapattis and sharing the hopes and plans of young Rahul for his brand-new baby and young Moosa for his brand-new career. India's on the move, they seemed to be saying, and we are moving with it.

Then there was some other movement afoot. That night, the wife bubbled, there'd be traditional Rajasthani dancing in that courtyard.

'Come see!' she bade us. 'Everybody will be there. So many people!'

Hmmm. The touring was tiring. Rahul was waxing a bit rich for the blood. In a word: "no". But her face was so eager and Rahul and Moosa so animated that we found ourselves nodding those tourist nods and smiling those tourist smiles as we took our leave to view some moth-eaten Rajasthani horses grazing in a field and to traipse through the obligatory shops, where Moosa would clearly get a cut if we bought a miniature of some elephants prancing on silk with a lot more gusto than the live grazing horses. How could we refuse? And if we wanted

Way out in India

some whisky for the evening ahead, Rahul could take us to a good bottle store. No problem with that.

THE MOON WAS laughing and the courtyard buzzing when we arrived, shivering, in our winter coats and sat round the bonfire amid the varied throng. The French tourists, a pair of women of a certain age, jabbered away gutturally with their slight and campy Indian guide, a natty dresser easy on the ear. The American travellers gushed about the date, Christmas night, offering cookies to all, shaped like stars and angels. The Indian clan got right down to business, wolfing down a meal like the one we'd had at lunch, while we mingled with the miraculously present miniature purveyors along with Rahul and Moosa, all of us crunching Bombay mix and beginning to need that whisky.

It seemed that Rahul needed it more than the rest of us, with Moosa having a tiny one to be sociable, shrugging off his Muslim customs – just for the occasion.

Other snacks arrived fresh from the frying pan, along with other guests until at long, lo-o-ong last it seemed time for the show. While the rest of us huddled round the bonfire, the husband of the house rigged up two speakers in the concrete courtyard for the event, leaving their cables trailing in a way that would make a dancer leap. Then the music began: strictly Bollywood with some scratching from the speakers, but without a traditional instrument to be heard. Then the music played some more and still the concrete stayed empty, with the whisky bottle in Rahul's hands vying with it for that status and nary a sequin nor flared skirt in sight.

Until one of the Frenchwomen, casting off inhibition as might happen under the spell of an Indian Christmas night, took to the cracked cold surface and began to sway. Soon she was joined by the nifty guide, swinging his supple hips with a rhythm and panache that could only come from practice. In an eye blink other figures were on the floor, all bopping and boogying to the Bollywood beat, until Rahul decided it was his turn and that I should be his partner.

Shiny eyed and a touch lusty by then, he needed a chaperone in my opinion, in the form of none other than my husband. And Moosa? Well

Of Palaces and Protests

it would have been rude to have left him alone.

Which was how we spent the rest of that memorable evening on our feet – the traditional dancers long forgotten – with Rahul bowling and batting phantom balls to the music between Usain Bolt lightning gestures in my direction. Moosa, goggle-eyed, flapped his long arms as if out of his depth and Arnie, swinging to the national smash hit, "Kolaveri", altered the lyrics to "Kolhapuri, Kolhapuri", his favourite Indian sauce. I, in my practical walking shoes and functional jacket, beheld the scene between light steps and folded over, giggling, then unfolded upwards, backwards to the laughing moon.

IT WASN'T SO funny getting through the traffic of the Old City of Jaipur with our slim and comely guide at pains to point out the beauty of the place the next day. Well, yes. It must have been astoundingly beautiful once, being as it had been such a novelty: a planned city in the primitive eighteenth century, its patron the inestimably wealthy Maharajah Jai Singh II. His capital's population at Amber nearby had been burgeoning, testing its water supplies. So with his passion for science, regulation and conquest, though not necessarily in that order, the maharajah had set about building his new capital, the splendid new city of Jaipur.

Waving her slender arms around the Suzuki, our guide in her pink salwaar-kameez pointed out the once lovely avenues that partitioned the city into rectangular bazaars, each assigned to a specific craft. But it was as hard to detect the elegant order in all that racket, pollution and population as it would be on the boulevards of a bursting Paris painted pink, with hawkers and vendors spilling off the crumbly pavements in a ruckus of hooting and a haze of smoke and diesel.

Old Jaipur is seriously pink, from its imposing gateways and fortifying walls to its buildings, courtesy of a later maharajah who decreed that every structure in the city be slathered in this colour of hospitality to welcome the Prince of Wales in 1876.

'And now it's still painted pink to welcome you,' the guide smiled in a way that looked like she cared.

Veering off a main road suddenly, we found ourselves in the surreal grounds of Naila Bagh Palace whose reception hall drew gasps from both of us. Elegantly opulent and filled with frescoes, it kept our eyes roving over the chandeliers and intimidating portraits of maharajahs and their wives. Lapsing into the plushness of chairs carved in colonial times and clustered in groups of four or five, we shrugged at each other, struck into silence until we were ushered through the dining room. Its stained-glass fanlights left coloured patterns on the floor while its ceiling hung as a canopy of local woodblock-printed cotton.

A glorious swimming pool above the ground met us next, an obvious modern addition, but from then onwards touches of The Best Exotic Marigold Hotel began to encroach on the splendour.

'How do you get this thing to open?' Arnie turned to the porter, handing him the hefty padlock to our room's French doors that had warped, and now hung in skew hunger for new hinges while thirsting for a coat of varnish or two.

Nailah Bagh Palace, whose owner was the prime minister of Jaipur in the 1870s, also owned our previous lodgings in Nawalgargh, Roop Niwas Kothi. One Thakur Fateh Singh Ji Naila, he was a man under whose tenure things tended to move and shake. All that pink paint, for example, was his business during the prelude to the royal visit of 1876. Electricity was introduced to Jaipur on his watch, as were new road systems, underground water systems and administration systems befitting the well-heeled capital of Rajasthan. To this day, his successor and the current owner of the hotel is known as "thakur", a rough equivalent of the British title of "lord".

Following the tour guide around the Jantar Mantar later, I wondered if she had some kind of Indian lady title, the way she wafted about with her nose raised, rattling off facts and figures at this curious World Heritage Site. Built by none other than the creator of the city himself, Maharajah Jai Singh II, in the eighteenth century, it is an observatory whose huge instruments are geometric constructions with precise curved or slanting surfaces. Sundials and carefully graded stairways, seemingly to nowhere, are other instruments that cast shadows at particular angles.

All these, the guide explained at record speed, measure and calculate celestial movements such as the positions of the stars and the times of eclipses. Neither a whizz at maths when it counted nor a fan of the subject, I gazed at the astronomical scales formed by regular notches carved into marble around a mammoth dial and felt my head begin to spin in three-hundred-and-sixty-degree whirls.

Distracted by the fat guard in khaki storming up and down blowing his whistle to depose the locals from their perches on the various astronomical instruments, I found myself itching to offer the guide a tissue as she sniffed every hundred and eighty degrees or so. Still holding her nose in the air between sniffs punctuated with regular jingles of her Bollywood ringtone, she guided between chatting on her phone, rather than vice versa, until the itch in my fingers became intolerable.

More scratchiness was to come though at the City Palace, a wonder to be lingered at but, which stuffed with Sunday crowds, became unbearable. The unfortunately named Welcome Palace, an outlandish structure combining too many architectural styles got my gold for Most Unsatisfying Tourist Experience. Displaying royal finery of varying grades of opulence, many garments encrusted with pearls and gems, it also displayed some Rajput royals' gluttony. The sizes of some coats and robes impressed, but none more so than that of Sawai Madho Singh who stood two metres tall and weighed in at two-hundred and fifty kilograms. Picture how much silk and encrusting that would take – then take some ginger and mint tea for nausea.

Outside in a courtyard some other objects of mammoth proportions caught the eye. They were the bulbous silver urns that Maharajah Madho Singh, a Hindu, filled with Ganges water and took with him to England in 1901 for King Edward VII's coronation. To date, they hold the record as the largest silver objects in the world.

These two exhibitions of extravagance underline one of the reasons for the decline of the princely states of India. During the Raj, the maharajahs had become allies of the British who compensated them more than handsomely for running their states' internal affairs and keeping their subjects under control. The maharajas, imitating the blue bloods of Britain, developed a taste for whisky, for polo, for international travel and many other delights on a fabulous scale. Over time, though, they burned through the bounty until at Independence even a wealthy state such as Rajasthan had the poorest health and literacy rates in India.

Naila Bagh Palace, though, fully intent on preserving the glory of the Raj, supplied cane chairs to the guests in its front garden as peacocks roamed the property and liveried waiters in turbans and jodhpurs served gin and tonic at sunset.

'Or, perhaps, Sir would like to try one of our fine whiskies.'

To enhance the experience, a musician roved the grounds fully costumed from his turban to his coat that flared like a frisbee when he twirled – which was often. He played several instruments in turn, one a sarangi with a bow, between various flutes, while his ankle bells tinkled under his white trousers tapered perhaps to display them.

His eyes danced, too, in the direction of the guests, which made it as difficult to watch him as the evening chill made it difficult to stay there.

'Well let's go inside then,' Arnie suggested.

'Let's escape,' I corrected him as we fled to the dining room, ensconcing ourselves happily at the window.

It wasn't long, though, until the maudlin strains of a flute crept around the building, accompanied by a soft jingle low down. Then there he was outside the window, fiddling and twirling, piping and stamping until one of the guests, whom the Indians might call a Britisher, lamented: 'Oh, I do wish he'd put a sock in it!' to the tittering of the English speakers and the perplexity of everyone else.

Unable to stand the insult to the musician or the insistence of his music and its obvious object any more, I wandered out as discreetly as possible to replace the tinkle of ankle bells with the rustle of rupees, then sighed to the sound of that flute finally fading away.

TWO THINGS MUCH bigger faded away the next day, one in the form of profound hope, the other in the form of an elephant, or more precisely, an elephant ride – a much vaunted highlight of our tour to Amber Fort on a mountainside just north east of Jaipur. The excitement of Rahul and the guide about the prospect of sending us up to the site on these wretched beasts of burden had made it seem rude to refuse the opportunity. But we had even less heart for the experience after the news on the car radio of Nirbhaya's death from her injuries during surgery in a Singapore hospital that day.

Thankfully, fate or karma intervened then to keep us grounded there, while the nation grieved and Delhi exploded into further rioting.

'Oh, yes!' I whispered to Arnie on our arrival at the fort, where the queue for elephant rides up its ramparts wound its way to eternity, causing our guide-in-pink to tear up, gulp a remedy and resume sniffing before quarrelling in her pale and frail state with Rahul about their opposing proposed start times for the day. Accusations flew in Hindi. She'd arranged our schedule around her children's school times, he claimed and she didn't care about the guests. Of course she did, she frowned, banging her delicate fist against the thickening air of the Suzuki.

We were interested in the magnificent fort, which has nothing to do with "amber", but is quite coincidentally, a colour which could be described as such. More than five centuries old, it was built by the Mughal Emperor Akbar the Great as his capital city of Rajasthan, about two centuries before the city of Jaipur was created to take its place. Amer, he called it, which was corrupted to Amber.

Chugging up to the Sun Gate in our noble Suzuki, I imagined the welcome Akbar's victorious armies would get as they rode up the ramps bearing their war booty to be shown in the massive courtyard later and viewed by the ladies of the court from behind latticed screens upstairs.

My reverie was broken by the welcome we got, from an endless procession of miserable beasts plodding up to the site, their fraying caparisons and discoloured skin unnoticed by the braying tourists hopping off on to a carpet of elephant shit.

Things looked up at the fort's glorious palace with its grand scale and artistry, the elephant-headed columns of its Audience Hall stretching into an optical delight, the tiny inlaid mirrors of its Victory Hall kindling lamplit imaginings, the Hall of Pleasure with its channel streaming cool water along its length and the zenana or harem intriguing with its discreet corridor reserved for the maharajah who could visit any woman's apartment unseen by the others.

We wanted to see the fort, too. Would that be possible? The guide balked, sniffing.

'Well, it's a very long walk up the hill to see it and it's closed for renovations.'

Undaunted, Arnie glowed. 'A walk! Great. Let's go.'

The rocky ramparts were not the guide's cup of tea, she being so delicate and unused to physical exertion. And the fort was closed. But

Way out in India

the discussion was open between us, two women talking about marriage and particularly arranged marriage in India.

'Oh, it's still very popular here,' she smiled, throwing her filmy scarf over her head against the desert sunlight. 'Unlike in your country, I suppose.' Then as the third or fourth Indian to do so, she asked if ours had been a "love marriage".

Check.

'Really?'

It seemed to surprise Indians no end that a couple could have cobbled a marriage together in their youth and still be smiling thirty years later.

'We have a very different system here.'

Which turned out, generally, to be a much looser arrangement than in days of yore, when a non-negotiable partner was selected by the parents and the marriage ensued – for better or for worse.

These days, across many strata of Indian society, the children have a far greater say in choosing a partner, including even the right to reject parental choices. From talking to our host Tommy in Kerala, who was about to begin discussions with a prospective bride's family for his son, and from chatting with Rahul our driver, the process seems to follow roughly the same path, with some variations, of course, among the billion and more Indians.

'So how does it work?' I asked our guide as we rested on a low stone wall at the roadside for a while.

'Well, when the parents and child decide that it's time for marriage, the parents either start making enquiries among family and friends about a suitable match or they start advertising.'

'Advertising?'

'In the matrimonials.'

These, the matrimonial ads in the newspapers, are an Indian art form. Often shameless self-endorsements of the advertisers, their particulars may surprise the Westerner, as may their stipulations. Specifying the religion, caste, education, status, income and appearance of both parties as they do, they leave no doubt as to what is offered and sought.

Here's one as a taster: '*Cultured status family seeking alliance for tall, handsome son with Hons. Computer Science and MBA degree working in American IT company. Based in comfortable bungalow in Mumbai.*

Salary $120 000 per annum. Travels regularly to America. Girl should be fair, slim, beautiful from a respected family, aged between 20 and 25. Should be professional with a university degree.'

The word "fair" is prevalent in these searches and sometimes substituted by "wheatish". Either way, a mammoth cosmetics industry based on this ideal has grown fatter in recent times by feeding on the insatiable Indian demand for skin-lightening creams.

The guide, perhaps not such a fair lass herself under her make-up, went on: 'Or people might also advertise on something like Shaadi.'

'What's that?'

'Shaadi.com. It's a website – I think the biggest in India – devoted to matchmaking.'

Either way, matchmaking is a major project for the family and one in which discretion is the key. Approached the more traditional way, the process is as follows: word goes out to trusted family members and friends and a search ensues as widely and silently as a fishing net cast before dawn. The aunties get busy on the whispering wire, identifying a list of "boys" or "girls" for the candidate.

'Is he settled?' they may ask, angling if the answer is affirmative, for information about other details, down to what Shaadi.com calls "mother tongue" and the boy's accustomed cuisine.

'Yes, but didn't his father's brother have a mental breakdown when his business failed?'

'He did, my dear, but it was perfectly reasonable. It was a huge business. I don't think there's any other case of mental illness in the family.'

Once a partner is identified as prospective, a matchmaker is engaged – someone older, well connected and, above all, circumspect. In many traditional communities, such a person is the local barber.

The matchmaker then approaches the potential partner's family, armed with a photo of the suitor – or suitress – his or her horoscope and a résumé detailing biographical details, achievements and virtues.

Should the family bite, a meeting is arranged by the matchmaker between the two families, usually at the bride's home, where she appears all dressed up to serve refreshments once the company is settled. All the while, both families are aware that this meeting might be only one of several similar ones, but etiquette dictates that questions on this score are strictly omitted.

During the family visit the couple are allowed some privacy to talk to each other, at which point in Rahul the driver's case, he came up with a minimal response to a prospective bride's equally frank 'Yes or no?'

'No.'

'Why not?' she asked.

'Because you're fat.' He'd turned to us in the Suzuki's back seat to relate the crux of the issue: 'I no like fat girls. I no accept.'

In the case of our Jaipur guide, though, matters were rosier. 'It was definitely love at first sight,' she recalled with a wistful twist of her scarf around her wrist. 'He was so handsome…'

If the match has potential, the matchmaker pursues the matter on behalf of both families and the engagement buzz begins. The couple get acquainted on dates, or, in more conservative families, through phone calls.

At this point, an important and delicate matter has to be dealt with: the careful conclusion of discussions with unsuccessful partners. Back go the photographs, horoscopes and résumés to their owners along with assurances of mutual respect and reminders of the role of karma in joining souls for life. All evidence of previous discussions thus removed, the families go their separate ways.

'And do these marriage arrangements have any legal status?' I asked the guide.

'None whatsoever. They're customary. That's all. But customs change. These days some people find their own partners and then ask their families to get involved to approve each other and the match. This we called a self-arranged marriage.'

'Whatever works,' I shrugged. Even an oxymoron.

The match between Rahul and the Jaipur guide had not been a good one and for the remaining sights of the day we drove in silence. Then, suddenly, at a seemingly random spot in the middle of the Old City, he stopped, she left and we wondered why there?

But the spot was not random at all.

'Look,' beamed Rahul, pointing diagonally upwards across the road.

And there it was – the Palace of the Winds, which is not a palace at all but rather a magic castle in a dream, all pink and flimsy, whimsically windowed and latticed throughout as a five-storey screen. Built by the maharajah in 1799 for his royal women as a place from which they could view the life of the busy street below unseen, it's called the Hawa Mahal and it's probably the most famous building in Jaipur. For its elegant uniqueness, rightly so.

Throughout our wanderings through all this architectural magnificence, a question kept nagging at me and bothers me still. If their forebears were able to build so splendidly, why are Indian buildings so shoddy today? Why does a yoga mat in so many hotel rooms fail to square up with the walls? Why do batteries regularly roll off worktops and damp spots bubble through paint and plaster? Is thoroughness simply not a priority?

What is a priority among Indian parents are their children's weddings, on which they commonly spend lavishly. With an entire area of the Jaipur bazaar devoted to wedding finery and accessories, the seriousness of these unions crystallises in the mind. Money is literally hung around the neck of the groom in the form of a garland of tinsel and rupee notes in various denominations. To our astonishment as our new guide Akshat led us through this maze, these hang from the ceilings of market shops and no one dares to steal them.

Less elegant than the marriage bazaar, the rest was a riot of trade and colour, even spilling out into the street in the form of locksmiths, copper pot sellers and one man who'd set up shop in a parking bay, squatting barefoot a hair's breadth from the traffic, repairing cooking pans by smelting them on a brazier fire.

Inside the bazaar the country women, shopping for fabric cross-legged on the floor opposite the traders, bought only the kind of brilliant colours you'd associate with Gypsies. Amazingly enough, technology has now proved their origins in north-western India, from which they began to migrate to Europe about fifteen-hundred years ago. Probably spurred by their defeat by Muslim armies, they packed their caravans and, with their nose rings and sequins glinting in the sun, they began the long trek westwards.

Delicious smells of street food drifted around the Jaipur bazaar, one being entirely irresistible. That was kulfi, a sweet treat more solid and creamy than ice cream and more exotic, too, by being flavoured with

Way out in India

cardamom, rose water, saffron or pistachio. Only the red-bummed monkeys running about on the awnings above us threatened the appetite, but not for long.

In a short cul-de-sac we came upon a puzzling gathering of men mingling in a quiet crowd.

'What's that all about?' Arnie asked the Akshat.

He lowered his teardrop shades and his voice. 'Gem trading. A long tradition in Jaipur.'

'But is it legal?'

Akshat shrugged. Better not to ask.

Then suddenly we were off the street in the courtyard of a haveli, un-frescoed but humming with the life of the "joint family" who shared it, their laundry proclaiming like bunting over every balcony, that the house was inhabited.

'About thirty-five people live here in all,' smiled the jeweller who led us inside his family's cramped quarters.

There we sat on a mattress, which became his parents' bed at night, while he produced from a creaky built-in niche-cupboard his pieces of the utmost refinement. His art was enamelling – difficult, traditional in Jaipur and extraordinarily masterful in his hands. A tray of tea was brought by a little girl before we left the haveli to encounter a different kind of enamelling on the street below.

Two gentlemen sat at their low street stall in fezzes. Their wares on display between them bit the grimy air with perfect, pearly smiles. The gents were not smiling, though, perhaps because few matches had been made that day between their dentures and the Jaipuris. It was a tense attempt at banter with them then, tight, unwelcoming.

In short it was time to move on.

TO AGRA THAT was, enduring that suffocating fog and the flatulence of Rahul every nerve-wracking kilometre of the way. Unbelievably in Agra, in addition to the Obvious Taj, a sight called the Baby Taj pops up on travellers' itineraries.

'Can't imagine why,' I muttered to Arnie, pushing my surgical slippers into my pockets by way of preservation for the event, at the end of our visit to the Obvious Taj. 'How can anything compete?'

But compete it did, not in scale but in the richness of its gemstone inlay work. Also a tomb, but built before the Taj Mahal and suggesting elements of style for its future Big Sister, the Baby Taj is literally related to it, being the tomb of Empress Mumtaz Mahal's grandfather. Built by his daughter, it's a treasure chest of gems in a peaceful garden without the collective mania that seems to cloak the Taj Mahal and a good place to wind down from a visit to it.

There was one last monument on our tour of Monumental India, the glorious sandstone Agra Fort full of the history and splendour that by then was making me nauseous. Only its bittersweet view of the Taj Mahal from across the Yamuna Riva soothed me like a cup of tea, but thoughts of the broken Emperor Shah Jahan gazing out at it dragged me into a sadness that stooped towards thoughts of escape.

I'd seen it all now, I decided. I wanted to go home.

But then a guard with shifty eyes approached our guide. Did we want a secret tour off limits to the public? The empress's bathhouse? We'd pay the guide who'd pay the guard – strictly and discreetly in cash.

'Serious?'

Spirited through a side door into an unimaginable experience, we found ourselves in a series of dark anterooms whose ceilings and walls were carved marble reliefs. Geometrically designed, they were inlaid in inconceivable abundance with miniature mirror chips, so that when a match was lit – just one – a spectacle of golden reflection glittered throughout the space. The baths, marble of course, would provide a hypnotic ritual for any lady lying in petalled water amid a million lamps flickering from the mirrors and the finest fragrances of oils and incense drifting about her.

The guide and the guard waved two cigarette lighters about for a taste of the place, while the group of Malaysian schoolgirls with us, struck into silence, circled their heads with ours to follow the glimmering arcs.

'No wonder they call it The Golden Triangle,' Arnie whispered as the Malaysian teacher struck up two lighters to drizzle dazzle upon dazzle – a fitting end in that dense-aired cloister to an intimate journey with the history shapers of India.

8
Of Passengers and Puffings

TO BE A PUKKA Indian traveller you have to take a train. Long distance. Okay, you still qualify if you choose first class – or what's called AC 1 in India, the AC part denoting the air conditioning. We did, admittedly, in a fit of wimpy softness.

But we weren't the only ones. Slinging ourselves into our compartment on the Radjhani Express from Delhi to Darjeeling, we found ourselves in the company of Mr and Mrs Middle Age from the remote northern state of Himachal Pradesh. They held high positions in school education and bore not a jot of cop-out guilt. On the contrary, they were proud to be travelling in this class and assured us that only the best people did.

Besides our cabin attendant, that was, whom Madam ordered around shamelessly to ensure the comfort of her new Western companions.

'More tea,' she announced with a head waggle by way of dismissal.

There were two other companions with us, one being temporary: our tour manager, at whom we had to fling the last of the money owed him before the train pulled out of the station. There'd been a miscalculation of our bill, leaving the poor man to risk his life leaping off a departing train, clutching his precious haul in a plastic envelope to his chest. The other companion, a large flat-screen TV set, was permanent and less dramatic, snuggled up close to Madam's berth for the journey. It was a long journey in a box, beginning as it had in Singapore where Madam's and Sir's son had welcomed them to share the successes of his life for a few happy weeks.

It was hard to settle down on the Radjhani Express after the tortuous haul through the Delhi traffic, exacerbated by the populace, agitated, angry and out on the streets in thousands since the death the previous day of Nirbhaya, the young woman who'd been gang-raped on a bus.

Of Passengers and Puffings

It would have been hard to settle down anywhere with that disturbing event hanging over the city and country, but harder still with Madam's staring at me in that close, upholstered compartment.

It's a feature of Indian travel, this sustained staring, as unashamed to the Indian as it is unnerving to the Westerner. And it's often accompanied by the kinds of questions your mother told you never to ask – after she'd hissed 'Stop staring!'

'How much did your handbag cost?'

'Did you put the blonde colour in your hair?'

Frankly, it was hard to remember the price of my handbag when a girl had been raped and had died so horrifically and it was harder still to sidestep the question politely with those brown eyes boring into mine. To top it all, I was sickening after one monument too many in the chilly mist, I was hungry and my chest hurt.

Nevertheless, the compartment was cosy in a lived-in way, the leatherette seats having taken as much of a beating as the rest of the train and the tracks, the way things do in India. Things take a beating everywhere they're used, but the Western way is quicker to replace than repair them. There was a sense of comfort, though, in knowing that the tracks we were travelling on had supported so many journeys and that the teapots holding our tea had clinked their way to wobbliness over so many years.

Our driver, Rahul, had prepared us for the twenty-hour journey by warning us against the dangers of Indian Railway food and taking us to one of Delhi's rare delis for "English food" – fortifying cheese wedges and the like.

With our hamper bulging, we began offering to break crackers with Madam and Sir, who just smiled at our folly.

Let's get something straight: class AC 1 on Indian Railways is a feast! The cabin attendant comes around at regular intervals in his dapper cap and waistcoat, with what in India are known as "menu cards". Then he sets up TV trays from the 1960s on the spongy stuff in red that's Indian Railways' version of carpeting and in whooshes a procession of meals as warm and abundant as any from an Indian mother's kitchen. Oh, and there's ice cream in little cups – one of the major perks of travelling AC 1.

Way out in India

As if that wasn't enough, Madam had a stash of her own that she insisted on sharing: fresh home-made chapattis with her special mango pickles, a boost so delicious that my eyes closed and chest opened at the first hint of chilli.

Sated, we all settled down to reading, Sir with a newspaper that I ached to borrow, since my paperback, as absorbing as it was, just didn't cover my face. And that staring was starting to rattle me.

At my squirming limit, I decided to make a break for it, to the bathroom – a desperate measure in India – even if my slippers emerged from their bag into a wallop of scrutiny and interrogation. Disappearing through the compartment door under heavy surveillance, I emerged into the passage only to be gaped at by two gents in turbans rocking gently there for no apparent reason, their eyes as riveted to me outside the compartment as Madam's had been inside it.

With her eyes fixed to the door for my return, her eyebrows rose in question.

'It was dirty,' I reported, too depleted for niceties.

Forthwith the cabin attendant was summoned and dispatched to get the bathroom cleaned up.

Unruffled and silent, he acquiesced. This manner had no doubt aided his selection for class AC 1, which was no small matter, for among the 1.65-million employees on Indian Railways, only the cream would earn and keep this job and its benefits.

Madam smiled then, as satisfied as the proverbial cat, but studied me like an owl until her attention was drawn to a series of burps that erupted from her in dramatic increments. Like her stares, though, they were not embellished with any embarrassment. While Arnie blushed, Sir read his newspaper, apparently unperturbed by his wife's Vesuvian impersonations.

Then, without warning, he began a few renditions of his own in the form of alarming and serial snorts, accompanied by a distressing technique of pinching his nose to wiggle its cartilage, which emitted a cracking sound. This percussive symphony continued for some time, augmented by Sir's rattling newspaper and Madam's occasional swigging from a bottle of anti-burping agent.

Then, as suddenly as it had started, the symphony died. Mesmerised

Of Passengers and Puffings

finally by her discomfited subject and the train's rhythm, Madam flopped over on her berth and fell asleep. Sir, nodding into his newspaper, dozed off with his glasses hugging his nasal cartilage into a gently snoring narrowness.

'Phew,' was all Arnie could say as we stared at each other for a moment and listened to the clacking of wheels on tracks, turning our gaze to the windows.

Outside an endless mist seemed to float over endless fields of crops farmed by hardy men and women in the almost total absence of machines. Squatting, stooping, hauling and working with whatever manual tools their forebears had used, they presented scenes of pastoral peace; until the train would slow and the tented camps of the migrants would present a wretched view, or the lines on a thin and weathered face would become more clearly defined. Passing by reflecting on the hardship of their lives, I wondered how they defined them if they knew nothing else. I pondered, then, the concept of relativity with regard to life's ease or difficulty.

When Madam's and Sir's awakening interrupted my thoughts, it turned out that they had a lot to say. They were genuinely nice. They were interesting and they made me glad we'd travelled by train. They'd been married for forty years and had been posted to Himachal Pradesh to work as young teachers. There were many benefits to rising up in the education system as they had done, to principal and inspector, respectively; but the price was staying in this remote and snowy place far from family and friends for decades.

'No matter,' Madam sighed, smiling. 'Sir has already retired – last year – and I'll be retiring after one year more.'

'And it's very beautiful, Himachal Pradesh,' Sir added, 'with mountain peaks and snow and it's not so polluted or corrupt or urbanised as other places.'

'But it's right next door to Jammu and Kashmir where there is so much trouble,' Madam interrupted, wobbling her head.

We talked cricket after that and parenting and politics – theirs and ours – as we passed through agricultural India, lush and expansive, while hours and hours rolled by.

By mutual agreement, as night deepened, the gents would sleep in the top bunks, the ladies below, but it was the work of all four of us to unwrap the brown-paper parcels of fresh bedding and figure out how to tuck in the sheets.

Once sprawled out on them gazing at Arnie's bunk above, it didn't matter whether they were crumpled or not. We'd taken a long-distance train in India, which was now rocking us to sleep, connecting us with millions of others who'd done the same and with all the travellers who'd travelled on the eleven-thousand trains that day provided by Indian Railways. And, in the morning, we'd wake up initiated as pukka Indian travellers at the hem of the Himalayas.

9
Of Peaks and Pine Trees

THINK DARJEELING AND you think romance, tea, British and cool – in that order. The cool brought the British and the British brought the tea; in which case you'd assume the essence of the place to be cool. There you'd be right – and wrong. There's a lot that's cool about Darjeeling, including the climate, but its underside is dark and spiky, like a mountain range at night. Like the business end of a soldier's rifle. Like the bark of a policeman's voice on the square. Like the face from Nepal – defiant, bitter. Like the signs above shop doors. "Gorkhaland" they say. That is all.

You forget this mostly, while the steam twirls from your teapot at Glenary's and you tuck into your fusion Cornish pasty harbouring veg curry between its crusts. The prickly bits of the town vanish, ironically, at the smell of pine trees on a tingling uphill stroll. And the chief trick of the place is to banish all gloom by presenting its Himalayas with the kind of spectacular splendour that can make you weep.

Imagine, then, the delight of the British officer and official in 1829 on their way to Ontoo Dara in the region – no kidding – to resolve a border dispute between the locals, when they encountered Darjeeling. The site they stumbled upon was a Buddhist monastery, Dorje Ling, where monkeys now swing from rainbows of prayer flags flapping on lines in the wind and where concrete lions in yellow welcome you to the peace on their sacred hill amid the shrines.

The two British gents must have felt the cool, beheld the view, understood the strategic and health benefits of the place, turned to each other and said 'By golly!' before reporting to the brass.

The brass must have responded 'By George!' with a colonial gleam in the eye about a minute before the local *chogyal* or monarch ceded the

Way out in India

area to the "Britishers", who got busy establishing their hill station there with its gasp-worthy views. The point, first and foremost, was to build a sanatorium there for their compatriots suffering from a nasty affliction called hill diarrhoea.

It didn't take long before the place began to sprout all the storybook features of a pukka British village, complete with a Hill Corps to keep an eye on the restive locals and to protect its countrymen who, hearing of how healthy the air was, began a genteel stampede up the hills far from the raging city summers down below.

The relief of the cool in the dizzy air must have bubbled into decadence, since the town earned a discreet notoriety in its heyday for the White and not-so-White mischief that ensued there between crustless sandwiches. Among the British and the Indian elite from the princely circles of the time, cooling down from city summers on the plains, a little G and T on the veranda before dinner might have led all sorts of ways to be whispered about – and often did.

And, still now, though traffic-blackened, crumbling or facelifted into astonishing hybrids, the contemporary architecture bears witness to the time when the British built Utopia in the hills far from home. And although the decades have dipped it in India with all its adopted neighbouring peoples, its traffic, garbage and colour, it has never been totally submerged.

The road that winds up from the plains is British, even if embellished with pure Indian English en route warning motorists that "Hurry burry spoils the curry" and "Looking for survival? Do not believe in fast arrival."

The narrow gauge railway line that plies the same route is British, with the little steam train fondly called "The Toy Train" still puffing and tooting up and down the hillsides, having earned itself World Heritage status a while back and gaily offering passengers like us its "Joyride" for a flavour of its history.

THE JOY OF the Joyride certainly didn't begin at the station, a heritage building in the workhorse mould, rather than the thoroughbred. The little engine didn't bother. Cool in royal blue, it steamed away happily,

Of Peaks and Pine Trees

its minders tending its antique parts with obvious care amid the throng bundled against the chill.

The ticket officers were a different breed from the steam engine workers. Caged behind their grille, they snapped at any passenger who dared to approach them.

'Fill up the form!' Passports were passed to them and tossed back with the requisite sneer 'n snag, the Indian official's favourite sport. But finally we were on our way, wheezing along the tracks a hair's breadth from shops and homes en route to the next town, Ghum, showering butchery stalls, fruit stalls and the general populace with soot. At Ghum, the conductor swung off and bestrode the platform.

'Look!' Arnie pointed. 'The Fat Controller!'

'Who?'

'The Fat Controller from *Thomas the Tank Engine*.'

And there he was, puffing like the train in his suit, with its three silver buttons pulled to popping point, his pen in his breast pocket, his shoes as shiny as his smartly parted hair.

It was a miserable station, Ghum, with nary a comfort for the traveller besides a thimble of sweet tea from the kiosk and a moth-eaten museum of the Darjeeling Himalayan Railway's history. Much more engaging were the cherubs on the platform, their caps of bright yak wool ending in ear flaps with plaits close to those rosy and pinchable cheeks.

On we shuffled round the Bastia Loop, a feat of early British engineering. While its spiral shape provided a gentle gradient for the train, its altitude provided astounding views of the town and Kanchenjunga, the world's third-highest peak. Finally, its Gorkha War Memorial provided a looming Darjeeling shadow in the form of an obelisk with a point – as sharp and cold as Kanchenjunga itself.

From the lounge of the hotel with its picture windows, the peak flared into afternoon pink, mirroring our faces warmed by the coal stove squatting among us and our afternoon tea. Our companions were a young British couple very much in love.

'So you went on the little blue train then?' Matthew asked us.

'Oh, yes.'

'So you saw the Fat Controller, then?'

'Who?' That was his girlfriend, Rachel.

'The Fat Controller. *Thomas the Tank Engine.* Remember?'

You only have to crack up once with strangers to turn them into buddies.

They were great to walk with in Darjeeling. They were fit and funny and their accents rolled us into its history. You have to be fit to benefit from Darjeeling. The roads are steep and narrow and the air is thin; and as is true everywhere, you miss places like The Hot Stimulating Café in a vehicle.

Gloved and padded, we moseyed down the Mall, the town's main shopping street, stopping to gaze at the mock-Tudor hotels weakly warmed in the late afternoon and the old wooden fittings of a pharmacy with its timber fretwork and its grandfather clock still ticking away in the chemical smell as it has done for the past century or so.

Past the Christmas crowds and feral dogs we ambled, towards Chowrasta, the main square, where we found the whole town and its pigeons en fete at the The Tea and Tourism Festival, an endearingly inclusive affair that smelled of fried foods and continued for days with the locals providing many of the acts on that stage hung with paper stars.

Indian faces, Tibetan faces, wrinkled faces of Nepalese grannies in matrons' aprons passed us by, along with kids on ponies delivering smelly challenges to the strollers who yelled: 'Watch your step!' in so many languages. Petite oriental girls with glossy hair and high heels gossiped in gaggles while their boys roamed in packs crowned with crested haircuts. A young mother smiled at us as Arnie's camera and permission request to click were pointed at her little son. Wrinkled into his oversized suit he stared, his mother's hand on his head, trying to keep her lips closed for the camera, but her pride burst through with her buck teeth anyway.

Ducking into an old bookshop on the square, we browsed its fustiness housed in creaky shelves along with other festival goers eager for quiet. It's a bookish place, Darjeeling, known for its educational institutions, some of which, like the grey and Gothic St Joseph's School high on a hill, were modelled on British public schools and meant for the children of the Raj's colonial officials. And where else in the world would you find the sole statue on a town's main square being that of a poet all in gold? But there he stands on Chowrasta, perpetually impervious to the pigeons, Bhanu Bhakta, the Nepali poet in his tunic and sash, armed with a robust tome.

It's a musical place, too, Darjeeling, its festival having given any kid with a guitar instant street cred as he wandered the hills towards the unique gathering of six-hundred plus guitarists who'd attempt – and fail sadly – to create a Guinness world record of the biggest guitar ensemble in history, playing John Lennon's "Imagine".

It was an emotional event, dedicated as it was to Nirbhaya, who'd died in Delhi that week.

Rachel had a very British solution to the situation: 'I think what we all need is a nice cup of tea.'

The setting was Nathmulls, one of the oldest tea shops in town.

'So 'ow do we choose?' Matthew asked the assistant, waving his hand over the fifty or so teas available. I wandered off to peruse the teapots, cosies and strainers on display for the tea connoisseur.

Strolling away from the spangles and racket of the festival along quieter roads, the wind blew the piney fragrance about as we stood on a hillside looking out over the town. Its town hall was a feast of incongruity – an elegant British bastion of officialdom sporting a strange dome on its clocktower and a fancy fountain dedicated to the goddess of art and science, Saraswati. We smiled – only in India – wrapped our coats tighter and headed downhill to dinner.

The Christmas lights hung across the street invited the ghosts of Christmases past out to play, blurring the shabbiness of the Gymkhana Club, the Planters' Club and the hospital, which glowed so Victorian in the early evening as to entice one of our party in – me.

"We pray for your health", a motto on an entrance archway declared ominously, sending me and my chilling spine back out into the street, panting about the discovery to the group stamping its feet in the cold.

STILL ON THE British trail, Arnie and I decided to explore its last bastion in full daylight – the famous Windamere Hotel. Once the original boarding house for English and Scottish tea planters, it evolved into a hotel just prior to World War Two. With its neat pathways and red postbox, with its picket fences and brass plant pots, with its pines and firs, its high tea and roly-poly puddings and with its hot-water bottles in rooms of hospital spotlessness, it feels unequivocally misplaced in twenty-first-century India. But even aspic must have a shelf life, not to mention demographics, reflected in the little framed sign placed on the lounge mantelpiece amid its photographs of past guests.

ATTENTION VISITORS

it said,

Visitors are respectfully requested not to move around furniture in this room in order that comfort may be shared in fair proportion by all.

*Also, visitors are requested **not** to take off their footwear, or put up their feet on the furniture, or lie supine on the hearth, or sleep behind the settees, lest unintended offence be given to others – Windamere Hotel*

There were no prizes for guessing who'd put it there. Outside an English voice that could shatter glass skewered us from across the veranda.

'Excuse me. May I help you?'

Its owner, a formidable matron in a military tent disguised as a shawl, looked anything but helpful.

I chose the charming option. 'Well, we were just looking around...'

'This is a private property. You can't do that here.'

'...to see if we'd like to come for dinner perhaps, or high tea. We've heard you offer a wonderful high tea!'

'Ah.' Her tent deflated somewhat as she directed us towards the reception area for the relevant bookings.

'See you soon,' I grinned as we left, flapping a pamphlet about scones and cream, which we tossed in the nearest bin. And we were the supposed upper crust in these parts. Imagine the generations of those who were not.

They'd either lived in the district under their chogyal, prior to his ceding it to the British, or they'd come from neighbouring Nepal or Bhutan or Sikkim – another Indian state – when they'd heard there were mansions to be built, post offices and banks. They'd fled from worse conditions at home – under tyrants or poverty or both. They'd heard that the sahibs and memsahibs of the Raj would need roads and railway tracks, ballrooms and boarding houses and so they'd come, essentially, to serve.

Labyrinthine political streams have run through the district since then, floods of Tibetans have found refuge there after China swept into their country, wars have been fought and treaties signed; but still there is a rankling among the district's people who call themselves Gorkhas. Nepalese-speaking Indians they are, who agitate for their own Indian state they call Gorkhaland as they have done for decades. At issue are the rights and opportunities they believe are theirs as Indians, even if their language and ancestry are Nepalese.

The passion of their belief has clashed ferociously at times with that of the Indian government, especially during the 1980s – and still the matter finds no resolution. As late as 2013, the town was shut down for weeks by thousands of Gorkhas standing their ground on the road that leads into and out of it.

Hence the bristling military presence all over the area. Hence the policemen as jittery as they are numerous. There are other reasons, too, for all the guns and clenched jawbones of Darjeeling: Big Brother China sprawls just beyond the border, as do Bangladesh, Nepal and, less ominously, Bhutan.

Add to that a town housing a population thirteen times the ten-thousand for which it was designed and the pressure builds. Hear that population babble a multitude of demands in as many languages. Watch as mountain forests make way for more dwellings and consequent monsoon landslides and understand then why the grip of the men in laced boots clenches so hard on those guns.

IF YOU'RE THE wandering breed of traveller in Darjeeling, you'll find many roads that lead to the military. One such was the road to the racecourse, which seemed like an interesting relic to explore. Visions of Mr and Mrs Winterbottom having a flutter on their steed sprang to mind as we set off, winding down hills where housewives washed pots in roadside water channels and sifted the day's rice in flat baskets. It was all quaint and rustic until some excrement came floating by and my husband developed his new game, "spot the turd".

The modus operandi of finding the racecourse was to amble along in the dust, bleat "racecourse" to any passing local at a fork in the road,

Way out in India

watch him waggle his head in both directions and then guess.

When we did find it, finally, after a two-hour amble, it was not a racecourse at all, but a military base with a shooting range next door, from which shots banged out in disquieting proximity. So there was no perusal of the racecourse that day, or even its former site, since the moustached gents in camo – best left bristling among themselves – were not in the friendship business.

An uphill walk met a similar fate at the top of a road that happened to lead high up to the Gothic surrealism in grey that is St Joseph's School. Nearby a sudden barrier of guns at the guard hut turned us back and it was all downhill from there.

THE MYSTERY OF Darjeeling downhills is that they sometimes prove to be uppers – that then drop you into the darkness when their sheen wears off. At the centre of one of these roller coasters was a strange little woman who stepped out to greet us on a pedestrian visit to a tea plantation.

'Can I help you?' She planted herself in our path outside her little house, her wrinkled Nepali face squinting into the sun, her jersey screaming yellow against the green of the tea plants.

We were seeking the tea tour – dutifully – having entered the estate through its back gate where a sign proclaimed it a supplier to Harrods.

'Yes!' The woman's chins wobbled. 'The tour is here.'

'In her house?' I whispered.

Arnie shrugged.

A two-roomed affair as frilly and fakely flowered as any you've ever seen, it was hers in return for long service on the estate. From it she ran a little shop, too, selling sweets and snacks to estate workers and the odd passing tourist.

Getting down to business, she seated us on her rug-strewn benches beside her forest of teddy bears, bustling out and back equipped with a smile for her Darjeeling tea ceremony.

Bowls of dried leaves were offered and smelled; fresh tea flowers handed round and explained, the best teas coming from the 'tippy toppy leaves', she assured us. The pot tilted, the steam twirled, the cups clinked and the rupees rustled as various packets as bright as highlighters were squashed into a bag of success for both parties.

'With all the instructions,' the little woman beamed, with her delight fanning out at the corners of her eyes.

I examined a packet – just to make sure.

'Boil fresh water in kettle. Do not under boil, if you want five second leaves three times you can reuse.'

No problem.

And then, the ceremony over, her mask dropped. The question cutting it loose surrounded her children – all gone searching for greener pastures.

'They don't want to do this work anymore,' she lamented. 'The young women don't want to stand in the sun all day with baskets strapped to their heads for such low pay. They get their education. Then they go to the cities. My son's in Doha. He works for engineering company. My daughter's in Kolkata. A schoolteacher.'

'And do the original families still own the plantations?' Arnie asked.

She sighed. 'Hardly any. It's all corporations now. It's all changed. All the traditions of Darjeeling are dying.'

'That's a sad thing, a bad thing,' I ventured, sipping the last of my tea.

A sunray on the woman's face revealed the depth of her wrinkles. She shrugged. 'What is bad? What is good? All things die for new ones to be born.'

BETWEEN OTHER LOOPS betwixt darkness and light sat the Tibetan Refugee Centre, a solid walk from the town centre. The light illuminated the self-help aspect of the place, the shadow loomed on the reasons it was there.

A cluster of buildings all craving plaster and paint, it housed inhabitants craving their home. Some had been there since its inception in 1959 when the Chinese had swept into Tibet. Crooked, old people they were, lined up at their looms or spinning wheels in work halls as chilly and gloomy as the cost of power dictated. Some were younger women weaving bright carpets. A crèche, school and an orphanage lent the place its vibrancy, and a shop full of crafts its delectable colours. It

Way out in India

was a happy-sad place, this, which left us rolling upward and downward, too, on our way back to town.

Whether up or down, wherever we went the porters of Darjeeling shuffled, wretched men bent double in rags, their straps across their crowns and under their loads. Wood planks, gas canisters, tourist luggage, rice sacks and furniture weighed down on these human donkeys with anaesthetised eyes whose vistas in this splendid place had contracted to the patch of pathway immediately before their feet.

Even Kunga's, the cheery little sanctuary full of aromas that served up such comfort with its noodle soup, offered no relief from the thoughts of the porters the first day we discovered it. Even with its wall scrolls rolling out inspiration along the pine panelling from the Dalai Lama himself, the disturbing images lingered.

At the next table in knee-brushing distance sat a party of young Buddhist monks robed in saffron. Their teacher, a jolly man sipping yak-butter tea, discharged smiles in our direction.

Hot momos dipped in achar warmed our bodies as we smiled back, but the chill remained at heart level with thoughts of those pack animals on two legs.

'Tell me,' Arnie leaned an elbow on the table, 'about the porters we see here? They suffer so much.'

The man grinned, raising a chicken morsel in his chopsticks. 'They all come from Nepal origin.'

'Does that mean that they have to do this kind of work their whole lives?'

The question drew a brief chuckle from him. What kind of Western thinking was that? 'It's their karma. What can a person do about that?'

NOT EVERYONE IN Darjeeling was so fatalistic. Indeed the entire careers of some residents were dedicated to reversing destiny's tricks. The town's long history of intervening in the course of hill diarrhoea was an early example and had led to a vibrant health sector, especially in the area around the district hospital, where a field of garbage flourished and a host of private doctors practised. Their offices, many with kiosk-style pharmacies attached, bore colourful nameplates detailing their services.

One in blue, yellow and white belonging to Dr Krishnabahadur Ghale, MBBS (Cal) MD (Skin), read as follows:

SKIN SPECIALIST

Consultant dermatologist, venereologist, leprologist and cosmetologist dermatosurgeon – Surya Chatterjee Medico, opp. District Hospital, Darjeeling, Gorkhaland

'What's a leprologist?' Arnie murmured absently.

'Three guesses.' I strolled a few steps ahead of him, then turned around to see him frowning at the sign, shaking his head.

Another sign in smart navy and white proclaimed Dr VJ Vasai to be MD (Gynae) with a separate sign to advertise his skill upgrade in red capitals.

Now works on IVF **(TEST TUBE BABY)**

Others in Darjeeling who work passionately to change the cruel course of fate are attached to the zoo there.

'A zoo? In Darjeeling? I'm not going to any zoo thanks.' That was me, a veteran of zoo avoidance in many lands.

Arnie sighed. 'Okay. Look, we don't have to look at the zoo, but we do have to go through it to get to the mountaineering thingy.'

And we were both so pleased we did.

The zoo in Darjeeling – The Padmaja Naidu Zoological Park – an excellent one, houses its animals in sensitive enclosures full of trees and rocks and breeds endangered species. Some of these beauties, like the snow leopard and Tibetan wolf, leave one goosebumped and paralysed at the sight of them. Others, like the black panther – sleek, silent, potent – absorb the gaze the way a unicorn would.

The glorious pelt of the clouded leopard captivates the admiring eye – and unfortunately that of the Asian "medicine" market – as do its teeth and bones. This creature is not alone in suffering such a fate. The organs of the Himalayan black bear are as desirable, while the vanishing habitats of so many of these rare animals tighten the screws on their futures.

One fascinating species bred by the zoo is the red panda. With its little cat-like face and bear-like claws it lies on tree branches, flicking its raccoon-like tail, totally oblivious to its luck in being bred here and even released back into the wild.

Way out in India

But probably the most intriguing of all are the humans who visit this immaculate zoo. In the presence of signs requesting silence all around, they charge about, clapping and jumping in front of the enclosures, yelling for attention from each other and the royalty of the jungle, who gaze away in disdain, their rich animal smell proclaiming this their territory.

And, as is the case among the four-legged animals, some of the human ones are more interesting than others, Homo Westernus being especially enthralling for its relative rarity in these parts. Take me as a specimen, for example, compared with the tiger nearby playing hide-and-seek amid the foliage of its enclosure, the sun dappling its stripes and spotlighting its astonishing yawn.

Presented with that, would you glue your gaze to a granny-aged matron in a beanie and functional shoes? Would you find that bulky jacket more alluring than the tiger's coat or those glasses more glamorous than the gold in its eyes?

I rest my case, but felt restless there as a school group surrounded me, then a family group, staring into my ear canals at close range and jostling for a view of my sneezing performance. A workable strategy here is grace under pressure: a smile, a few photographs, a wave and a brisk stride upon departure, right through the zoo, for example, to the Himalayan Mountain Institute to ponder the life of its founder.

One of Darjeeling's sons who beat the karmic odds and earned fame internationally was Tenzing Norgay Sherpa. It was he who founded the esteemed institute and remained its director of field training until his death. At its unusual location in the grounds of the zoo, the institute includes the Everest Museum. At its entrance a relief of fake rock features the silhouettes of two climbers, one pulling the other to the peak by a rope.

Following the historic summit of Mount Everest by Edmund Hillary and Tenzing Norgay Sherpa in May 1953, the British, so recently relieved of their imperial jewel that was India, were obsessed with establishing Hillary as the first to have summited the world's highest mountain. The international press was aflame with the story, but the modest New Zealander insisted to the end that he and Tenzing Norgay had reached the peak together.

The relief at the Himalayan Mountaineering Institute hinted otherwise, inviting visitors to draw a different conclusion and to be photographed beneath those silhouettes, in a recessed niche built for the purpose.

Inside, the museum is as orderly and immaculate as a well-planned expedition, with a certain quaintness of 1950s design and a smell of floor polish. Through cabinet windows smudged by noses and fingers eager for proximity to adventure and glory, visitors gawk at equipment from various Everest expeditions. Yellowing typed labels curling at the edges tell their stories.

And then there are Norgay's own artefacts: his windproof jacket, his ice pick, his furry calf-length boots, all looking remarkably modern and ready for him to step through the back of the cabinet, suit up, open the window and step out on to his beloved mountains.

But, sadly, he is gone, his cremation having taken place at the institute. On its site a granite plinth now stands, stating that *"the Himalayan Mountain Institute was his favourite haunt"*. A high bronze statue of him stands victorious nearby with goggles raised, right arm raised, prayer flags raised in smiling triumph. Its citation reads: *'Tenzing Norgay Sherpa along with Edmund Hillary became the first man to climb Mount Everest.'*

Fascinated by this man who lived most of his life in Darjeeling, we set out to find his home – not an easy task amid the winding roads and locals who seemed puzzled by our quest. When at last we did find it, it turned out to be a smarter house in a smarter area than we'd expected, with the odd beauty parlour and boy carrying a guitar signalling its status. With no sign that Norgay had ever lived there, we were about to give up, when a small decal on the outer wall of a house featuring two crossed ice picks and the date, May 1953, caught Arnie's eye. Imagining that tourists might be welcomed, I mounted the stairs, only to be met by two chained and snarling dogs with impressive teeth.

'I wonder why they don't make it a tourist site,' Arnie lamented from the street.

I wondered how fast I could escape and what the gentle Tenzing Norgay would have thought of that kind of greeting at his home.

Way out in India

SURROUNDING ALL THE drama of karma in this fascinating place, the Himalayas stand as indifferently in their beauty as they have done for time unimaginable, Kanchenjunga the queen among them as the world's third-highest peak after Everest and K2.

The thing to do in Darjeeling is to view her by sunrise in all her roseate glory, for which enterprise the deal is this:

You get up in sub-zero temperatures at 3:45 am, plunge into the street, hail one of the ubiquitous Jeeps waiting there for this purpose, haggle over the fare, agree finally to the high fare requested for a half-empty car. You do, after all, want to make it to the sunrise spot ahead of ten-thousand shamelessly jostling others, not to mention the sun. Then you bump and bounce your way upwards in the dark for about half an hour to the viewing pavilion and choose at which level you wish to view the sight: General, Deluxe or Super Deluxe, all increasing in price in twenty-rupee increments, the most costly per person equating to about sixty American cents.

This exercise, of course, proves merely theoretical, since the Super Deluxe viewing deck, supposedly heated and probably providing thicker red velvety stuff on its plastic chairs than its poorer relatives downstairs, is already jam-packed.

So you land up, if you're lucky, in the Deluxe model fray of predawn masses wrapped in shawls and blankets edging their chairs forward into each other's space, a concept shrunk to millimetres in the setting for the sole purpose of staring through the windows into the icy black sky. All the while the strident bawls of chai sellers, blanket sellers and Himalayan knitted-cap sellers resound down below, eager to catch the unprepared, shivering and willing to pay anything for a modicum of warmth.

Finally, the night sky lightens and a wisp of gold appears, to the delight of the gathered company who whistle and cheer accordingly. The crowd heaves to the eastern side of the hall, commanding each other to sit down and elbowing each other in a manner that would leave a drunken buffet crowd in pursuit of roast beef blushing.

Meanwhile, on the western side, totally unobserved by anyone but my husband and me who've planted ourselves there, the peaks of Kanchenjunga and its siblings appear like cloaked pink ghosts, with radiant matching clouds above. Suddenly someone on the eastern

Of Peaks and Pine Trees

end notices and a stampede rushes west, shoving and determined to photograph this wonder at all costs.

'Arn, someone's balancing a camera on my head,' I felt compelled to report to my husband in the circumstances, my neck on an interesting diagonal.

But my husband, deafened by his rapt clicking at all that rosiness, offered only a grunt by way of protection, before once again I felt the urge to relate the fact that I was being surrounded, nay embraced, by some long male arms with the attached hands pointing a camera out west towards the mountains.

A husbandly stare of horror did nothing to abbreviate the episode, which I realised would cease – soon – assisted by the rapidly shifting colours of sunrise. At the first hint of blue-white replacing the rose, the man was off and everyone else with him, the throng of dawn viewers trampling each other to get down the stairs and the hill in every rickety four-by-four imaginable.

It was an icy roll downhill from there, through fields of frost to the Ghum Monastery. Think pagoda in bright paint. A few monks wandered the courtyard, a prayer wheel turned and I fled gasping with Arnie in steaming pursuit after an attempted visit to the holy site's toilet, which to this day holds my distinction for the Most Disgusting in India.

This, however, should not dissuade you from visits to the region's other monasteries. Many are clean and orderly, one even boasting a sign specifying '*Parking for Devotees Only*'.

THE NEXT MORNING, Rachel, the lovely Brit, shambled into breakfast looking tousled and pale. And was she trembling perhaps?

'Are you okay?' I asked when Arnie went off to replenish his tea.

She gazed through the picture window at Kanchenjunga, nodding unconvincingly and murmured: 'I am, but we got up very early this morning to watch the sunrise over at the viewing pavilion.'

'And?'

She turned her head back towards me. 'Well, Matthew popped the question over there.'

'*The* question?'

She nodded, sighing the steam off her tea.

'*And?*'

'Well, it was a bit traumatic. I was shivering and we were pushed up in a corner with a family jumping up and down and Matthew had been acting strangely since we woke up and the sun had come up and it was time to leave and then…'

'*Yes?*'

'Well then he popped the question.'

I could barely stay in my seat. I took her hand and squeezed it. 'So what did you say?'

'What?'

'What did you say?'

'I said, "What?" I couldn't believe that he would choose that moment.'

'I believe congratulations are in order,' I smiled at a rumpled Matthew plonking down with an omelette and toast.

'Thank you,' he smiled wearily.

'And I believe it was quite a moment up there at the viewing pavilion.'

'Did I miss something?' Arnie smiled, his eyes flitting among us.

'Matthew proposed to Rachel. At sunrise. This morning.'

Arnie's gaze roved among us, his truth sensors primed. 'Well – I'm speechless.'

Matthew cut open the omelette and grinned. 'Precisely, thank you, Arnie. Quite honestly it was a bit rough you see because when I chose the moment back in England, I didn't exactly have in mind a fridge full o' people pushin' and shovin' up against us, y' know.

'I had romance in mind, the sunrise, the pink mountain, me Mum's engagement ring in me pocket. And I started to panic when the sun had come up and there was no let-up from the cold or the crowds or anythin'. So I just went ahead and proposed.'

Arnie turned to Rachel, cup poised in mid-air. 'So what did you say, Rachel?'

She suspended her fork above her plate, smiling wanly with Matthew drawing nearer to her.

'I said yes – eventually.' Thawing out from the cold, she cast her eyes down and giggled – contagiously – until we all joined her with the warm smells of buttered toast and marmalade wafting in the steam from the teapot.

And there was Darjeeling before us: all the romance, tea, British and cool we could have wished for.

10
Home Run

'TAXI?' HE SEEMED A wildcat sort, the driver, zipped into a faux leather jacket, his collar turned up and his shades sleek in the weak morning sunlight outside the Embassy Hotel in Siliguri. And the car blinked chrome like a wink against its shiny black body.

'Airport?'

We nodded – uncertainly – bracing ourselves for the journey, as had become a reflex in India.

Twitching as he clasped the gear lever, I clutched my backpack to my chest, squeezing my eyes closed. But without the slightest bump we rolled out on to the road clogged with morning traffic.

As he reached for the radio, Arnie's fingers curled into a fist. But only the dulcet plucking of a sitar blossomed forth with a bow drawn over some sweet strings.

'You like this music, Sir?' the driver smiled, turning towards us.

Arnie's palm bloomed open. Yes. We liked the music very much.

'This Indian classical music. This Krishna song. My name Krishna, also.'

'Very good,' Arnie sighed, while I flopped backwards and Krishna negotiated the barging, growling throng with the dexterity of a dancer.

The music had a complex quality, rich and so exotic to the unaccustomed ear. It felt jumbled and glittery simultaneously – a lot like India itself.

But then Krishna raised a hand heavy with chunky rings to pinch some notes from the air.

'This sitar instrument,' he announced in the rear-view mirror. 'You know sitar, Sir?'

Sir's eyebrows rose like the crests of question marks in my direction.

'We do,' I assured Krishna.

'Every note of sitar sharp. Clear. Listen, Sir,' he smiled. 'Very beautiful.'

It was.

Then his arm waved to draw an airy bow over some invisible strings.

'That is sarangi. You know?'

'Mmm – maybe.'

His arm swayed in a rhythm then, like a conductor's, to weave some of the beauty of India around us, while threading through the traffic and its ghastly fumes.

'And that's the tabla – t-t-t, Sir. Play tabla drum with fingers. T-t-t. Drum sing. You hear, Sir?'

In this way, we were transported through this busy little city with its peculiar name, towards its airport with one even more curious: Bagdogra.

Then, after what seemed but an eye blink, Krishna turned a hundred and eighty degrees and drew to a smooth sort of halt.

'Airport,' he announced, turning to grin at us as the music tapped and sparkled.

'Already?'

A Glossary of Indian Terms

This glossary excludes those more common Indian or Indian-related words and terms listed in the *Oxford Dictionary of English*.

aarthi: in Hindu religious ritual, the component of puja in which light – normally from a wick soaked in ghee (purified butter) or camphor – is offered to one or more deities.

chaitya: a Buddhist shrine or hall for prayer and worship, usually with a stupa at one end; a stupa is a hemispherical mound containing Buddhist religious relics – usually the ashes of deceased monks.

chogyal: a form of monarch (like a raj) in the former kingdoms of Sikkim and Ladakh; the chogyal was the absolute ruler of Sikkim between 1642 and 1975 until the people of Sikkim voted in a referendum to abolish monarchy in favour of making their homeland the twenty-second state of India.

dabbawallah: a person in India, most commonly in Mumbai, who collects hot meals in canisters in the mornings from the homes of the people who prepare these meals and then delivers them to customers in the workplace; the dabbawallah is responsible for collecting the empty food canisters and returning these to their owners who prepare the meals.

gopi: a milk maid – some of whom are famously associated with the life and teachings of Lord Krishna, the Hindu avatar or deity whose teachings are contained in the seven-hundred verses of the Bhagavad-Gita.

juttis: a pair of embroidered or similarly decorated handmade leather shoes found in northern India and neighbouring regions; some juttis feature an extended curved or curled tip known as a *nokh*.

kettavallam: a large, wooden, barge-like boathouse – usually between

A Glossary of Indian Terms

twenty and thirty metres in length – with a palm-thatched roof found the southern Indian state of Kerala.

koki: a distinctly flavoured Indian wholewheat flatbread often eaten for breakfast.

momo: a Nepalese and Tibetan-style white-flour dumpling containing a cheese, meat or vegetable filling.

paddekar: a traditional coconut picker such as one found in Goa in southern India.

shirodhara: a form of ayurvedic therapy that entails gently pouring a liquid such as milk, buttermilk, coconut juice or plain water over someone's forehead, depending on what is being treated.

upma: a thick, seasoned breakfast porridge made from dry roasted semolina; the dish is popular in southern India, particularly in the south-western state of Karnataka (formerly Mysore).

xacuti: a complexly spiced Goanese curry containing, among other delicacies, poppy seeds, coconut and dried red chillies and usually prepared with lamb or chicken.